Dancing in the Kitchen

Dancing in the Kitchen

A Woman's Remarkable Walk in Faith

Pam Stewart

Pleasant Word
A Division of WINEPRESS PUBLISHING

Pleasant Word (a division of WinePress Publishing, PO Box 428, Enumclaw, WA 98022) functions only as book publisher. As such, the ultimate design, content, editorial accuracy, and views expressed or implied in this work are those of the author.

Unless otherwise noted, all Scriptures are taken from the *Holy Bible, New International Version®, NIV®*. Copyright © 1973, 1978, 1984 by the International Bible Society. Used by permission of Zondervan. All rights reserved.

Scripture references marked KJV are taken from the King James Version of the Bible.

Scripture references marked NASB are taken from the New American Standard Bible, © 1960, 1963, 1968, 1971, 1972, 1973, 1975, 1977 by The Lockman Foundation. Used by permission.

ISBN 13: 978-1-4141-1003-5
ISBN 10: 1-4141-1003-0
Library of Congress Catalog Card Number: 2007902788

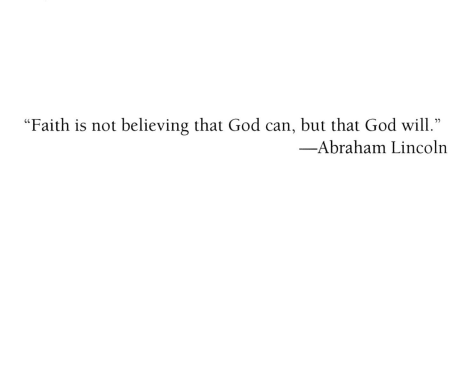

"Faith is not believing that God can, but that God will."
—Abraham Lincoln

Maurie S. Comenzo, PhD, LPC
Upward Solution
10209 North 37th Avenue
Phoenix, Arizona 85051
602-332-6115

I am honored to provide the introduction to this wonderful, true-life story. It is written by an extraordinary woman who serves an extraordinary God!

Although I am blessed to know Pam personally and have watched as she marvelously battled through some of the "seasons" she describes, I could not help but be amazed to read such intimate details of her heart and soul experiences. Most of us would never risk being so "real." Yet Pam's willingness to do so is for one purpose only. She longs to share the powerful truth of how God miraculously came through even in the most terrifying, devastating moments of her life.

Pam's incredible ability to trust God in the midst of each insurmountable circumstance will give you the hope to trust Him in your own situation. She will captivate your heart and lead you to a new step of faith. If you are struggling with the hellish nightmare of a loved one's addiction, you will be inspired to keep believing and not give up!

When most people would have cracked, Pam pressed in harder to seek God's will, prayed more fervently to enter into His presence and forced herself to be still and listen for His leading. As you read, you will learn how she did this.

May you be encouraged by her faith, humbled by her transparency, and blessed by her willingness to share the very personal uttering of her soul. Ask God to open the eyes of your heart and reveal His divine purpose for you as you read. Get ready for a journey that will impact your faith forever.

I love you Pam. I am so grateful for your friendship...

—*Maurie S. Comenzo, PhD, LPC*

In The Beginning

For years I threw pages of my diary into a desk drawer not understanding why I felt so compelled to keep the worn-out paper that chronicled my life. One day I pulled opened that long-forgotten cabinet to watch hundreds of recorded memories explode onto the floor in front of me. Should I throw them away? While gathering the unruly stack of thoughts about days gone by, I asked the Lord to answer a simple question. "Lord if you want me to keep this journal, then please give it a name." I smiled at the ridiculousness of my request while cramming the account back into the drawer.

The phone rang. With one leg I shoved the drawer shut while I picked up the phone. It was my dear neighbor, Laurie. She was going through a painful divorce in those days. Her tone told me she needed an answer to an important question.

"Pam, why is it that in the middle of all the pain, all I want to do is…dance in the kitchen?" Her question took my breath away. I understood it completely. Her heart wanted to dance because she was living in victory long before she would ever see one. Her question was my answer. "Laurie," I said right before we hung up, "I just have to thank you. You just named the book I am going to write." And so it has been for me, through all the years of pain our wonderful Lord has helped me keep focused on the unseen victory. I keep my eyes on Him while I just keep….dancing in the kitchen.

Table of Contents

CHAPTER 1

The Long Wait

He was gone. We immediately decided to get into the car and search for him. What if he was hurt lying on the side of some road with no one to help him? This was *our* son we were talking about. Jim put on his shoes and pulled the car keys out of his front pocket while I grabbed my purse. Our hurried steps clicked on the tile until we stopped at the laundry room door. Jim looked at me with the agony only a father could know. I pressed my handbag into my chest trying to keep my heart from smashing onto the ceramic floor.

We stood motionless, fixed on the wordless questions that continued to explode around us. What were we suppose to do? Where would we search? Why did our son run away? What caused him to be so full of rage? The answers never came. Jim backed up from the doorway and walked into the family room. I watched as his hand carefully placed the keys on the cold slick surface of the granite counter. He stood staring at the nonsymmetrical heap of gray and yellow metals. The laundry room door still held most of my attention. This was the door to the next door to the final door that could potentially begin a journey which could lead us to our son. I could certainly not let go of *that* door.

It was such a strange series of moments. I watched Jim and felt as if I were somewhere else experiencing the paralysis of a frozen second. "Pull yourself together," were the words that kept racing through my head. "Oh Lord!" I cried, and in that instant the door released me from its enormous pull. I ran into the family room toward Jim. The ache in that moment dictated our next move. We cried.

When tears no longer offered comfort, we sank into the overstuffed couch in the family room. Jim called out to the Lord from the very bottom of his soul. We prayed and begged the Lord for a plan. This was all so new to us. We had no idea how to handle this desperate situation. I ran to Justin's room and began calling out every number I found scratched on old fold-worn paper while Jim punched the numbers into the phone and prayed for our son to be safe in someone's home. No one knew where he was. We had already called everyone on the planet, we thought, and yet we just knew there had to be one more series of digits left undiscovered. The phone calling went on for hours. We had lots of frantic conversations with strangers who seemed not really to care about our concern for our son. One woman told me in a sarcastic tone, "If you had done a good job as a mother when he was young, you would never be in this situation today." Those words stung.

Jim was once again barefooted and cross-legged with one arm over the back of the couch. His other hand was intensely rubbing his forehead as if trying to massage an answer out of his brain. I finally asked the question out loud. "Jim, what happened?" The question broke open the floodgate as we each took turns pointing the finger at our own inadequacies as parents. Jim anguished over the inconsistency of our family devotions. His impromptu times praying with Justin no longer seen as special moments from the Lord, but markers of sporadic Christianity. Jim's heart ached as he wept through all the imperfections he saw in his walk with the Lord. I listened and wept too.

The truth of the matter was quite different. Jim was an extraordinary dad. He loved our children. Justin was our first. We had spent hours and days trying to decide on a name. Jim loved the name Justin. It came from the root word Justice, the character of God. So our son would be named Justin. His middle name was Jameson. It was the name given by a proud father to his precious son. On that most wonderful day in 1978, we met the child we had prayed over for months, Justin Jameson Cox. Jim daily lifted up the heart of the boy to the heart of God. The praying went on every day for years.

Looking at me was not like looking at Jim. I was controlling and stubborn. It was often hard for me to maneuver within the set of expectations I assigned for myself. Life was in constant flux, often leaving me a bit off balance. Jim was a commercial pilot which meant our lives were not very typical. He was gone a lot and I found myself walking through difficulties alone. It was during those times, I saw my most glaring flaws. No matter how inadequate I felt, I knew one important thing. Crisis was best handled on my knees.

How strange it seemed to have Justin run away while Jim was home. My mind scanned back through the years of Justin's life. The thoughts indicted me for what I should have done better. If there was someone to blame, it was I. I looked over at Jim and watched him as he sat completely submerged in thought, his bare feet rested in perfect stillness on the coffee table. My heart pounded so loudly I wondered if it disturbed the otherwise soundless moments. Our little dog Hayden, a Shih Tzu, hovered around my feet rubbing his fuzzy face into my legs. "Hayden," I confessed, "Justin has run away and I know it is my fault."

There I said it. I felt it. For the first time, I heard my own accusations as they were finally set free to bump into each other in the air. Maybe I had gotten too close to Justin or maybe not close enough. Could I have been so busy trying to impose my agenda on Justin I forgot to look at his? It was such a foreign concept for me even to entertain the notion of an "agenda" for example. My "agenda" was to honor the Lord. Now that strange word struck at me like an ax splitting dry wood. I rubbed Hayden's fluffy body as water ran from my eyes. Jim bent over to scratch Hayden's ear.

"Pam, this is *not* your fault! If it is anyone's fault, it is mine. You have always been here with the children spending countless hours loving them and teaching them how to love God." His words didn't help. I just felt guilty before God. Justin was a gift from the Lord and somehow I had blown it! Tears kept rushing out of my eyes. Hayden didn't seem to mind the rainfall as his motionless frame reveled in all the attention.

"Oh, Lord," I called out, "please forgive me." It was in that moment the Lord revealed the heart of Justin to me. I knew so much more about him than his great voice, flair for drawing, and handsome face. There was such depth in him. He was clearly "Justice," the one who wanted things right for all people. This story came to my heart.

When Justin was in the sixth grade the basketball coach asked me to come to practice—something parents were routinely discouraged from doing. The coach said my presence at the practice would definitely be an exception to his rule because he needed my help with Justin. The problem was simple. There was no keeping Justin's attention on the game. I went to the practice and watched all the kids running up and down the court to the screech of the coach's whistle. All the heavy-breathing boys responded but one. It was Justin. My eyes followed his as he tried to discreetly look in one direction without being detected. I smiled when I realized the reason for Justin's disinterest in the game was right in front of everyone's eyes all the time.

The coach had a small son with Downs-syndrome who loved running up and down the bleachers. The coach had forgotten about him, and none of the other kids remembered him either. But that little boy was all Justin could think about. While still smiling, I put my hand up and nodded to the coach who quickly blew his whistle for a short time-out. The problem wasn't really a problem. Justin would rather be watching out for the little boy making his way up and down the bleachers. The coach smiled when he realized how obvious it had been right along. He was genuinely touched by the heart of a disinterested basketball player, my son.

So many memories flooded my mind that night. I squinted my eyes in an effort to check the time on my watch while I reached for the box of tissue which sat undisturbed at the end of the coffee table. It was nearing 8 P.M. The phone had not rung once. Daylight had disappeared, reminding me to turn on the outside lights. I flicked the switch in the hallway and opened the front door just enough to make sure none of the bulbs had burnt out. Jim sat stoic on the couch, obviously deep in thought until I disturbed him when I sat back down beside him blurting out more of my guilt. I started a pile of used tissue on one end of the couch while trying to keep one hand playing with the furry boy at my feet.

"Jim," I finally had the courage to say aloud, "How could God let this happen?" Even with all my flaws I had always believed that the Lord would stand in the gap for me. He would be to my children what I could never be…perfect.

Jim looked at me as if stunned by the boldness of my question. He didn't say a word. "Do you remember when Justin was a very little boy and spoke of his love for Jesus?" I said. Jim affirmed my memory with a barely audible "Yes." "How about the time when Justin flew on the corporate jet with you and the chairman of the board?" Jim chuckled quietly through a mask of tears. I relived that day, while twisting the white tuft of fur on top of Hayden's head between my fingers.

Jim had been a corporate pilot during the first 10 years of our marriage when we lived in Wisconsin. The small flight department was always ready to meet the rigorous demands of a very active chairman of the board. They traveled everywhere. Jim even flew around the world twice. Children were not considered important cargo to carry on any trip. It was said they would certainly interfere with the exuberance of the business discussions anticipated on a "good" flight. It was different with Justin. The chairman of the board, John, really liked him. When we traveled on the corporate jet, we were always invited to bring Justin. He was the only child almost always approved for travel.

One time we went on a flight to Tennessee. Jim's dad was in a Nashville hospital facing a serious diagnosis. John immediately granted us permission to travel with him to Tennessee and, of course, Justin was invited as his guest. That was such a unique blessing. We boarded the GII. Passengers included; John, Justin and me. That was it. The only other person, outside of the two pilots, was the flight attendant. I took my seat in the back of the airplane trying to be considerate of John. Justin was to sit in the chair facing me. That was all changed. John took Justin's hand and plopped him right down in the seat directly in front of him. As the airplane took flight into the clouds, I watched a five-year-old boy completely captivate the CEO of a huge corporation. It was not hard to hear Justin's high-pitched voice over the whirring sound of air rushing over the wings, though I wasn't always able to make out every word. It was time for lunch and the flight attendant had spent some time arranging a lovely stuffed tomato on a plate lined with fresh fruit and vegetables. John asked Justin what he thought about the lunch. His response was an unabashed "gross." John chuckled and suggested Justin pick the food on the menu. Justin quickly volunteered his favorite things—peanut butter sandwiches and an apple. The flight attendant dug around trying to make that menu happen. She found all the requested items and presented the new lunch on a shiny silver platter. I munched on the lovely plate of food earlier prepared by the flight attendant while the man and the boy chatted over gooey peanut butter and crispy apples.

Then the question of all questions came out of nowhere. "John, are you going to heaven or hell?" I was stunned with the casualness of the question. Then I was gripped with fear, after all he was talking to *John*. In between sips of his drink and patting his mouth with the cloth napkin, John said "Justin, I think I am going to heaven, what about you?" Without skipping a beat Justin answered "I'm for sure going to heaven. Do you know Jesus?" John didn't respond quickly, it was clear he was either thinking about the question or determining how he was going to change the subject.

I desperately wanted to jump into the conversation, "Everything OK up there?" I managed to get out.

"It's all fine here," John answered. Then he said, "Justin, I know about God." Justin picked the skin off his sliced apple while he said, "That's good, but you need to know Jesus or you will go to hell, John."

I remember thinking that I would never, ever forget that moment on the airplane. Justin had just told the head of a multi-million dollar mega-corporation that he was going to hell. I held my breath. "Well," John replied, "I know about Jesus. Is that enough in your opinion?"

"John," (Justin was calling this man John, that alone made me cringe) Justin boldly spoke, "If you don't know Jesus, I hate to tell you... but you are going to hell." Yes, Justin really said that. All of a sudden the airplane became entirely *too* small and my lunch lost its appeal. Maybe John would finally cast Justin to the back of the airplane where I could wield some control.

"Tell me about Jesus," John said. This little child told of the wonders of Jesus. How Jesus had saved me and his dad and now him. We were going to live with God for all of "e-turd-ity."

John never said another word about Jesus on that flight. When we landed, though, John took Justin into his big arms and gave him a kiss on the cheek. "Quite a boy you have here Pam... quite a boy." As I spoke the last detail of that unforgettable trip, I looked over at Jim who was smiling.

"Pam, I can't believe what Justin so easily said to the Chairman of the Board." Jim put his hand up to his face as if to hide the broadness of his smile, obviously a bit uncomfortable. I laughed out loud while shaking my head. Jim rested his back against the overstuffed couch and closed his eyes. I scooped Hayden up into my arms and put him in my lap. "Where did that little boy go?" I asked myself while gently stroking the head of the now sleeping little dog.

In some ways Justin had become a stranger to me, and now he had run away. Where did his gentle heart go? Where was that boldness we saw in him on that flight to Tennessee? It boggled my mind to think about all the possible reasons that now crowded into my head. I looked over at Jim who was still resting his head on the back of the couch, eyes closed. What had gone wrong? Hayden yawned and stretched one last time before settling back into a cozy sleep. He snored softly while I played with the long black and white hair that covered his ears. It struck me how peaceful our home appeared in the midst of such internal turmoil. "Oh Lord," I sighed almost inaudibly, "where is he?"

I thought about his safety. The one thing I knew was that even though I didn't know where Justin was or what he was doing, I knew where he was going. He was going to heaven. I thought about Justin's salvation and how often that confidence brought me comfort. Justin was barely four when he claimed to know Jesus personally. He was a Christian—after all Jim and I were both Christians. Oftentimes though, throughout the years, I had wondered if Justin really knew Jesus. And over the past few years it became more and more apparent that maybe he really didn't have a personal relationship with Jesus Christ. How could that be? Was it possible for Christian parents to have an unbelieving child?

I looked over at Jim who still had his head propped up against the back of the couch with his eyes closed. "Jim," I whispered hoping not to awaken him if he had gone to sleep.

"Yes," Jim replied as if he had been sitting straight up in his seat waiting for conversation.

"There is something I have been wondering about for a while. We have always been taught that Justin is a Christian because ...well...basically because we are Christians. It is as if I gave birth to Christians. Do you really believe that?"

For many years we sat confidently under that teaching. There was the place in Acts where Paul told the jailer, "He is saved, he *and* his household." That passage was the spiritual safety net I depended on to save my children. But in that moment, when I needed unshakeable assurance, it was not there. Had I misunderstood the Scripture? It seemed a strange thing to want to discuss at that time in our lives. I grabbed my Bible and flipped to Acts and right there were the words I had counted on for so many years. I read and re-read the passage over and over. Did I really believe that? I looked up at Jim to find that he was waiting for me to say something.

"Jim, I don't believe that teaching is right?" His look told me to keep talking. "Well," I said, "I know what I am about to say will probably not seem encouraging, especially now, but I really believe we have been deceived by hanging on to a wrong teaching."

Jim kept his eyes glued to mine as I explained what I now believed, without doubt, was the truth. Yes, I knew it would have seemed more uplifting for us, especially then, to think Justin was just messing up and that his confession of faith as a small boy proved he was a Christian. For the first time I was convicted to push past what was comfortable and stand on what I knew was the truth.

"Jim," I said while he pushed his glasses back up on his nose not breaking the gaze he had fixed on me. "The Bible teaches that God is the only One who can make Christians. I honestly believe now that I gave birth to lost people." It was clear Jim was processing every word I spoke. I quickly continued, "Now that is not to say they will always be lost. God in His grace and mercy saved us. He could easily choose to save our children, but that is His decision. I don't believe our children are Christian by birth."

Jim took off his glasses and began rubbing his eyes, "Pam," he said, "boy that's a hard thing to look at now. Yes, we have assumed Justin and Ashley are saved because we are saved. But the only One who can make someone a believer is the Lord."

While he was talking I shuffled through the thin crackling pages of my Bible until I found what I knew was there. I found it in John 6:4," No one can come to me unless the Father who sent me draws him, and I will raise him up at the last day." My fingers traced the words over and over. How would this passage become a comfort to us? Why was I questioning something I had believed my whole Christian life? The truth had been exposed and in an odd way a new overwhelming compassion welled up in my heart for my son. I ran my fingers over the verse one last time before closing the Bible. The reality of my own salvation unexpectedly brought me to tears. For some unknown reason, God, the Almighty Sovereign Lord, chose me to be His own.

I began sobbing so hard, I could hardly catch my breath. Jim leaned over and gently put his hand on my arm. "It's going to be OK, Pam. Justin will come home." I smiled, knowing he didn't have any idea what caused the tears. Yes, I thought, it is going to be OK, not because Justin will come home, but because we serve a God of grace and mercy. He was at work in Justin's life.

"Oh Lord," I silently prayed, "please give me the privilege of knowing that You, most holy perfect Lord, chose my son too."

It was 11 P.M. and still not a word from Justin. The front door seemed to call me to stand in front of it one more time just in case the doorbell had rung and somehow we had missed it. The absurdity was clear, but it didn't matter to me. I pressed my ear up against the slick varnished surface of the wood door and only heard the odd screeching of the neighbor's garage door as it closed for the night. I was compelled to linger for a moment longer. Where was Justin?

Our daughter Ashley, almost six years younger than Justin, had finished dinner hours earlier along with the homework assignments she meticulously prepared at her girlfriend's house across the street. She was home by 8:30 P.M. and was now nestled in soft peach sheets and a puffy down comforter sound asleep. I pulled myself away from the front door to walk down the hall to check on her. Ashley always preferred her night light be kept off. It seemed strange to me that she liked having a nightlight in her room, but never wanted it on. She claimed it made scary shadows on her walls. I tiptoed into the dark room and leaned over to kiss her one more time. The devotional she read every night was again safely tucked inside the top drawer of her night stand.

Ashley always made my heart smile and with each "goodnight, peanut butter and jelly (my love name for her)," I thanked the Lord for the gift she was to me. I closed the bedroom door of the blonde-headed girl with the pink cheeks.

Ashley was so different from Justin. How often you hear that about kids. Two completely different children raised by the same parents in the very same household. It often boggled my mind when I thought about their differences. I walked down the carpeted hallway and heard the familiar tapping sound of a spoon as it hit the side of a ceramic cup. Jim squeezed the last bit of sweetener into his hot tea. He appeared to be staring into space while waiting for the powdery substance to completely dissolve in his cup. "Jim, do you hear something?" I said while I rushed past him on my way to the front door.

"*No*, Pam," he said. "It's probably just a neighbor?"

I kept hearing noises all that night. It was hard for me not to run to the front door every time I heard an unfamiliar sound. I just knew Justin had lost his house key and would need us to open the door for him. I wanted to be ready. Jim and I sat on the couch in the family room long into the night waiting for what never came. Jim had only a few drops of cold tea left when he glanced down at his watch. He needed to get some sleep for his flight in the morning. How would that be possible? We made our way to the bedroom.

For some reason neither one of us got ready for bed. We just sat on the couch in our bedroom and continued the vigil we had just left in the family room. In a very methodical way we began to go over every possible thing we could remember that might have been a red flag. Our lives had been upside down for so long we weren't confident in what we saw anymore. For years Justin went into rages without any warning. The mornings were the most difficult. There was yelling, cursing, slamming doors, and the pounding of his fist on whatever was near.

We had gone to our pastor, an array of counselors, and even a psychiatrist to help us figure out what was wrong. The doctor's called it ADHD— "an inability to filter out stimulation from the world." We had been warned repeatedly by many well-intentioned "professionals" that life as a teenager was going to be more challenging for Justin and us, due to this strange thing called ADHD. It proved to be true.

CHAPTER 2

The Ritalin Connection

Still not one word from Justin. I paced around the bedroom while thinking about the many things that had happened in his life. Jim had nodded off on the sofa in our bedroom. He was at least getting closer to the bed. I envied him for being able to keep his eyes closed. I wondered if he was asleep or praying. Either way, he looked peaceful. I climbed up onto the bed fully dressed, not even removing my shoes and just lay there. My eyes wouldn't stay shut, so I stared at the ceiling, focusing on a tiny spider web next to the air conditioning vent. It shook with each gust of cold air that blew over its threadlike lattice work. I couldn't relax. Where in the world was Justin? Why did he run away that day? There were no answers, just more questions. I stayed completely still and thought about the struggles we had with Justin throughout the years.

One of our biggest challenges with him had always been keeping him focused. The problem was really multi-faceted. Indeed, he had difficulty staying on task, but what troubled our hearts far more was that he never understood the relationship between actions and consequences. That disconnect deeply disturbed us. After years of searching we found a highly regarded doctor who specialized in behavior "challenged" kids. She gave Justin a series of tests and together with her associate agreed with clinical diagnostic assuredness that Justin was so far "off the charts" ADHD he needed Ritalin. The drug was purported to be the answer. I hated the idea of giving our son a drug. Jim and I painstakingly reviewed the results of each test with the doctor in an effort to get a handle on this thing called "ADHD." We had to be convinced this was the only remedy for him. I prayed constantly, begging the Lord to give us direction.

Often, I thought of the silly story about the man who prayed to God for help. The man's house had flooded and he knew if he didn't get help he'd perish. A boat motored by and stopped in front of the man's house. Those in the boat asked the man if they could give him a ride to safety. The man shook his head no. He was waiting for God to send help to him. Then a helicopter circled above the man and threw a harnessed line to airlift the man out of harms way. The man refused the rope because he was waiting for God to help him. In the end, the man perished. When the man got to heaven he asked God why He hadn't helped him through his great difficulty. God sadly shook His head and pointed out all the help He had sent. First He sent a boat and then a helicopter. God had sent the help to the man and the man in his foolishness didn't recognize it. In some ways I wondered if I was like that man, too foolish to consider "Ritalin" a tool God would use to help Justin. It took a great deal of prayer and several more meetings with the doctor before we reluctantly filled the prescription.

For a while, the drug seemed to have a positive effect on Justin according to the teachers and Justin himself. We, very begrudgingly, continued giving it to him. Jim and I were very respectful of the fact that Ritalin was a drug and kept it hidden. We wanted to make sure we were the only ones with access to it.

One afternoon, after Jim and Justin had just about finished running errands, they sat frustrated in the parking lot of Fry's grocery store in a car that just wouldn't start. Thank God for AAA. Jim left Justin for only a few minutes while he used a phone to give directions to their stranded vehicle. In that short time, we later learned, Justin shoved his hand way under the front seat of the car and retrieved the newly-filled prescription of Ritalin. He managed to take a half the bottle of pills and re-stash the bottle without Jim's notice. AAA came and jump-started the car. Jim thought the dead battery was the biggest event of that afternoon. Little did he know that something much more serious had happened.

I remembered the events of that next morning as if it was yesterday. Jim dug the newly-filled prescription bottle out from under our mattress while we chatted about our plans for the day. I was drying my hair while talking with Jim. I had just retrieved the hair spray from under the sink when I turned around and watched Jim dump out the Ritalin pills on the bed. Only a few pills bounced on the quilt and settled into the cracks of the tightly sewn seams. I put the can down on the bathroom counter while I watched Jim as he carefully picked up the small pills that had formed a line on the bed.

"Pam, we have a problem." Jim sat on the bed staring at the remains of what had been a full bottle. Where did the rest of the prescription go? Jim looked at me and spoke in a very serious voice. "Justin has somehow taken 15 pills. I just filled this yesterday. How did he do it?" The only time the drug was unattended was when Jim had left Justin for a few minutes to call AAA. That made sense. We asked Justin about the Ritalin and he was quick to deny any knowledge of the "missing" pills. It was clear, Justin had stolen the Ritalin. Obviously it wasn't helping him with the ADHD. We started the search for help, again.

Research led us to a psychiatrist who suggested something else. It was just another drug. We said no. This doctor, like all the others, assured us Ritalin was not addictive. She told us kids with ADHD feel "normal" when they are on the drug and kids who don't have ADHD don't feel anything with the drug. If that were the case, than why in the world would Justin steal 15 pills? It is a "harmless" medicine she repeated over and over in an attempt to comfort us. Alternative drug options were offered to us, but we had lost confidence in the drugs and the doctors. Those were such difficult days. The rhythm of the blasts of cold air that shook the silky fibers of the spider's web finally lulled me into an almost relaxed state. I tried to close my eyes to give sleep a chance.

Jim sat up straight on the couch and cleared his throat interrupting my feeble attempt at rest. I opened my eyes when I heard him stirring. "Pam," he said, not realizing I had been in my own world of deep thought, "do you think this all could be related to the Ritalin?"

His question spooked me. Could that be it? We had taken him off Ritalin months earlier. The fact that it was even a remote possibility suddenly felt as if we had found the root of all the bizarre behavior. Was this connected to the use of Ritalin? I thought the unthinkable. It was the worst thought a parent could ever have about their child. Jim said what ran through my mind. "Is Justin using drugs?" I watched Jim as he shook his head in utter disbelief. The thought was bigger than the moment. It literally took our breath away.

Jim grabbed a piece of paper off the small end-table beside him. I jumped up from the bed and sat on the floor in front of him. Very methodically we revisited every possible detail of that day, again. Jim scribbled the events down on the yellow lined paper:

He went to school. We discussed it thoroughly. Yes, Justin was grumpy that morning, but that wasn't anything new. We considered his irritability a normal part of his day. He came home from school on time. If something had happened at school he certainly would have missed the bus. His attitude hadn't become more unpleasant that day.

Jim continued with the list. Justin ate a sandwich. Not exactly. I corrected the inaccuracy. Justin ate only half of the sandwich. That was different. He usually ate like a vacuum, sucking up anything that came into his path. Could that be it? We weren't convinced the wasted half-sandwich offered any clue. I even recalled the conversation Justin and I had about his French class. He enjoyed French and was conjugating verbs with the best of them, and that afternoon enjoyed demonstrating his obvious aptitude. That was probably our best conversation in a long time.

After taking apart the events of the entire day, point by point, we could not find one thing that would make that day stand out from any other. Why everything had fallen apart the way it had, baffled us. Dinner appeared to have been a pleasant time of family conversation. It was when Justin had just finished shoving his last bite of Italian bread into his mouth that he announced he was going out. When we asked him to simply give us a few more details about his plans, he went into a rage. Ashley, Jim, and I watched the scene completely dumbfounded. His anger reached a fevered pitch. He stormed out of the kitchen before we had a chance to say one word. The front door banged as it slammed against the entry wall. Jim and I stood up from the table and rushed to the doorway, confused by what we had just experienced. Something was seriously wrong. But what?

Finally, at 1 A.M. Jim put down the list. We didn't understand what had happened that day. It just didn't make any sense to us, at all. We collapsed onto the bed ready to jump up in a moment's notice. I began to pray out loud. Jim prayed for Justin to come home safely. I asked the Lord to bring someone into Justin's life who would take care of and love him in his desperate time. The hours were excruciatingly long. They had to be billions of years disguised as minutes. We remained steadfast in our communication with God and opened our eyes to find that the Lord had ushered us past the darkness into the light of a new day.

It was the sound of birds chirping outside our window that woke me. My eyes hurt from lack of sleep. Jim was already up and in the closet packing his bag for his upcoming trip. It was hard for him to even consider leaving home. He tucked his shirt into his neatly pressed navy blue pants and adjusted his belt. With one hand he took his uniform jacket off the hanger while grabbing his hat with the other. I snatched the opened devotional from off my stack of reading and encouraged him with its words while he wheeled his bags down the hallway. He loaded his suitcase and flight bag into the trunk of the car. I quietly watched. As he backed out of the garage, I mouthed the only words I could think to say. "No matter what it looks like, God is good, always."

CHAPTER 3

The Battle Plan

Somewhere between washing the kitchen floor and taking the clothes out of the dryer, the root of the problem became clear to me. I wished Jim was home so I could tell him. Justin did not run away from home because we failed as parents. It was not about imperfect devotions or my stubbornness. The problem was much more important, more menacing. It was about spiritual warfare. We were living what we knew happened all the time. Pointing fingers and living in the world of "if I had only done this or that" would never help us in this battle. It was time to take our stations and prepare for the fight.

I ran to Justin's room and began scouring his room for things that needed to go. Rap CDs and handwritten phone numbers stored under his desk blotter were the first to get tossed. I wiped the dust off the books stacked untouched on top of his dresser. The bottom book was the Bible. My eyes stuck to these words when my hand quickly flipped to Ephesians 6:10-18:

> Finally, be strong in the Lord and in his mighty power. Put on the full armor of God so that you can take your stand against the devil's schemes. For our struggle is not against flesh and blood, but against the rulers, against the authorities, against the powers of this dark world and against the spiritual forces of evil in the heavenly realms. Therefore put on the full armor of God, so that when the day of evil comes, you may be able to stand your ground, and after you have done everything, to stand. Stand firm then, with the belt of truth buckled around your waist, with the breastplate of righteousness in place, and with your feet fitted with the readiness that comes from the gospel of peace. In addition to all this, take up the shield of faith, with which you can extinguish all the flaming arrows of the evil one. Take the helmet of salvation and the sword of the Spirit, which is

the word of God. And pray in the Spirit on all occasions with all kinds of prayers and requests. With this in mind, be alert and always keep on praying for all the saints.

Those verses took me back to the days when I taught Sunday school in our church. I had all the little children parade around the classroom clad in armor. The visualization of five year olds wearing oversized plastic and cardboard "armor" made me smile. Yes, it was cute then, but how was I going to make this real for me today? I looked at the verses one sentence at a time. I was being called to…be strong in the Lord…put on the full armor of God…stand firm…take up the shield of faith…take the helmet of salvation and the sword of the spirit…pray and be on the alert.

My mind took me to the young boy named David in the Bible. David was a small boy, not a big powerful man. God used him to demonstrate His strength against the giant Goliath. David knew he could trust the Lord for the victory, and so he did. In 1 Samuel17:45-47, we read David's response to the giant Goliath:

> David said to the Philistine, "You come against me with sword and spear and javelin, but I come against you in the name of the LORD Almighty, the God of the armies of Israel, whom you have defied. This day the LORD will hand you over to me, and I'll strike you down and cut off your head. Today I will give the carcasses of the Philistine army to the birds of the air and the beasts of the earth, and the whole world will know that there is a God in Israel. All those gathered here will know that it is not by sword or spear that the LORD saves; for the battle is the Lord's, and he will give all of you into our hands."

What confidence David had in the Lord! As a tiny boy he understood what was happening in front of him. The battle was not really about David and Goliath. It was between the Lord and the enemy of the Lord. That was why David knew the victory was certain. As I sat on the edge of Justin's bed, David looked so much bigger than me. He knew beyond any doubt the battle would end in victory. I wanted David's faith. My hand paged back to Moses in the Scripture Exodus 14:13-14:

> Moses answered the people, "Do not be afraid. Stand firm and you will see the deliverance the LORD will bring you today. The Egyptians you see today you will never see again. The LORD will fight for you; you need only to be still."

I reveled in the thought of the Lord fighting this fight for us. We were to hold our peace. Even though I knew I was reading powerful stuff, it still didn't seem like much of a battle plan to me. I re- read the verses over and over. The battle plan was simple. All I had to do was believe the Lord for His victory, stand firm, and stand still.

I found myself sitting on the edge of Justin's bed while my mind raced back to recall other great warriors in the Bible. Joshua came to mind. Joshua lived under the teaching of Moses and was revered as a great leader and strategist. It was easy for Joshua to put together a successful war campaign. How strange it must have been for Joshua, the warrior, to engage in the seemingly absurd battle plan God told him to use.

God told Joshua to march around the city of Jericho for six days in complete silence. On the seventh day he was to march around the city seven times with the priests blowing their trumpets, and in the final long blast of the ram's horn, all the people were to let out a great shout. The walls of Jericho would fall down and the city would be theirs. That plan didn't sound like a plan at all! It sounded completely crazy! It must have been difficult to accept what appeared to be illogical nonsense, as a serious battle strategy. What happened was amazing. Joshua was obedient, going against everything he knew. He abandoned his military tactics and believed the Lord. It worked exactly as the Lord had promised. The city was captured. It was clearly the perfect battle plan.

OK, I thought, it was time for me to re-assess the unbelievable plan I saw before me. Yes, the Scripture laid out the perfect course of action for me. I was to look to the Lord for His strength, to believe, to put on, to take up, to stand firm, pray, and be on the alert. Sounded nuts as a strategy, but it came from the Word of God, so it would be exactly right.

Thursday afternoon came without a word from Justin. It had been three days. Jim got home from his flight hoping to hear there had been a call, but there was nothing to report. I had been glued to the phone, never farther than earshot away except when I had to take Hayden out to go potty. Ashley had been her most delightful self while Jim was gone. She spent hours reading and working on homework while enjoying "Saved by the Bell" and "Full House" on television.

Jim wheeled his flight bag into our bedroom and quickly got out of his uniform into his comfortable clothes. Ashley had already finished dinner and was eating apples smothered in peanut butter as dessert. She gave Jim a big hug while filling him in on what he had missed while he was gone. There were the funny stories about her teachers along with detailed updates of all her friends. Jim leaned against the back of the family room couch completely involved in her stories. She offered him a bite of one of the pieces of apple she had dipped in peanut butter. He bent down and took a big bite of the gooey apple. Ashley laughed so hard she almost lost her grip on the plate. I balanced the makings for sandwiches with one hand while I closed the refrigerator door with the other hand. It was our habit when Jim came home late in the evening, to have a sandwich instead of a big dinner. Jim pulled his chair up to the island so we could talk while I layered the bread with meat and lettuce. He noticed a pile of papers stacked on my opened Bible at the end of the island.

"Pam, what's all this?" I hurriedly slapped the mayo and mustard on the bread so I could tell him about what I had found in the Bible. Jim picked up one half of his sandwich after we had brief prayer. I began paging through the Bible to find the verses that had popped out at me during the day.

"Jim," I began slowly, "yes there is a problem and I don't know the full scope of it. I do know, however, that it involves spiritual warfare. Justin is in the middle of a battle. The enemy wants him." Jim quit eating and put his sandwich down on his plate. "This is war," I continued. Jim nodded while fingering the napkin I had tucked underneath one side of his plate. I began reading Ephesians Chapter 6. God wouldn't leave us stranded. He provided the perfect plan of attack. We needed to believe in the Word of God, to stand firm, put on the full armor of God, pray, and be on the alert. Jim continued to nod his head with every word I spoke I closed the Bible and pushed it in front of me, forcing my plate with the uneaten sandwich to slide almost to the edge of the counter. I sighed and thought about the plan.

"Pam," Jim redirected my attention, "there is one more thing that is needed to make this plan work. You need to press on. I know it feels impossible for you, but you have to find a way to keep living." I was stunned by his words. I thought I had been pressing on. "You need to keep walking and doing life with all of its activities."

I couldn't believe he had just told me to do stuff I could care less about. His words felt like sandpaper scraping across a raw heart. It was true. I had, if I were really being honest with myself, stopped living for days. The place of isolation and introspection was becoming more and more comfortable to me. Jim put his dirty dish in the dishwasher and stopped in front of me. He leaned over and kissed my cheek as if to say he knew how hard life had become for me, for us. I couldn't help but notice how his concern had etched deep lines into his face. I threw my uneaten sandwich into the garbage disposal and listened to it grind while reminding myself that God was at work in Justin's life. "Stick to the plan, Pam," I said while I flipped off the disposal and left the sink.

The phone rang. I raced to pick it up only to find it was a neighbor making sure I would be at the monthly "bunko" game scheduled for that night. I tried to bow out of it gracefully saying something had come up at the last minute. I even volunteered to find a sub to take my place. Ashley walked by me with her plate sporting a small blob of peanut butter and the remains of an apple. She scraped the uneaten bits into the garbage while asking me what I was searching for in the bottom of, what I called, the bill drawer. I was still on the telephone, so with one hand over the receiver, I told her I was looking for the sub list.

She put her hand with freshly painted fingernails on top of the list I had finally put my hands on. "No, Mom," she said firmly, "Daddy is right, you have to keep going." And with that comment, I put away the sub list and went to bunko that night.

Friday morning was beautiful. The sun exposed a royal blue sky. The air felt crisp and refreshing. While Jim repacked his bag for another flight, Ashley raced around the house getting ready for school. I sat at the kitchen table pretending to be relaxing while savoring my hot morning coffee. In actuality that couldn't be further from the truth. I was busy. My mind was sorting through my never-ending list of possible places to find Justin. In the end I always came up empty. Ashley could tell I was preoccupied, but she went right on pretending everything was all right, just like I was. She sighed while she pushed her heavy books into her backpack. It was comical to watch her stand on the edge of book-bag while wrestling with the zipper. Often she'd looked up at me and smile. I knew the purpose of that little grin. It was intended to assure me Justin was fine.

I got up out of my chair and hugged her, trying not to let her see my tears. She had lots of theories about Justin and shared every one of them on her way out the door. He was probably at one of his friend's house, a friend who lied about him when we called. He might even be in the neighborhood sleeping under a tree. I smiled at her attempt to make me less concerned, and for a moment I borrowed both of her theories. It helped.

Ashley ran back to her bedroom to grab a sweater. I waited for her in the kitchen. It wasn't long before she was back standing in front of me trying to cram her sweater into her already overstuffed pack. Somehow she managed to find a place. She hoisted her big load onto her back and made her way to the front door almost running into Jim as he wheeled his flight bag out into the hallway. He bent down and hugged her and called her his "dolly" which always made her giggle. She left for the school bus with her lunch box and kisses goodbye. Jim left right after her.

I watched Jim drive slowly down our street out of the subdivision. Ashley waved at him before he disappeared from sight and soon they both vanished. I felt the emptiness of the space around me. It was so desolate. "Lord where is he?"

CHAPTER 4

The Runaway

My eyes caught a glimpse of the bright numbers on the microwave. It was time to face the day with a new resolve and "press on." I kept moving while I grappled with the truth that I really didn't want to get on with the business of living, at least for that day. What I really wanted to do was climb back into bed so I could be undisturbed while I figured it all out. I dismissed the temptation that beckoned me. It wasn't an option. My friend, Sue, had invited me to hike with her that morning. Staying in bed would have to wait for another day.

I threw on my clothes, hardly noticing what I was wearing, got into my car, and headed for her house. My mind taunted me with excuses I could easily have used to bail out of the hike. I even rationalized that they weren't really excuses. After all, the right thing to do would be to search the streets for Justin. He had to be somewhere. My friend would certainly understand my reasoning. I considered calling Sue on my cell phone. It would be easy for me to dig it out of my purse while I was driving. Hey, maybe that line of reasoning had even come from God?

I started to punch the numbers into the phone when I heard that unmistakable small voice speak my name. "Pam, be still and know that I am God." It caught me by surprise.

"OK, Lord." *Re-focus, Pam.* I thought. The battle plan resurfaced in my mind. I needed to believe. Stand firm in the truth of the Bible. Stand still. Be at peace and press on. These were my marching orders. I had to trust them.

I saw Sue's waving hand as I approached her and wondered how I would be able to "stand still" while "pressing on?" While I turned into her driveway, I silently begged the Lord to show me how to live out this new, uncomfortable way of life. She jumped into the passenger side of the front seat of the convertible, throwing extra water and supplies onto the floor in the back. We prayed and cried while I shared with her the pain of missing Justin. The wind blew in our hair as we made our way to Squaw Peak.

The mountain proved to be an excellent reminder of the majesty of God. Sue prayed out loud calling upon the Lord to return Justin home safely. She even took a picture of me while we were resting on a bench halfway up the trail. "One day, Pam," she said "You will look at this photo and remember the goodness of God. He hears us when we cry out to Him." I longed for that day. While she prayed, I silently mimed the same words over and over. "Lord, if I could just have a minute when I don't live in the pain of the worry about Justin."

I knew I was not supposed to worry. We are commanded in the Bible not to worry. I learned why. It was of absolutely *no* value. But did realizing how unproductive worry was keep me from worrying? No! Then, as we made our way down the uneven path, my foot caught the edge of a jagged rock and I tumbled to the ground rolling several feet before coming to a complete stop. My knees were split open by the knife-like points of seemingly harmless pebbles. The pain from the fall captured my complete attention leaving no room for any other thoughts. I sat motionless for minutes trying to reckon with the agony of throbbing knees. Then it dawned on me, in a very weird way the Lord had answered my prayer. I had not thought about Justin for even a second since the fall. It was a relief to be finally free of him. What an unusual exchange, one pain for another, and in it I found a bit of rest. Sue helped me hobble to my car ending the trek. I treasured our time together.

The morning disappeared into afternoon far too quickly. I packed ice and smeared Neosporin all over my damaged knees. The unrelenting ache kept me from getting the housework accomplished. I sat on the couch anticipating what had to be done, bad knees and all, and what could wait. It was time for me to go to the police department and file a "runaway" report.

Getting up from the couch to the driver's seat of my car was quite an ordeal. I drove to the only police station I remembered seeing in our area. The sound of flags flapping in the wind greeted me when I pulled into the parking lot. I laughed to myself while I debated the necessity of putting up the top of the convertible and locking the car door. I was in front of the police department. The car should be safe here. I pushed myself out of the front seat of the car and stood propped up against the hot surface of the driver's side facing the front of the building.

The ominous glass doors of the police station were completely uninviting. I dreaded going inside. After one deep breath, I got the nerve to face the unpleasant conversation I knew awaited me inside. My weight pushed the doors open. I limped across the beige colored tiled floor and spoke to a disinterested man through a secured glass window. He had so many questions. I had only two facts for him. 1. I had not seen Justin in four days and 2. God was in control. It felt strange to reduce everything into only two facts. The policeman concentrated on the first not willing to even approach the second. I was in a fog while I tried to process his interrogation.

"You don't remember what he was wearing?" was the indignant question thrown in my face. *Wait a minute, I* thought, while trying to collect myself. Yes, I *did* remember what he was wearing. He had on dark blue jeans and a white T-shirt with yellow and blue horizontal stripes. Justin wore brown-rimmed glasses. As I said that, I wondered if he still had his glasses, as we had replaced so many lost pairs over the years. I handed the uncaring uniformed man a recent picture of Justin. It would go into his file. A small card was pushed through the window identifying Justin by number as a "runaway." I stuffed the card between the dollar bills that lined my wallet and quickly shoved it back into my purse. The nod of the policeman told me our meeting was over.

The walk out the front door of the police station was the longest walk I had taken in a long time. My knees continued to make it impossible to escape the reality of my injury. The heavy glass door was even harder to push open on the way out. I pulled opened the car door and awkwardly angled myself into the seat, trying to convince myself I was in less pain than was really the case. Hot sun beat down on my head. The steering wheel felt like it had just been taken out of a fiery kiln and was certainly not ready to be touched. My once beloved convertible became a weapon of great discomfort.

I sat for a moment trying to collect my thoughts. It struck me how odd it was that I had come up with two facts. I wondered why I had blurted out "God is in control." It didn't need to be one of the facts and certainly it proved to be completely unimportant to the policeman. My mind fingered the words "God is in control" as if the once-familiar words had become a series of meaningless syllables. Was this a fact to me, really? I knew I had proclaimed it as true.

The sun pounded on me while I drove over the heat-softened tar of the road home. Cars around me offered no distraction from that one thought, that single inescapable thought that captured my complete attention. Did I really believe God was in control?

I drove into the garage and parked my car beside Jim's. I was so glad he was home. The front door of the laundry room opened in front of me. Jim greeted me with a look of alarm, "Pam what happened to your knees?" It was obvious the fall had been more serious than I had the time or inclination to indulge. He held my arm as if he needed to become a crutch to get me safely inside. We walked into our bedroom and I sat on the edge of the bed so I could almost stretch out. He sat on the couch and watched me silently dump the contents of my purse onto the bed. The brown leather wallet landed beside my hand. I unsnapped the clasp and my fingers sifted through dollar bills to recover the card—the "runaway" card. Jim carefully eyed every movement without saying one word. I held the identification card in my hand delicately as if it was what connected us to Justin.

Jim read the long list of numbers. There were so many numbers I wondered if there could be that many runaways? I unloaded all my feelings about the whole police station experience, except for one thing. I never mentioned how my statement "God is in control" sent me into a serious examination of my own beliefs. It didn't seem like the right time to bring that up. We put the card on the mirror and discussed how incredible it was to label Justin a "runaway. " I touched that card often. Somehow, it kept Justin close.

More days passed and still not one word from him. We called the people we knew to be his friends again. They offered us no answers. Some thought they saw him on the campus of his school. All the information was vague and filled with inconsistencies. It was another difficult week. I found it hard to do even the smallest things from grocery shopping to forcing down the meal I had spent hours preparing. This thing called "pressing on" was so tough that sometimes I wasn't absolutely sure I would be able to get through another day of it. I knew I needed to press on…really to press *in* to the Holy One. Daily I searched the Bible to find "how" to press on. I was reminded in Philippians 3:12:

> Not that I have already obtained all this, or have already been made perfect, but I press on to take hold of that for which Christ Jesus took hold of me.

I had no idea what that would mean in my life.

Another long weekend was made even longer because of a holiday Monday. When Tuesday finally showed up, I called the school again to deliver the same message. We had not seen Justin. The counselor interrupted me while I regurgitated the same unchanged report.

"Mrs. Cox," she said firmly, "Justin is standing in front of me as we speak." I found myself shaking while I held the telephone closer to my ear. There was a silent pause between her last word and Justin's first. He didn't have much to say except that he was sorry for making us worry and that he would be home that night. That was it. I never had a chance to ask him all the questions I had collected over all the days. Why did he run away? Why hadn't he called us?

I sighed into the receiver while the counselor told me not to worry. Her tone was consistent with her words, "Everything was going to be OK." I repeated her words aloud. For one instant I decided to believe everything was going to be OK. I shook my head in affirmation of a statement I just couldn't make it a fact, no matter how I tried. Life seemed better. I knew Justin was alive and seemingly doing all right. I breathed a giant sigh of relief while I peered into the refrigerator at the leftovers. The old potato salad seemed much more appealing than it had just minutes earlier. I was going to make a wonderful dinner that night. Our "runaway" would come home.

I had forgotten it was Tuesday. For the past months I had taught ladies Bible study on Tuesday nights. My first thought was to get on the telephone and cancel the study. It seemed the best decision as all my notes for the class were still scattered on a table and I was not quite ready for the study anyway. I excitedly started collecting them and stuck them into a notebook having convinced myself to call it off. I hurriedly went back to the refrigerator to determine what ingredients I would have to pick up from the store to make Justin a special homecoming meal. My finger tapped on the chrome handle while I surveyed what I would need to make the recipe happen.

In the quiet of that moment I heard a small voice speak to my heart. "Pam, are you pressing on?" In that instant I resented the question. Wasn't making a wonderful family dinner a way to press on? I backed up from the refrigerator and leaned up against the kitchen island. "Lord, isn't this pressing on?" I asked out loud. It didn't take long before I realized how "pressing on" was an act of obedience to the Lord. The sweet voice continued in my heart. "Ladies Bible study is what you need to do tonight." Even though I continued to silently protest, I knew I needed to stop making excuses and do what I knew was the best thing. OK, Lord, I smiled in halfhearted submission. I brought out the neat stack of papers and briefly went over my notes. The material I planned for that night no longer mattered to me. "Oh Lord, what will I teach? I have nothing to say." Matthew 10:19, popped into my head: "But when they arrest you, do not worry about what to say or how to say it. At that time you will be given what to say."

That particular night the lesson was exceedingly more meaningful to me than it had ever been before. We studied a subject that had become intimately familiar to me—pressing on. It was a special teaching, especially designed by God just for me. Justin didn't come home that Tuesday night.

Morning came in a moment, like the closing and opening of the shades. I took the "runaway" card off the mirror and held it in my hands. As I fingered the long list of numbers on the card, I felt close to Justin. It was as if his whole life had become flattened and concentrated into one very limited rectangle. I held it tightly in my hands close to my heart. The Lord spoke gently to me as I pressed new creases into the once-perfect card. He reminded me of my own teenage years.

I had lived my life without the Lord, running from one scenario to the next. I expected life to simply find a way to turn out right for me. I was 23 years old when He saved me. It was as if I had been a runaway too those first 23 years, running from the Lord. The numbers on the top of the card reminded me how personal the Lord was to me. I couldn't help but smile when I reflected on the fact that the Lord knew everything about Justin, even the number of hairs on his head. It was no surprise to God that Justin was a runaway. My friend Nancy once said, "A person is either running to something or from something." I wondered if that was true of Justin. Could he be running to a new faith or was he running from a faith he just couldn't shake? Either way, I knew in my heart Justin wasn't really running from our family, regardless of what it looked like. The bottom line was clear. Justin was in a battle, unaware of the victory he could only know in a personal relationship with Jesus.

The days continued to pass without a word from him. Jim, Ashley, and I prayed for him almost all the time. Somehow the corners got dusted and the clothes got washed, but it was all just a distraction to me. My mind was centered on one person, my son. My prayer life was exhausting as I played tug of war with God. One minute I was at peace, completely confident I had handed over my troubling thoughts to the Lord, and the very next minute I ripped those worries right out of God's hands convinced they belonged with me. Life was a struggle. A small number of close friends and family members saw the turmoil in my life and prayed faithfully, day after day. Their commitment reminded me of Moses in the Bible. He needed help to hold his hands steady in the midst of the battle. Exodus 17:11-12 says: "As long as Moses held up his hands, the Israelites were winning, but whenever he lowered his hands, the Amalekites were winning. When Moses' hands grew tired, they took a stone and put it under him and he sat on it. Aaron and Hur held his hands up—one on one side, one on the other—so that his hands remained steady till sunset."

I daily pressed into the promises of God and with my hands lifted up, like Moses, and waited for God to prevail in our family. When I was tired, others rallied around and held my arms up even higher.

CHAPTER 5

Unanswered Questions

Late one afternoon, after I had settled into the space between faith and worry, Justin appeared at the door. It was an awkward encounter. He didn't have anything to say. It was as if all the days he had been gone were merely a blip on a radar screen. Jim stood silently in front of him, unsure of what he should say. I had a million questions and yet I knew I needed to stand back and wait. Jim stood with his arms folded and head looking down. In silence Justin leaned up against the wall in the entry way and twisted the belt on his trench coat between his fingers. I took deep breaths trying desperately to hold back the deluge of questions that rested impatiently on the tip of my tongue. In the complete quiet of those moments, I ordered all my thoughts. He said he was going to come home the Tuesday I talked with him when he was at school. What happened? Where has he been all this time? Why did he lie when he didn't have to promise me anything? The most overwhelming question I had was not even one directed at him. Why did I just want to forget all the questions and throw my arms around him and hold him?

Jim broke the silence. "Son, your mother and I have been so worried about you. Why did you run away? What made you so angry you had to disappear for all these days? What is going on? His voice was soft and gentle. Justin looked disinterested in the conversation. The only thing he managed to say was that he didn't know what happened to make him want to leave. Jim threw out questions as they popped into his head. Justin simply shrugged his shoulders. I couldn't contain myself any longer. I desperately wanted to run up to him and grab him up into a big hug, but I held back.

"Justin," I said sternly, "we have been worried sick about you. Where have you been?" He looked up at me and glibly stated that he had been at his friend's house. It was someone Jim and I didn't know, he said.

Jim interrupted. "Justin, what are your plans? Are you going to live with those friends?"

Justin responded so quickly it took me by surprise. "Oh no, I plan on staying here. Are we done talking yet? Can I go to my room?"

Neither Jim nor I knew how to respond. We had lots more to say but it all seemed to pale in light of the fact he had finally come home.

Things were not what they appeared to be. Justin looked like he was home, but he was somewhere else. He was still a "runaway." Turmoil punctuated every mealtime. He cursed us at every turn and slammed doors so hard the door jams no longer held them closed. He punched holes in the walls and even the eight-foot bathroom mirror cracked under the pressure of our angry son. His contempt made our life almost unbearable. I continued to remind Jim we were under attack. Spiritual warfare was crashing into every safe corner of our lives. We went back to our pastors, counselors, friends, and family for help. My stomach ached most of the time, but I was compelled to keep moving forward in the promises of God.

Time after time friends of mine who were not Christians called my concern about Justin "unfounded." They calmly stated he was "in a phase." Their counsel gave me a false sense of hope. There were times I clung to their optimism. After all, if it were just a "phase" it certainly would be over soon. A part of me desperately wanted to believe they were right, even though I knew they were wrong. It wasn't about a "phase." It was about rebellion and a spiritual battle. I knew from my own life how many long years "a phase" could last before being resolved at the Cross. I had to be ready for the long haul. I stopped indulging in the world's fruitless thinking and took my battle station, at the feet of Jesus.

Things went from horrific to even more horrific. Family life was nothing like I had imagined. I felt like a private investigator, warden, and policeman. Like clockwork I searched Justin's backpack, his drawers, closet, shoes, every pocket of every pair of jeans, and every single corner of his room. He hated it. I told him he had my permission to search every part of my room. I had nothing to hide, so the thought of him rifling through my stuff was certainly not a threat to me. Things began to show up in his desk drawer, on his night stand, and in the very bottom of his backpack. I didn't understand what I found, but I knew it gave us clues about what was happening. I found empty casings for BIC pens and plastic straws cut in half. Jim and I brought these strange findings to Justin. Why would you have empty BIC pens? What was the purpose of a straw cut in half? Could these be related to "drugs?"

I began to read everything I could find about drug paraphernalia. There was nothing about pens or straws. Jim and I prayed and begged God to help us help Justin. Our prayers always included a plea to *not* let the problem be drugs. I talked to everyone I knew who might know anything about drugs. I called "D.A.R.E." at the police department. They all said there was a possibility he was using drugs, but even after hearing all the "evidence" I had collected, it was not their absolute conclusion. They advised us to keep on asking if he was using without accusing him of anything. It would be unproductive to alienate him. Our pointed, yet careful questioning, brought only denial. He was steadfast and had almost convinced me that I had the problem. In the deepest part of my heart I knew it had to be our worst fear. It had to be drugs.

My suspicions continued even though the evidence appeared to be dwindling. Life seemed to calm down for a brief time. Justin didn't stay out late anymore. He had a job, and by all accounts went to school. He even participated in the activities of the church youth group. It was not an unusual thing to hear him rave about his summer experience at Hume Lake Christian Camp. His good humor didn't remove my gut feeling. I patrolled his room in search of anything that might flag a "problem." The BIC pens weren't around, nor were the straws, but the nagging wrenching in my stomach just wouldn't go away. There was something seriously wrong. Justin was so good at twisting conversations that often I walked away wondering if I had somehow dreamed up my concerns. He continually pointed the finger at me. I was the one with the problem.

The phone started to ring at strange hours of the day and night. The short muffled conversations began and ended before I had a chance to hear any of the exchange. The late night callers were not people I had ever spoken to before. Justin started taking long walks around the block in the late evening hours claiming he was eating too much and needed the exercise. It just didn't make any sense. I often asked him if I could walk with him, but he always had reasons why that just wouldn't work. He even put on sweats at times, to make it that much more difficult for me to join him while he "ran around the block."

Many evenings I'd watch him leave our house all decked out ready for his nightly "run." My eyes followed him down the street into the wash—his shortcut to the main road. He always walked with such determination, as if he had an important destination. Once I followed him, trying to stay far enough behind him that he couldn't detect my presence. He turned into a street where his friend lived, a family we really liked. I walked up to the front door and the sound of laughter from inside the house made me question my purpose for being there at all. Justin kept telling me I was paranoid and my drug research was warping my view on life. I almost bought his thinking. Day after day I begged the Lord to reveal the truth. He did.

CHAPTER 6

Our Worst Nightmare Confirmed

It was Friday morning, November 22, 1996. The stifling uneasiness in our home was like a heavy, thick black blanket draped over the box we called home. We had come to accept this as a way of life. A sick routine had developed. We asked questions that always led to untraceable stories. Every encounter with Justin was hostile. Hate-filled words were thrust at us like grenades, constantly blowing up all around us. We lived in a mine field. But that day was different from any other.

Justin had gotten up early, very early, that morning. He had taken a shower and gotten completely dressed long before the alarm had awakened me. I poked my head into his room with my usual "good morning" and found him lying on top of his comforter all dressed for school. He even had his scruffy basketball shoes on with the laces tied and double knotted. I invited him to have some breakfast. The anger started to spew out of him like the overflow of a plugged toilet. I became disgusted and backed off while his voice erupted in the words, "When are you going to finally figure out that I don't eat breakfast." My heart began to pound. Something was going on and I didn't know where to turn for an answer.

The hallway became my safe space from the assaults. I could still see him from where I stood, sprawled out on his bed completely still. Something was wrong. "Oh Lord, please help us uncover the truth," I prayed as I walked back down the hall toward the sound of the whistling teakettle. Jim and I sipped Earl Grey tea in the kitchen while Ashley chomped on crunchy cereal. My ears strained to hear if there was any activity in Justin's room during the lapses in Ashley's conversation about the upcoming events at school. Jim and I took turns hugging and kissing Ashley while she collected her lunch bag from the counter. She smiled and yelled "I love you" right before we heard the sound of the heavy wooden front door shut behind her.

I tiptoed down the hallway so I could watch her walk down the sidewalk to the bus stop. That was my routine. I loved watching her blonde hair dance across her shoulders as she almost skipped down the street. I delighted in her. For some reason in those moments I felt compelled to pray over her like no other morning.

When I finished, I crept past Justin's room and found Jim gazing into space while he held his almost empty tea cup up to his lips. He turned and looked at me as if he had something important to say, but just couldn't quite get it out. I turned my head and looked towards Justin's room. I knew what Jim wanted to say, but wasn't saying. We had a problem. After swallowing the last sip of tea and quietly resting the cup on the counter, Jim headed for Justin's room. It was absolutely "last call" or he would miss the bus. The covers flew off the bed and without much of a "goodbye," Justin snatched his lunch from the kitchen counter and ran out the front door.

"Jim," I said "something is so very, very wrong." I watched as Jim fumbled through some drawers trying to find the phone numbers we had called once before. Maybe this time they would help us get some answers. I called the D.A.R.E., officer at Justin's high school. We had talked many times before, so I felt comfortable calling him with concerns. My question was direct and to the point. "Do you think Justin is using drugs?" The answer came quick.

"Pam, Justin may have a problem. I just don't know." We didn't know either, and that was the problem. I wouldn't hang up until I had presented all the "evidence" I had collected over the past months. The D.A.R.E. officer patiently reiterated it was a possibility, but not a certainty. Keep talking to him, was the advice. I hung up.

I took a deep breath and tried to redirect my thinking, desperately wanting to give my brain a reprieve from its obsession. Jim and I had made a plan for the day. We'd go out to lunch and see a movie. I put the breakfast plates into the dishwasher while Jim paged through the newspaper to find out what was playing. For a minute it almost felt as if we were on vacation, doing something we hadn't done in a long time. We laughed while trying to pick out the movie. It would be a good day, we thought.

We were just about ready to leave the house for the morning when Jim remembered he needed some insurance paperwork out of the safe we stored in our closet. I stood in the garage assessing all the organizing that needed to happen when I heard a shriek. What was wrong? It sounded like Jim had screamed. Why would he do that? I bolted back into the house and found Jim sitting on the edge of the bed moaning. Empty velvet pouches were stacked on one side of him.

"Jim?" I picked up the pouches. All the jewelry Jim had bought me throughout the years was gone. The "emergency" cash envelope was empty. We dropped to our knees. It was drugs. It no longer mattered to us what anyone else thought. I shook while I wept. Everything became clear to us for the first time. The lies now *looked* like lies. This was definitely a battle and the enemy was using a powerful tool to keep Justin running. The enemy was using drugs.

Jim ran to the car and I followed close behind. We drove straight to the school. The receptionist knew me so well that I felt she was probably saying, "It's her again, "when we walked through the main part of the building to the attendance office. A nice lady quickly checked the roster to give us Justin's room number. The class had taken a field trip. Yes, we had known about it but had forgotten in our panic. In unorthodox shorthand, the directions were jotted down on an old attendance sheet. We drove frantically to the cross streets on the piece of paper. It was easy to find Justin. He was the one who stood on the peripheral of a group of boys all bunched together. The closer we got, the more I could see the man who stood in the center of the circle. My guess was that he was talking about the pro's and con's associated with "leasing" a car. I remembered that much from the permission slip I had signed.

Jim pulled up behind a truck on the side of the road in front of the dealership. Justin saw us and began to back away from the group in anticipation of Jim's next move. From my angle Justin looked so very thin. His jeans seemed unusually baggy. I even wondered how they managed to stay up and why I hadn't seen his gaunt frame before. The sweatshirt he had on looked as if it was draped over a thin wire hangar. As my eyes traveled up his body, I caught the sight of an earring sparkling from the bottom of one of his ears. Was it one of the diamond earrings he had just stolen from me? I waited in silence with only the sound of the car's clock ticking softly in the background.

Jim brushed past Justin on his way to speak to the teacher. Her nod made me believe she had given Jim permission to take Justin home. Justin shoved his hands into his pants pockets and started his slow walk to the car. He got into the back seat without saying a word. I twisted my head around to get a good look at this boy. It *was* one of my diamond earrings that glistened from the hole in his ear. That was quite a surprise. He sat scrunched down in the seat as if he didn't have the energy to hold himself up. His hands were busy picking at his body. It was as if he couldn't control the urge to dig into the bleeding pock marks that now covered his face.

He caught me staring at him and stopped his unrelenting pursuit. He shifted back and forth in his seat, unable to sit still. I watched him as he dug at the sores on his arms. I gasped at what I saw for the first time. Huge red scabs covered most of his very thin arms hidden under the sleeve of an oversized sweatshirt. His fingers drilled into the wounds until they bled. The sight was so upsetting I couldn't manage to say a word. Jim climbed back into the car having been granted the appropriate dismissal for Justin from the teacher. (Little did I know it would be the last time Justin would be in school.)

I leaned over to Jim and whispered for him to look at Justin's face and arms. Had he seen anything like this before? Jim looked at Justin as he backed the car out of the parking space. He put the car in park while he almost choked from the sight. I saw the same questions I had, appear on Jims face. What had caused all those sores? Why was he so obsessed with scratching himself? It had to be related to some drug. I closed my eyes and began thanking the Lord for revealing the problem. The truth was evident. No more guesswork. We saw exactly what we had hoped and prayed against for such a long time. Justin was deep into drugs.

We drove home without speaking a word. My mind kept attacking me with the same taunting questions. How could I have missed it? Why did I believe all the lies? How stupid. How could I be so unbelievably stupid? The traffic and road home was nothing more than a blur to me. My brain raced to figure out how all this had happened right under our nose. Life was out of control. I found myself blinking hot waves of tears down my face as I wordlessly cried out to the Lord. I begged God to show Himself to me in this nightmare. Philippians 3:20-21, pushed through the pain of my heart into my thoughts:

> But our citizenship is in heaven. And we eagerly await a Savior from there, the Lord Jesus Christ, who, by the power that enables him to bring everything under his control, will transform our lowly bodies so that they will be like his glorious body.

Yes, the Lord had total power to subject everything and everyone to Him. The Lord knew what was going on in that car that day. He could at any moment change all of it. That comforted me. Justin was not a boy abandoned by God. The Lord knew about this moment before the beginning of time, and none of it had slipped by Him undetected. God, the almighty God of the universe, had allowed this to happen in our lives for some reason. I knew at that moment, I did believe. God was in control.

The humming of the automatic garage door opener brought me out of my thoughts and into the moment again. Justin stumbled into the house and stood directly in front of the kitchen sink, his hands supporting his bent body. His knees swayed back and forth as if he was fighting the force of an undertow dragging him unwillingly out to sea. Jim went over to Justin and lifted up the baggy sweatshirt so we could see what was underneath. We stood aghast at what our unveiled eyes saw for the very first time. Thin pale skin stretched over large bones about to poke a hole through the too-taut covering. His chest and stomach looked like someone had thrown a blanket of blood red measles over a skeleton. It was obvious Justin's life was hanging by a thread. The panic in our faces kept our mouths paralyzed, unable to utter a sound. We stood frozen.

Jim broke loose first and picked up the phone while I thumbed through the yellow pages in search of a hospital for serious drug use. The voice on the other end of the phone identified himself as the director of the hospital. He agreed to evaluate Justin immediately. A staff member took the phone from him and asked for more details and delivered the instruction to pack a bag in the event they decided to keep him in the hospital. Justin walked to his room and slowly sorted through T-shirts and socks, as if only certain ones would take this journey. His bag was packed.

I watched Jim and Justin climb into the car and slam the doors. Justin stared out the front window vaguely registering the happenings of the moment. Jim forced a "don't worry, Pam" smile at me and waved as he backed out of the garage. The garage door shook as it hit the cement floor to its close. I busied myself with housework. I had worked myself into a sort of unconscious robot-like motion as I folded, dusted, and put things away. It was when I looked on the counter in the kid's bathroom that I found myself experiencing a wave of pain so intense that it caused me to cave to the floor. My eyes focused on the only thing left sitting on the bathroom cabinet. A squeezed tube of toothpaste lay opened right in the middle of the counter. Fingerprints had made an interesting pattern of dents on the tube. I picked it up as if I had come upon a great treasure. Justin had gone without his toothpaste. The tears poured out, unleashed by a silly tube of toothpaste. I began a non-verbal conversation with the Lord. "Oh Lord, I want to believe that you are in complete control of all things. Lord, help me to believe more."

The doorbell rang. I stood motionless wondering if I should pretend no one was home. The doorbell rang again. I used my sleeve to wipe the mascara out of my eyes while I peeked through the slats of the shutters. It was a friend. He was holding a parcel wrapped in newspaper and tied with a string. I decided to open the door. The time it took for me to release the lock, gave me the moment I needed to collect myself. My voice cracked under the strain of trying to disguise my deep grief and could only force out the word, "Hi."

"Pam," he began, "I felt compelled to buy this for you and bring it to you now." He excused himself with a quick good-bye and a promise to pray for me. I closed the door a bit stunned, and carefully began to unwrap the gift. It was a picture, an artist's rendering of what appeared to be the Lord Jesus. The shadowed form of an angel was positioned just above the Lord who was kneeling. This Scripture was written across the bottom of the picture. It grabbed my heart. " 'Father, if you are willing, take this cup from me; yet not my will, but yours be done.' An angel from heaven appeared to him and strengthened him" (Luke 22:42-43).

My fingers traced every word. Those were my feelings. I desperately wanted the Lord to change my circumstance too, and yet I only truly wanted a change if it would be right in the sight of God and for His purposes. A disturbing question penetrated my thoughts. Was my desperation for change greater than my desire to accept this circumstance in my life for the purposes of God? My eyes surveyed the image of Jesus in the picture. The answer to that question eluded me. The notion of "change" versus "acceptance" seemed like an unfair pairing.

"Lord," I cried out, "please, please help me walk this out to Your glory." I meant it. The words in Luke invigorated my soul. I just needed to read them again and again. My index finger quickly raced by the first line, as if I honestly didn't want to be reminded of my flawed desire to bypass the pain of my circumstance. I felt my heart pumping hard as I came to the second line. "Now an angel from heaven appeared to Him, strengthening Him." That verse was just for me. The Lord God would send help. It was no surprise to God that I was inadequate to walk this trial alone. I needed help. I loved the reality of an angel especially assigned to me for such a task as this and to think God had already assigned an angel to walk this with me. I smiled while I explored the idea that there was an angel in our home sent by God to strengthen me. I wished I knew more about angels.

So what were angels about? Angels were beings I had never spent much time understanding. Department store folklore and New Age nuances kept me stuck to what I thought I knew about them—very little. I pulled out my Bible to refresh myself about what Scripture says about angels. God created several forms of beings: human beings, angels, seraphims, and cherubims. There are more than 12 legions of angels (see Matt 26:53). According to my Vine exposition of words, one legion is more than 5,000. There are lots of angels in heaven. Yes, angels lived in heaven (see Matt. 18:10) although they had been known to show up on earth quite often, especially in Old Testament days. They never married, nor did they die (see Matt 22:30; Luke 20:35, 36). They spent their time worshiping God (see Psa. 103:20, 21).

Angels were designed by God for two purposes. First, they were charged by God to act as His messengers. The word "angel" itself came from the Greek word *angelos* which meant "messenger." Secondly, angels were purposed to act as servants to those called by God to be saved (see Heb. 1:13, 14.) Angels looked to those who loved God for an understanding of the wisdom of God (see Eph. 3: 8-11). We are told angels protected those that love the Lord (see Psa.34:7). These beings would even have some role at the time of our death (see Luke 16:22). There was a lot to know about angels. And to think, God had assigned one to strengthen me. I closed my Bible and sat amazed.

There was still not a word from Jim about Justin. I held the shiny chrome framed picture of the Lord and His angel, while I sat on the couch and waited for the phone to ring. My mind wandered through hundreds of possibilities, none of them good. Why hadn't Jim called? Did they even make it to the hospital? If they did make it to the hospital, what if they decided they weren't going to admit Justin?

"Oh Lord," I sighed. What would we do at that point? When I was just about convinced something terrible had happened, the phone rang. I sprinted to get it before it could even get to the second ring. It was Jim. The hospital had admitted Justin into their intensive two-week detox program. He would be safe there. Jim told me he was on his way home.

It took a few minutes for my heart to stop racing from all the "what if's" I had needlessly lived through. I shook my head while I wondered why I always seemed to go to that place of despair first. I sat back down on the couch trying to pick up where my thoughts had left off before I had let them run wild. Oh yes, I remembered the question that had just begun to take shape in my thoughts. Was I willing to accept this trial, no matter how it turned out, to the glory of God? I wanted to say "yes," but somehow it lacked sincerity. "Please Lord," I prayed, "help me to walk this trial for Your glory."

The next morning our home felt different. Ashley got ready for school in the unusual quiet of a peaceful home. Jim and I even laughed about something dumb he had read in the paper. I found myself literally dancing in the kitchen. The glasses clanged together as I loaded them into the dishwasher while humming one of Steven Curtis Chapman's songs. I stopped when uncomfortable questions welled up in my heart. Was I joyful because Justin was out of our house? Could it be that I was experiencing more a sense of relief than real joy? Was Justin's absence from our home something to be celebrated? The questions deeply disturbed me. I silently begged God to provide the answers. The dishwasher banged as it shut. I twisted the knob and stood in front of it while the sound of the motor kicked on and forced hot water against the door. The still quiet voice spoke into my heart,

"Pam you are dancing in the kitchen because you are celebrating a victory. Justin will win this battle by the blood of Jesus."

I smiled. Yes, I completely believed it. From another part of the house the loud sound of running water as it gushed into the washing machine caused me to redirect my attention. Jim stood in the laundry room separating the whites from darks. I walked past him and went directly to our bedroom. Neat stacks of dirty clothes formed lines at the foot of the bed. I tiptoed around the piles and threw myself down on the comforter allowing my kitchen thoughts to continue to preoccupy me. I had to face the truth. A part of me was happy because Justin was not in our home. What was that saying about me as his mother? Guilt made an attempt to pry into the moment and disassemble any encounter I had with anything close to joy.

I reached for the television remote and began surfing my usual news channels. My brain registered the presence of words on the ticker tape running along the bottom of the screen even though I had no idea what it said. I knew on some conscious level that I had heard the tone of a woman's voice as she detailed world events, but my mind remained distracted by my destructive thoughts. What kind of horrible mother was I? I dropped the remote next to me as it was clear that trying to watch television was a pointless exercise.

Jim briskly walked back and forth from one part of our bedroom to the other as if he had discovered a hidden spurt of energy. He didn't speak while he emptied his suitcase and collected his final load of wash. I wondered if he was feeling guilty too! I never asked him because I didn't want to know. I leaned on the bedpost basking in the calm. The tension was gone and quiet dominated every corner of every room. It was as if "quiet" was the guest we had been awaiting for years. Now she had come, and we wanted her to stay with us forever. I reached for the remote and clicked the television off and just enjoyed "quiet's" visit. A gentle voice brought life back into clear focus.

"Pam," my heart whispered, "who is your true source of joy?" What was my source of joy? I had hoped as I dug into my heart that I would retrieve a valuable answer. Was my circumstance the root of my joy? Yes, Justin was safe in a hospital, but was that fact the foundation for the smile in my heart? No, I had learned my circumstances were always changing. I could not rely on them. One minute it appeared things were all right and in the next minute it seemed our family was going under for the last time. Circumstances had become mere trappings of the "smoke and mirrors" of life. Joy had nothing to do with my circumstances. I knew that for certain.

The joy had always been there at some level as I had seen traces of it in the most unexpected moments in my life. I shook my head while I tried to rid my mind of the guilt that almost derailed me. The reason for the joy was the same yesterday, today, and tomorrow. His name was Jesus.

$\mathcal{D}etox$

Justin had to be in the program for three days before we were allowed to visit. The psychiatrist told us that he was withdrawing from "meth" with the help of another drug. She was very upbeat and saw this as a "turning point" for him. When we did visit, I saw Justin standing just outside her office, his eyes locking on mine when he looked through the beveled window of her door. Finally, while we were saying our goodbyes to the doctor Justin exploded into the room full of excitement.

"Mom," he said with a face that made the moment important, "I met this woman, Marge. She is an alcoholic and needs to go to your Bible study." I nodded a yes, of course, even though my complete attention was directed to the boy in front of me. His eyes sparkled. He tried to playfully pick up Jim as he grabbed him up in a hug. I laughed when he scooped me up and threw me over his shoulder. People chuckled as we walked down the hall toward the dormitory area.

"Put me down," were the words I must have said a million times before he finally let my feet touch the ground. That was definitely a different entrance for me. Marge greeted us with a handshake and began to tell about the great encouragement Justin had become to her.

A small crowd had gathered around us giving me a reason to excuse myself from the loud conversation. I wandered down to Justin's hospital room. I was curious. A nurse directed me down a long hallway. "The first door on the left," was the instruction. I stood in front of the strange doorway a bit perplexed as it didn't look like any hospital room door I had ever seen before. The heavy wooden door could only be opened by a strong shoulder pushing forcefully on its hinges, as there were no handles. After one big shove it gave way to the darkness of the small sterile bedroom. In the middle of the floor was a heap of dirty clothes. I laughed to myself when I realized in a strange way that this room with the piles of dirty clothes looked just like Justin's room at home.

I bent down and gathered the grubby garments into my arms. After I finished collecting the last filthy sock off the floor, I heard the Lord speak so clearly to me I had to look around to see if someone had entered the room without my knowledge. The voice said, "Pam, I want you to understand something. The dirty rumpled clothes you hold in your arms have a special meaning." I held the clothes tightly in my arms as the soft voice continued speaking to my heart. "Those dirty rumpled clothes represent the heart of your son. I am the only One who can do the cleaning. This is My work, not yours. Leave it to Me."

The dark room felt warm and safe. I dropped the soiled pile exactly where I had first found it. The time had come for me to stop trying to fix what I couldn't. My eyes searched for the crack of light under the door as I waded through the darkness to find my escape route. As the solid wood door became once again one with the wall, I walked to the noisy courtyard guided by the sound of laughing and talking voices. Justin was entertaining Jim and Ashley along with a couple of residents. His quick wit and penchant for impersonation made the atmosphere light-hearted and relaxed. The laughter was so loud and intense I knew their stomachs just had to hurt. What a good pain. The wrinkled shirt Justin wore caught my attention in a new way. His impressive impersonations of nurses and doctors caused quite a group of people to gather. Often Justin was slapped on his back for his "right on" imitation of the hospital staff while others had to wipe their eyes dry after he finished mimicking the facial expressions of one staff member. He was so funny, but it was his shirt that kept my attention. God was at work. He would clean what I couldn't, and I trusted Him.

On the way home from the hospital that day, while casual chatter filled the car, I checked out for a minute to a private place. I found I had gotten good at that. It was easy for me to appear to be in conversation, throwing in an appropriate word or two, while being somewhere else completely. I often ushered my mind to that other place. I was in the presence of the Lord, praising His name and thanking Him for His grace and mercy in our lives. The words of the battle plan continued to play over and over again …believe… stand firm…be still…be at peace, and press on. It was in His presence that the Lord continually breathed new hope and joy into my heart. Jim glanced over and recognized how deep in thought I was.

"Pam, you're praying aren't you?" I smiled.

Two more undisturbed nights passed. Jim and I talked about how exhausted we felt even though we hadn't done anything taxing. Where did the extreme tiredness come from? It seemed pointless to try to do anything productive that evening. We sipped hot tea while propped up on the fluffed pillows on our bed. I adjusted the volume on the television while Jim snored. The phone rang. I dreaded the sound of the phone when it rang late at night. It always meant bad news. It rang several times before I leaned over to pick it up. Justin was on the other end. Immediately I went into panic mode….Oh no. What was wrong now? Was he still in the hospital? What was the problem? The questions soon found answers. He was talking so fast, I could hardly keep up with all he had to say. "I understand, I finally understand, Mom," were the words he repeated. "Jesus is a personal God. I have a relationship with Him." I tapped Jim's arm so he would wake up. Jim leaned into the phone. This was big. Our greatest moment had arrived. Justin claimed to know the Lord personally. Jim quietly listened while Justin continued with exuberance to tell how he saw the Lord working in his life. Long after the conversation ended that night, Jim and I relived every last detail. It was our greatest moment with Justin, our best moment ever.

Finally, another visiting day arrived. We were glad to deliver the guitar Justin had requested. Several nurses and staff gathered around the nurses' station as we handed over the instrument and case for inspection. Each person had so much to say. They bubbled over with excitement as they spoke of Justin's musical talent—his extraordinary gift. He sang beautifully without accompaniment to their complete amazement and they looked forward to this new "devotional" hour as Justin had tagged the time. One nurse even said they would "miss" him when he left the hospital.

Her words brought me to the next reality. Justin would come home. Honestly, I completely dreaded the thought of that day. What would our lives be like this time? I refused to let my mind wander to that new place without first going to God. I prayed, "Keep me centered on you, Lord. This is the only day we have with Justin. Please keep me rejoicing in it."

Another visiting day began. Jim and I took our admittance passes from the nurses and began the long trek through the maze of locked doors and security until we once again arrived at Justin's unit. He was thrilled to see us and quickly got through the hugging and hellos to something he felt was far more important. There was a new resident he wanted us to meet. He was a heroin addict, the worst of the worst in the drug world.

The young man appeared from around the corner. His red hair and pleasant grin made it hard to believe he had almost died at the hand of the poison-filled needle. Jim respectfully answered his random questions about the perils of flying in bad weather. The conversation continued on that vein long enough for me to excuse myself to bring the six coveted cans of Coke Justin had requested to safety in his room. The heavy door seemed to push easier than the time before. *My exercise must be paying off*, I thought.

Once again the complete darkness of the room blinded me. There was not even one window to break the absolute blackness. It never dawned on me to turn on the light. My hand reached out and felt for the top of the dresser where I carefully placed the Coke. Finally, my eyes adjusted to the light-deprived space. There was something in a pile on the floor. I walked to the place where I thought I would be able to see it more clearly. There at my feet was a pile of clothes. I bent down to touch them. They were clean and neatly folded. I smiled as I remembered Justin's enthusiasm on the phone…yes… indeed… we *do* have a very personal Lord.

The familiar whisper of the Lord rose up in my heart, "Pam, I have loved him from the beginning of time, and now he is mine."

I knelt beside the clothes and thanked the Lord, from the heart of a mom, for saving this son… *my* son.

The youth pastor from our church visited Justin often. Staff members often accompanied him as they brought words of encouragement and a renewed hope for the future to him. He received their words with great anticipation and began talking about the possibility of going to Bible college. I loved listening to him while he spoke of his dreams.

The two week "detox" program had ended. Jim and I sat in the lobby waiting for Justin to gather all the mementos he had collected during his stay. The staff psychiatrist took us into a small office and began to unfold her strategy for Justin's new life. She handed us a prescription for medication, the key component of this successful plan. I held the scrip between my fingers hardly believing I was holding *more* drugs for the drug addict to use at home. Finally I couldn't keep the absurdity of it to myself any longer. "Doctor," I purposely stated, "why are we giving *drugs* to a person who has a drug *problem*?" She tried to console me by saying that Justin's drug problem was unrelated to this drug he would be taking. This new drug, given by prescription, was appropriate.

I asked what this would do for him. The vague answer involved words like "calming effect," "balancing," and even "regulatory." It made *no* sense to me. The prescription was never filled. The doctor nodded a "good luck" as she shook our hands good-bye. I was struck with the unspoken implication from the doctor that the difficult times were behind us. The pills and support groups would fill the gap and magically "fix" him. What a crazy solution!

Jim and I sat in the lobby waiting for the rest of our lives to begin. Two weeks in that hospital would never "fix" Justin; I knew that for a fact. My hope came from the "truth" not the "facts." Justin could be healed in a moment by the hand of God. The short life of a "fix" would never touch the power of being "healed."

Finally, Justin was ready to go home. He had two boxes and three bags of things he had been "blessed" with by other residents. We managed to carry it all, along with his guitar, in one trip to the car. While Justin climbed into the back seat, I prayed that what we were experiencing *was* a healing.

Justin liked being home—for a short while. Each day brought him further and further away from the hospital experience. Then old patterns showed up with old friends trailing close behind. It had only been three weeks since his hospital discharge when he decided not to come home one night. We were right back in the same place where we had been weeks earlier.

"But Lord," I kept saying, "I thought he was new?" The only words the Lord spoke to my heart were, "Trust Me."

Days passed and no word from Justin. A precious friend, Linda, learned from her son where we could find him. She gave me the address. Jim and I had many long and often heated conversations about what we should do "if/when" Justin pulled a disappearing act again. I was always quick to say we needed to get on the phone and call everybody. If that didn't get results then we needed to get into the car and drive all around the city until we found him. Jim wouldn't budge from his viewpoint. We were *not* to go in search of a boy who did not want to be at home.

Justin reminded me of the Prodigal Son in the Luke 15 Bible story we had almost had memorized. In those passages the father does not go after his son. Jim believed it was best for Justin if we waited until he came home on his own. I had to agree. After all, it was right there in black and white in God's word. It was the best thing to do. Had I forgotten we were in a battle? No I hadn't forgotten, not for very long anyway. In order to live out the principles of the Prodigal Son we needed to look to the Lord for His strength, to put on, take up, stand firm, pray, and pray and pray. The prodigal son was in a war.

One day, about a week after Justin left home, I kept hearing this voice in my head saying "What's the matter with you, Pam? You should be trying to make contact with Justin. He needs to know you care?" Those words hounded me all day. Jim was on a trip and we had agreed to stick to the plan outlined in Luke with the Prodigal Son. I entertained thoughts of defying what I knew was right and doing things my way. It killed me not to know what was going on with Justin. I had to keep the focus. God had a plan and I was determined to believe it.

CHAPTER 8

Disobedience

It was early in the afternoon. Ashley was still at school and Jim would not be home until late that night. I gave our dog one last treat (as if to bribe him into secrecy) and pulled out of the driveway. The paper with the address on it would lead me to Justin. The street was easy to find, but the lack of numbering on the houses made my mission a bit more difficult. I remembered hearing it was the third house on the right. I counted as I slowly drove by each one. My heart pounded so hard I knew it could be seen right through my thick cotton shirt.

I found the house and parked my dusty red car on the crushed rock driveway in front of the house. I prayed my way to the front door. There was no doorbell, so I pounded on the door with my fist. A boy answered. He looked to be about Justin's age. His bushy hair and grimy appearance made it apparent showering was not one of his priorities. It was obvious he was irritated with my intrusion and questions about the new resident. Yes, Justin lived there. Yes, he had been there all that day. No, he was not home.

A German shepherd appeared from out of the darkness and started toward me. The boy yanked at the dog's collar and with a short good-bye, he slammed the door in my face. That was it. I sat in my car for some time hoping to see Justin. Two hours passed. No Justin. It was time to go home. My car caused a cloud of gray smoke to form as I drove over the crunchy bits of irregular stones in front of the house. I had to ask myself the most basic and obvious question. What had I gained? Did I feel better, even the teeniest, tiny bit better? No, in reality I felt worse. Now I knew where he was staying, and it was darker and more horrible than I had imagined it to be. Justin was out doing something. His absence made my mind wander. Was he out… doing drugs? I searched my brain for a Scripture, anything, that would help me rationalize my behavior. I couldn't come up with one piece of Scripture or logic to soothe my conscience. I had done the wrong thing and there was no getting around that fact. It was amazing to me how often I knew exactly what I should be doing and yet walked in the exact opposite direction. Even more stunning, was the fact I walked in disobedience praying the whole way. Now that was nuts! The incredible thing about the Scripture was how it revealed God's perfect plan for our lives and yet knowing that, I still chose my own way.

On the way home I tried to justify what I had done. I could easily come up with at least three (that number gave me confidence) reasons why my actions were appropriate. As I pulled into my driveway, I heard the Lord speak to my heart "Pam, you are a serpent in your own home." The implication in those words stunned me. I shut my car off even before I entered the garage. My mind searched for the context of such a statement. It was all the way back at the beginning, in Genesis where Adam and Eve met the great "deceiver," the serpent. It was the serpent who had posed the logical argument, the justification, and persuaded Eve to trade obedience for the illusion of power and control. Yes, that *was* me. I put my head down on the steering wheel and wept. "Forgive me, Lord."

I entered the empty house just as Ashley appeared in the doorway with her backpack and constant smile, ready for her afternoon snack and discussion about her day at school. Carrots and ranch dressing appealed to her taste buds. She asked me about my day and I quickly interjected how much I wanted to hear about her day. It wasn't long into the conversation when she, between bites of carrot dripping in dressing, asked me what I had been doing all day. I really didn't want to go into what I had done. Every time I thought about the drug house and the hours I wasted there, I felt sick to my stomach. I certainly didn't want to confess my stupidity to Ashley.

She put her snack down on the counter and stood right next to me at the sink. "So what did you do today, Mom?" she said with an increased curiosity.

This time I cleverly looked down and commented how much carrot "stain" was all over my fingers.

She agreed and added, "You were about to tell me about your day, Mom."

Oh yes that was the dreaded direction she was trying to point me. I straightened my bent arms, as if I needed to do that before I could talk about the events of the day. She gasped when I told her I actually drove to the "drug house."

"Mom, that wasn't a safe thing to do. Daddy will be upset about that." Yes, I certainly knew she was right about that! I continued the conversation by confessing to her I had done the wrong thing. Jim had explicitly told me driving to that house "was not an option." I readily agreed with him at the time, but when it really counted, the idea of seeing Justin after all those days was impossible for me to resist.

Ashley scraped the last bit of ranch dressing off her plate and licked the drippings off her fingers. She stopped chewing and looked me straight in the eyes. I wished there were more carrots on her plate to keep her somewhat distracted. Her undivided attention made me feel worse. "Mom, why do you think you did that? Didn't you think doing the "right" thing was the "best" thing?"

She certainly had me there. I told her she was undeniably 100 percent right. "I did the wrong thing because...well...because I decided to take things into my own hands," I said.

"Did you lose blessings for doing that?" she continued. I thought for a few moments about how I would answer her question. It seemed to me the Bible's teaching had always kept me free from worrying about missing one single jewel God had intended for me to lay at the feet of the Lord. This act of disobedience didn't put any of those jewels in jeopardy, but I knew I had missed the personal blessing of completely trusting God. She sat perfectly still waiting for me to answer.

"Ashley, I certainly did lose a blessing for this disobedience. Before I went to see Justin I had some peace about the situation. I trusted God for Justin. Right now I feel very different. The peace is gone. I stepped away from the Lord's peace because I thought I could do it better. I really believed I knew me better than God. I was wrong, so wrong. Now that I have seen where Justin is living, I am so upset. I went up to the door of the house and a grungy kid answered the door. The place is dark and filthy. It all made me sick. On top of it all, Justin wasn't even home. I waited for a long time and he never showed up. Now I feel as if I know too much, and yet certainly not enough. It is such a terrible place to be in. If I had trusted the Lord, and had been obedient to what your dad and I had agreed to, I would not have any of these deplorable feelings right now."

"Mom," Ashley put her small hand on my back, "It's OK. You won't do that again!"

I smiled and leaned over and planted a big kiss on her forehead. The truth of the matter, however, was I knew it was possible for me to do that very same disobedient thing again. I couldn't believe I was even admitting that to myself. In the quiet space of my thoughts, I went to the Lord and thanked Him for loving me, even though I was disobedient and anticipated the possibility of a repeat performance.

"Help me, Lord; I can't be obedient on my own." That prayer became my mantra. I knew obedience could only be accomplished by the power of the Lord. I already knew I was completely unable on my own to do anything that pleased God. Ashley sensed I was lost in my thoughts and patted my back one last time before she backed away from the sink. I smiled as I watched that precious girl drag her crammed book bag to her room. She was such a blessing to me. Thank you, Lord.

Another sunset had painted the sky purple and still not a word from Justin. Jim came home from his trip with his usual "so glad to be home" grin. He wheeled his flight bag into our room and casually asked me what I had been doing while he was gone. He stood in front of the mirror after putting some water on his hair to get rid of the "hat hair" look. I took a deep breath and began my confession. It was obvious I was completely disgusted with myself, even though I just had to throw in my rationalization for making the trip to the "drug house." Maybe Jim would see some wisdom after all. Well, his response was no surprise to me. His grin faded fast in the details of my story and his disappointment in me became very clear. He wasn't going to "beat me up" about it, but there was no mistaking he was upset.

Jim looked at me and said, "Pam, I know this is hard to do." That was an understatement. Giving up control, was not *hard* for me to do, it was clearly *impossible* without God's help. I squeezed my eyes shut while saying to myself, "Lord, you heard me. I can't do this." The motion of Jim getting off the bed jarred me back to the moment. It was dinnertime. My bare feet slapped on the tile as I walked down the hall to the kitchen. The idea of dinner wasn't appealing, but I knew Jim and Ashley were waiting for something tasty to show up on the table.

I pulled on the handle of the refrigerator door and it easily swung open. My hands began shuffling food around as if my action would cause dinner to magically appear. Many thoughts went through my head while I pointlessly opened and closed the vegetable drawer. Two serious questions demanded recognition. Why was I having such a difficult time trusting God? Why didn't I have the faith it took to trust Him? Faith and trust are aligned very closely. I knew from the Bible that faith came from hearing the Word of God. "Consequently, faith comes from hearing the message, and the message is heard through the word of Christ" (Rom. 10:17).

My daily practice was to read the Scripture. So why was faith such a struggle to me? I shut the refrigerator door and sprinted over to the computer desk to look up the word "faith" in the dictionary. There it was in bold print, probably not written by a Christian so there would be no biases. Faith was defined by Webster as "belief and trust in God." I quickly pushed the dictionary between the other books on the desk and turned back to the real focus, dinner. The menu finally came together; chicken in cream sauce, asparagus, brown rice, and a salad. I knew Jim and Ashley would approve of my selections. I took the raw slabs of pink meat and covered them in herbs, bathed them in fresh garlic and olive oil and put them in the oven. It would be 45 minutes before I had to put everything else together. Jim was still in our bedroom and Ashley in hers. I now had time to do what I didn't want to do—think!

My mind raced back to the definition of "faith" I had just read. It seemed reasonable, based on that definition, to assume "trust" required "faith." Did I need 50 percent belief and 50 percent trust to demonstrate faith? That couldn't be right. I needed 100 percent of both. Where was I going to get it? I rushed to get my Bible. That's where I'd find more faith.

I dug around in the silverware drawer to collect the utensils to put on the table while I wrestled with my need to believe more. I had learned in my walk with God that faith never came from wallowing in my circumstance. Faith came from standing at the very throne of grace and mercy. It would be there that He would deliver what I needed. As I folded the napkins and slipped them under the forks, old memory verses about faith formed on the tip of my tongue. "Faith without works is dead." That Scripture verse stirred my thinking. Faith was an action word. I reflected on the battle plan Jim and I had adopted for this journey with Justin from Ephesians 6. We were to be strong in the Lord; put on the armor of God; stand firm; take up the shield of faith, the helmet of salvation, and the sword of the spirit. The "doing" came in the form of trusting and praying which would be a pointless exercise if we didn't believe.

"Then they asked him, "What must we do to do the works God requires?" Jesus answered, "The work of God is this: to believe in the one he has sent" (John 6:28-29).

Yes, belief was the greatest task to accomplish. I knew we were in a spiritual battle and that the weapons provided in the Bible were the exact tools needed to attack such an adversary. I just had to believe. With each plate I put on the table came a new sense of resolve in my heart. I took a deep breath and promised myself I would stick to "the plan."

The timer buzzed and the pleasant aroma of herbed chicken slipped out of the oven and into the rooms of Jim and Ashley. Jim arrived first, obviously weary from his long travel day, yet invigorated by such a good smell. The wrought iron legs of the kitchen chair scraped along the tile as he pulled it back. He sat down. I tried not to look at him while I finished putting the final touches o the meal. Ashley laughed when she announced from her room that the smell of roasting chicken was disturbing her concentration. It was time to eat. Jim offered the blessing and we all dug in.

Ashley was the first one done. She scraped the tiny remains of her meal into the disposal and put her plate in the sink. Her evening plan included PJs and her favorite book. She loved to read. Often times I wondered if reading was her way of living somewhere else… a calmer, happier place.

Jim and I did not sleep well that night. He tossed and turned all night and I got up to go to the bathroom three times. In between the restroom visits, I lay completely awake visualizing "the house" where Justin now lived. It still seemed important for me to uncover at least one good thing about my efforts to see Justin. I wrestled with every detail of that visit and finally got to the place where I completely admitted I was wrong to go to that house. You'd think with that confession I would have quit obsessing over that house knowing full well how pointless it was for me to go there. Thing was, I just wasn't able to stop thinking about it. Nothing about my thoughts offered me comfort, and yet I persisted in dwelling on them.

The night dragged on. Between the end of one hour and the beginning of the next, I'd pull out the Bible and try to find the focus one more time. I was reminded again and again of the battle going on around Justin. This was spiritual warfare. Justin had not slipped out of God's sight and that was a fact. God is, was, and would always be completely and totally in control of everything.

Daniel 3:17, kept me centered until dawn. "If we are thrown into the blazing furnace, the God we serve is able to save us from it, and he will rescue us from your hand, O king."

Morning came unannounced. I opened my eyes when I heard the Bible thump when it hit the floor. Jim was already in the shower and Hayden was standing at the bedroom sliding glass door ready to go outside. I grabbed my robe and took him out. The bright early morning sun caused me to squint as I watched Hayden water all the bushes. The sky looked sapphire blue and the air smelled fresh and clean. Hayden stood at my feet waiting for his treat for a job well done. I smiled and we both headed into the house. It was going to be a good day. God could do anything.

Ashley was already sitting at the kitchen table enjoying Jim's famous "cheesy eggs." She was busy applauding Jim and me for being the "best parents ever." Her efforts to deflect what was going on with Justin made me smile. With the last bit of egg gone, she got up from the table and balancing her juice glass on her plate, she walked over to the sink and carefully put her dishes down. I stood next to her, sipping the cup of coffee I had just poured for myself. She wrapped her arms around my waist and gave me a good squeeze while telling me how much she loved me. I kissed the top of her head. Jim was standing right beside us holding her backpack and lunch bag. She let go of me and threw her arms around his neck and told him that she loved him too. He kissed her little arm and helped her adjust the big load of books strapped to her tiny back. The last thing Ashley said on her way out of the house was, "Your favorite child is leaving now." I heard Jim chuckle. I laughed too.

I walked into the hallway, still holding the steamy coffee up to my lips and followed Jim as he walked toward the bedroom. He lifted his suitcase onto the bed and started neatly folding a pair of jeans and a shirt. "Pam," he said, while adding shoes and socks to his stack of things for his trip, "promise me you won't go back to that house. It's not safe." I put my coffee cup down on the nightstand. Jim stopped what he was doing and looked straight at me.

"Jim, I won't do anything that stupid again." He seemed relieved, though I could tell he wasn't completely sure I might not once again get caught up in the moment. I fingered the handle of my cup while contemplating a question that needed an answer. "What if Justin decided to come home, how would I handle that?"

Jim pulled out his Bible from the front zipper section of his bag. We were back in Luke with the Prodigal Son. That son was "repentant" and "asked for forgiveness." "Justin needs to be repentant, Pam. If he is really sorry he will want our forgiveness. If you don't see these things in Justin, than he just can't come home."

I nodded in agreement while Jim carefully tucked the Bible back into his flight bag, grabbed his hat, and threw his leather jacket over one arm. He kissed me goodbye and headed out the door. I reflected on our marriage.

Often people commented about our lives. Jim would be home for a few days and then he would be gone for several more. One friend speculated our lives must have been like permanent "honeymooners" always looking forward to re-uniting after time away. Others said marriage must be easier for us than for most because we had our time apart from each other. Though each assessment had some merit, the difficulty of having a "traveling" spouse never seemed to carry much weight to those spectators. It always amazed me how often people equated a "good" marriage with time of separation. Isn't that funny? But when you carefully looked at marriages with one of the spouses continually on the road, you'd find those relationships have their own unique stresses. As the wife of a pilot, I had to constantly be willing to "hand over the reins" of parenting every time Jim walked in through the door. You don't think that was hard? Try being a total "control freak" and see how easy it is to hand over anything? If that wasn't challenging enough, try to be affirming when your husband made a parenting decision you don't agree with and had to carry out when he was gone. That was tough! People forgot about the stress of life always on the "stop"/ "start" mode.

All my friends were familiar with the drill. When Jim was home, I didn't have lunch or do any real socializing with them. Friendships resumed when Jim took flight. That may not sound like a very difficult thing, but it certainly was, as friends often needed you at the wrong time. In other words, "traveling" would never be the formula for a good marriage. The true secret for a great marriage was simple. It was Jesus.

I put on the tea water while I quietly thought about Jim and Ashley. Jim had probably already begun tackling his pre-flight responsibilities and Ashley was possibly fishing through her backpack at school. The phone rang and interrupted the silence of the moment. My friend, Linda, announced she had just gone to the "house" and was with Justin. He was ready to come home. I listened carefully. What an interesting concept. Justin was "ready" to come home. What had made him "ready"? Her cell phone cut out before she had the chance to estimate how much time it would take to drive the distance from that house to ours. I guessed they were only minutes away and was surprised by how calm I felt. I thought about my friend, Linda. She was such a dear one. I knew she was trying to do her part to repair our family, but something about Justin being "ready" to come home just didn't feel right to me. I kept reprimanding myself for being so negative. My mind raced back to the front door of "the house." Why did Justin want to come home? I would soon find out.

CHAPTER 9

Stick to the Plan

Justin walked into the house with Linda right behind him. She wanted to know if she should stay. I smiled and thanked her for all she had done to help Justin and told her we would be fine working this out alone. During our exchange, he remained silent. I closed the door behind her and trailed Justin to the family room. He didn't have to say a word because his attitude said it all. A beige raincoat covered the thinning frame underneath.

"Are you home to stay?" I asked. He ignored the question as if it had not been spoken.

His hands stuck deep into the pockets of his coat as he plopped down on the couch. "Ya, I might stay."

They were the only words uttered by either one of us for some minutes. I sat across from him on the loveseat waiting for him to say something or look in my direction. He never made eye contact with me. I sat back into the couch and broke the silence by saying how glad I was to see him and hoped that he was glad to be home. Quietly, I reintroduced our simple house rules. It seemed important to me that Justin understand he was coming into "our" home again. Other people needed to be considered when he lived with us. His hands stayed buried in his pockets while he stared at the floor. I didn't know if he was listening, but I continued as if he heard every word. My voice was calm and gentle when I reminded him that he needed to be respectful of the people and property in our home.

Secondly, I continued without waiting for a reaction, we expected him to go to school full-time or work full-time. The final request seemed the easiest to me. He was to tell us where he was at all times. Justin looked up and while glaring into space called the rules "bull." His hollow glare made it clear he had no intention of following any of our requests. The rage in him exposed the same storm I had seen so many times before. My thoughts ran back to the Prodigal son. There was *no* repentance, and *no* sign of wanting forgiveness.

What had to happen? I knew the next step. Justin had to leave our home. That was the plan and I was determined to do what I knew was exactly the right thing. I told Justin it was obvious he did not want to be a part of our family so he needed to leave. I stood up and walked toward his bedroom volunteering to help him pack his stuff. It was clear he hadn't expected my response.

As soon as I got into his room I pushed my hand past the hangars to the bottom of his closet where I found his old, army green suitcase shoved underneath a stack of papers and a Doc Martin shoebox. I pulled it out and propped it opened on his bed. I struggled to get the top drawer of his dresser open. With one determined pull, I yanked the drawer from its stranglehold on its overcrowded contents. There were dirty and clean shirts all mixed together like an unruly salad. I moved the piles of clothes just as I had found them from the drawers to the suitcase. Soon the soft-sided luggage bulged with shirts and jeans. Justin stood in the doorway of his room completely dumbfounded.

I prayed quietly, begging the Lord to help me continue to pack this bag. It was the right thing to do and yet the impossible thing for me to do on my own. My fingers worked on automatic, folding and packing, while my heart stood silently weeping at the foot of the cross. Justin grabbed his favorite hat off the rack causing it to shake as it was temporarily dislodged from its place on the wall. I shook too. This was impossible! Was I really packing my son's clothes to send him off—somewhere? Where was he going to go? My hands trembled even though I tried to disguise the movement by constantly patting the clothes. "Oh Lord," I said under my breath, "I can't do this without You. Please keep talking to me."

The words of John 15:5, formed in my head. "I am the vine; you are the branches. If a man remains in me and I in him, he will bear much fruit; apart from me you can do nothing."

"Yes Lord," I continued the silent conversation with the unseen listener. "I don't want to do this, Lord. But I do trust You *in* this. So I will pack and take him away from this house. You are God. I know You have perfect understanding of what is going on. I rest in that, Lord."

I said those last words as I stashed the unevenly squeezed tube of toothpaste beside his toothbrush in the small front compartment of the suitcase. There was not a chance it would be left behind this time. All the packing was done and it was time to go.

The bag fit easily into the trunk of the car. He slid into the passenger side still appearing to be in shock by my behavior. He watched me out of the corner of his eye as I started the car. I thought he must have been wondering where were the tears he saw me shed so many times before. Why had I not pleaded with him to change and stay? It was all different this time. I was completely calm, no hysteria. While backing out of the driveway, Justin asked me to take him back to the drug house he had just left. I swallowed hard and had difficulty speaking with the huge lump that now stuck in my throat. What was he thinking? Was he trying to test my resolve? I looked over at him and struggled to get the word "yes" dislodged from my throat.

My mind began to second-guess the wisdom of my actions. What was I doing? How could I bring this son of mine to the "drug" house? What kind of mother was I anyway? Do you want him dead? The assaults got so loud in my head I couldn't find my focus. Finally, out of desperation, I said "Focus, Pam," aloud. My voice was calm and confident. Justin kept his eyes staring forward pretending not to hear what I had just said. We were in the car for a few minutes when he realized he hadn't given me the directions. "The house is off Cholla." I knew exactly where it was. After all I had not only in actuality driven there myself, I had driven to "Cholla" countless times while lying in bed faking sleep. It bugged me when I thought how the scruffy boy had not mentioned I had been to the house. I guess at that point it really didn't matter anyway.

We approached the house. The familiar crackle of the pebbled driveway announced our arrival. The German shepherd behind the front door barked viciously. Justin got out of the car and began collecting his bags. I asked if he would mind my going into the house with him. He immediately said it would be fine, but then gave me a bunch of reasons why I would be better off *not* going inside. I was going in.

The front door didn't open easily. Justin had to bang on the handle to get it to let go and swing open. The blackness in front of me made it difficult to know what room we had entered. The dog stopped barking when Justin called his name, but he continued to sniff and pace around us obviously unsure of our true intentions. Justin guided me from one room to another. We passed what looked like a living room. The overstuffed plaid couches sat faded and dirty in the middle of the floor. My eyes sifted through the haziness of stale cigarette smoke to find the television I had heard even before we entered. Two stick figure people stood at the far end of that room in hushed conversation.

Justin took their cue to remain quiet. He whispered, "Mom." I could barely hear him over the television. "They are heroin addicts." The words almost choked me. I felt my heart beating so hard it began to hurt the wall of my chest. I struggled to breathe quietly so as not to draw attention to this unintentional invasion of their privacy.

We kept walking and passed a small bedroom on the left. The house was poorly designed. The entrance to one bedroom was through another bedroom. A man sat in a wheelchair decorated in old stickers. His ponytail hung limp on his shoulders under the force of a shabby, ill-fitting camouflage cap. A thick ring of cigar smoke encircled his face. Justin signaled for me to move quickly past him.

Finally, we stood in what would be Justin's room. It was not a typical bedroom. He would share it with many people. Empty cans, big flat pizza boxes filled with stale uneaten crusts and "Taco Bell" food bags were strewn everywhere. My pounding heart prevented me from asking any questions. *Breathe and walk*, were the thoughts that guided me. Justin dropped his bag onto the floor and walked me back to the front door. All the way to the door I felt the heaviness of total darkness; the couple, the man in the wheelchair, and now my own son. How could this moment be happening? Was this really happening? This was the son we had raised in the light of the Lord. Now he stood in such a pit of darkness.

The depth of the despair that encased the atmosphere was inescapable. Justin read the fear he saw in my eyes and put his arm on mine to reassure me. A fragmented thought crept out of my scratchy throat, "Justin, aren't you afraid?" He smiled. It was the same smile he had at six when he rescued a bird from the side of the road. I knew my heart would rip through my clothes any minute. My breathing was heavy and slow and the tears couldn't be contained any longer. The force of the pain sent gusts of water down my face as if I were caught in a torrential rain storm. I couldn't see through the curtain of liquid.

We stood silently at the front door while I used my hands to wipe my eyes, clearing a small path of vision. Justin took my arm and walked me back to the car and kissed me on the cheek. He disappeared into the dark house. I kept my eyes focused on the task of starting the car and only allowed myself to glance one last time at the house that had stolen my son from me. There was Justin waving his arms trying to get my attention.

"Mom, tomorrow is Sunday. Would you mind picking me up and taking me to church?" I nodded, though completely surprised by the question. He put his hand up into the air while yelling a goodbye to me. I watched him as he walked back toward the blackness that seemed to beckon him.

The car drove home without any help from me. I got inside the garage and completely fell apart. The deepest wail I had ever heard came from the tormented space in the uttermost part of my soul. I pushed my car door open and fell to the floor, as if my soul had fainted. I moaned to the Lord from that newly-found depth of anguish "Oh Lord," I cried, "is this like the pain you suffered when you looked at the lost?" I continued, "Lord, this is *my* son."

The cold cement garage floor offered no comfort. A conversation started happening in my head. "Yes, Pam, I know the pain you are experiencing. Remember I watched *my* son, suffer…and die…for you." I was overwhelmed with the truth in that moment. There were no more tears to shed, just an unfamiliar sound from an ache-driven pain. "Lord, You are GOD, You knew what would come after that pain? What will come after this?"

A voice whispered in my heart. "I tell you the truth, you will weep and mourn while the world rejoices. You will grieve, but your grief will turn to joy " (John 16:20). I tenderly hid that promise deep in my heart while I scraped myself off the floor and walked into the house.

Our home was so quiet. Again I paced around the pool making conversation with God. He was such a good listener. "How can I show Justin how much we love him, Lord?" A situation came to mind. Jim's mother was in a special home designed for Alzheimer patients. When we were interviewing the owner of the home, I asked her how she would handle Jim's mom when she got into one of her very difficult moods. We called the familiar disposition "a funk." The woman didn't even flinch at the question for one minute. She immediately said, "I would just love her more. And who can resist that?" I had always embraced the heart behind such words, and now that advice seemed to offer comfort to me. How would I show Justin how much I loved him? I would just love him more. *Isn't that the Lord*, I thought.

Sunday morning came much faster than I had expected. Jim was coming home that afternoon after flying a quick turn around somewhere in Southwest's system. Ashley was all showered and smelling fresh, ready for church. I hurriedly got dressed and tried to make it look as if I was unaffected by our trek to the "house," even though I had to make a trip to the bathroom right before we left.

My stomach churned as we traveled to meet Justin again. The house appeared deserted. We sat in front for a few minutes. Nothing moved. Ashley looked at her watch and let me know Sunday school would be starting soon. I forced myself to get out of the car and walked to the ominous front door. I waited for the German shepherd to finally announce our presence. Several times I banged on the door with all the energy I could muster. The continued silence made my efforts seem futile. Maybe he wasn't there anymore.

I stood and examined the old neglected wood door. The sun had stripped it of all color. A small trail of dust indicated termites had taken the life out of it. I waited a good 10 minutes before I knocked on the door again.

Ashley yelled to me from the car. "Mom, he's obviously not here. Let's go." I shook my head and started down the sand-packed sidewalk toward the car. I turned the key in the ignition very slowly trying to stall for another minute or two. The sound of the house's front door as it slammed shut caused Ashley and me to turn toward the unexpected noise. It was Justin. He sprinted down the walkway while buttoning his shirt. "Mom. I'm ready," were the words we heard as he jumped into the back seat of the convertible. Ashley appeared irritated with Justin about the long wait in the car. She huffed when he spoke and was barely able to say "Hi" in a civil tone. I, on the other hand, was so happy just to see his face. One more day to point Justin to the One Hope I knew could save him from his tortured life.

I found a parking place near the youth building. Ashley and Justin went to their respective classes, disappearing into the crowd of young people. After church we all met back at the car. Justin had so much to say I didn't even put the key into the ignition. I just listened. It was obvious his new life had lost its appeal. He wanted to be back at home because he hadn't even felt safe enough to close his eyes for even a minute in that place. People had stolen some of his things which left him fearful of what else might happen if he drifted into sleep.

He complained about the exorbitant amount of money required for the communal food and how horrible it was not to know who actually lived there from one minute to the next. As I heard about all the self-inflicted difficulties, I reminded myself to not say a word.

Ashley glared at me, as if to tell me *not* to give in to him regardless of how pitiful it all sounded. I smiled at her to make sure she knew I hadn't fallen for the manipulation. Even though he said he "needed" to come home, that wasn't enough. There was no repentant heart. I decided to at least invite him home for dinner knowing Jim would be home.

Justin jumped at the chance and was thrilled at the prospect of maybe taking a nap on his clean sheets. I started the car and we headed home. Ashley was glad we were finally moving after what seemed like a long time to her.

Justin was in the front seat and played with the dial on the radio all the way home, never settling on one station. When we pulled into our driveway, I was relieved to see Jim's car already in the garage. Hayden greeted us with his usual excitement as we entered the laundry room. Justin sprawled out on the rug while he watched Hayden roll around on the floor in front of him. I tracked Jim down in our bedroom closet. He had just finished hanging up his uniform and had already changed into his well-worn jeans shorts and bright polo shirt.

"Jim," I didn't really know where to begin. So I just spit it out in one jumbled mess. "We picked Justin up for church today. He says where he is staying is dangerous and he wants to come home. What do you think?" It seemed like it took Jim only an instant to get the picture. I was caving and he needed to prop me up with the truth.

"Pam, was Justin repentant, even the smallest amount?" Jim spoke slowly and deliberately, making sure I did not miss one word of his question.

"No, Justin was not remorseful or repentant."

Jim shook his head while pursing his lips. There really was no need for any discussion about it; Justin was not ready to come home yet. I begged Jim to re-consider. Maybe things would be different this time. As a mother I just couldn't surrender him to that drug house one more day. I rationalized and threw out every possible scenario that popped into my mind. What if something horrible happened to him while he was in that hellhole? Would we ever be able to forgive ourselves? How could we help him if he wasn't living with us? I pressed Jim.

Against his better judgment Jim gave in to my pressure and granted permission for Justin to return home. I hated the fact that I had won. Jim was sick about the fact he let me win. It was obvious we wouldn't be able to fix Justin's "drug" problem with any greater degree of success this time than we had been able to do in any of the times past. I was sickened by my own manipulation, and yet unwilling to recant my twisted arguments. I knew I had made a mistake.

Justin moved back home. The nights got later and later before all the lights were off and everyone in bed. I never could even doze off if both children weren't safely at home. Their absence would always keep me awake. It was as if the house somehow breathed better when Justin and Ashley were sound asleep. In the late night stillness of a restless evening, I begged the Lord to give me clear direction. I heard the small voice speak to my heart.

"Pam, why do you keep begging for a plan? You were given two plans. One was the Prodigal Son. It is in Luke, if you don't remember. The other is the very specific battle plan laid out for you in great detail. It is in Ephesians. Why do you keep asking for a plan when you have the best plans right under your nose? Focus, Pam. Stay strong in the Lord, put on the armor of God. Stand firm. Take up the shield of faith, helmet of salvation, and sword of the Spirit."

I knew those plans, but I didn't want *those* plans, I wanted something better. Maybe what I really wanted was something easier.

Once again we tasted the bitterness of the days we lived before he had moved away. It was on Wednesday when I came home from the grocery store, my arms loaded down with bags, that I first noticed my damaging habit. Justin worked the night shift at a gas station, so he slept until late into the afternoon. I would always tiptoe whenever I entered the house, as if the sound of my footsteps caused the sleeping lion to awaken out of control. This meant taking off my shoes and scolding those who didn't follow suit. The other thing I did was more disturbing. Whenever I was away from the house for even a short time I performed a ritual that had become far too familiar, like flossing my teeth before bed. The practice was nothing I thought about on a conscience level, it was just something I did every time I re-entered the house. I took inventory. My eyes searched each room making mental notes of all the televisions, VCRs, stereos, and the like. It was as if I called out names and waited for each item to respond with "here."

This time this unconscious act found its way to the front of my mind. "Pam," I heard a very quiet voice speak to my heart. "What are you doing?" I kept walking to the kitchen trying to prevent the bags from breaking open on the newly mopped tiled floor.

"Lord, I'm doing what I always do." I looked for the closest chair and sat down. Somber words rose up in my ear "What you are doing is unhealthy. You are becoming as sick as Justin."

I replayed that last sentence over and over in my head. A noise coming from the direction of Justin's room caused me to get up and check it out. I took my shoes off and walked in socks down the hallway toward the bedrooms. Justin was asleep. The soft sputter of a snoring boy drew me into the room. I looked at the bunched quilt only covering one leg. The scene appeared so tranquil. How deceitful the image was to an unknowing onlooker. The counterfeit peace didn't fool me. I tiptoed back into the kitchen and started digging into the sacks and putting things away. Every time I put something in the refrigerator, I thought about the one statement I had never let enter my mind before now. The truth of it made it hard for me to escape. I was getting sick too.

It wasn't long before I recognized other disturbing patterns I had adopted and called "normal." I had become a master of avoidance. There were things I didn't talk to Justin about because they seemed to unleash an uncontrollable series of explosions. The list of things I would not discuss grew. My thinking followed this line of reasoning; if certain topics weren't addressed (and that included things that might only be remotely connected to the original subject); we probably would have less violent eruptions in our home. Daily, my mind scrambled for "safe" talk. There was no such thing.

The outbursts came unannounced and more violent with each encounter. The once-repaired stucco walls now revealed new assaults. Life was out of control…again.

CHAPTER 10

The Call

There are often special people the Lord puts in our lives to stand in the storm like a big oak tree in the middle of a hurricane. My sister was my oak. She held on to me when the winds of life blew with gale force ferocity into the once still parts of my heart. It was early one morning when she called. It was obvious to her that I was barely able to stand in this storm. My timid voice made it clear. I was trying to avoid the wrath of Justin. She knew all about it. I admitted something to her I had not even told Jim. Something terrible was happening in my heart. My feelings were growing cold toward Justin as I maneuvered through the tempest that constantly rocked at me. It was as if a piece of my heart had been torn loose in the turbulence and now lay on the ripped up landscape of my life, almost dead. There was a silence on the phone after I confessed to her about this new, despicable truth. I thought she was wondering how it had happened? How did the mother of a son with evidently a serious drug problem, love God and despise her son? What was wrong with me?

Karen interrupted me, "Titter (our pet name for each other)... it will be OK. Understand this; God is preparing you for something important with Justin. You don't despise him. You despise the hold these drugs have on all of you. Pam, stay strong in the Lord. Remember to put on the armor of God. Stand firm. Take up the shield of faith, the helmet of salvation, and the sword of the Spirit. Most importantly Pam...stay focused."

I was dumbfounded by her advice. She had repeated exactly what the Lord had continually spoken to my heart, day after day. God *was* at work in this chaos, not just in Justin's life but in my life too. I hung up the phone with a heightened awareness and a desire to stand in this pit...to the glory of God.

Days passed and I scolded myself each time I was tempted to slip into the senseless trap of taking a mental inventory. No more inventories. Often times I would purposely walk around the house and dare myself not to look at the stereo or the television. It took practice, but eventually I perfected a way of harnessing my mind before it choked me with its vice.

"Keep focused," I continually reminded myself. "This is not about you. This is about spiritual warfare." The words of 2 Corinthians 10: 3-5, came to my mind. "For though we live in the world, we do not wage war as the world does. The weapons we fight with are not the weapons of the world. On the contrary, they have divine power to demolish strongholds. We demolish arguments and every pretension that sets itself up against the knowledge of God, and we take captive every thought to make it obedient to Christ."

I took every thought captive, almost, and brought them to the Lord. I knew it was the Lord and His Word that would keep me from losing my mind. My hands searched through all of Justin's pockets, drawers, and his backpack every day. He called me "paranoid," saying I had been doing too much reading in my health books. His indictments caused me to read more books and talk to more people.

Our family was held hostage by the drugs. There was no freedom. One of us was always at home, "on duty." Dinner out with friends in the evening was a memory from days gone by. We were always surprised when an invitation to meet friends was extended to us. It had not been an option for a long time. Afternoon movies didn't happen much any more. We were on red alert 24/7. Life was miserable. The laughter in our home was replaced with Justin's fits of rage followed by my cracking into a million tears.

Praying was more than just a frequent occurrence around the perimeter of the pool. Prayer was my weapon—the only thing that kept my heart safe through Justin's daily drug-induced emotional beatings. I never took prayer time lightly. I found a special place to sit and have serious conversations with the Lord. At night I broke out of the fear-filled darkness to that quiet place. One small night light exposed the cold, marble surface which had become my most precious seat. I sat on the edge of our Jacuzzi tub and prayed. That tub had been a joke in our family since the day we had it installed. I wanted it and gave up other things in the house to have it. Oddly enough,

I never used it…ever. I always promised Jim someday I would use that tub. The Lord certainly had a sense of humor. That tub became a prayer room, in a way. It provided the perfect ledge to lay out all my hurts and worries before the Lord. I was so thankful for it.

Justin worked strange, unpredictable shifts. His work schedule was always confused and he never could really tell us what time he had to be at work or what time he would be done. It was always a matter of great uncertainty. One thing we knew for sure, he went to work or somewhere right after Ashley left for school. Whenever Jim traveled, I prayed the Lord would postpone the day until I could gather the courage to face it.

One morning I went into the living room and sat down. That was a rare happening for me. I had decided to simply enjoy a moment on the soft brown, leather couch. My eye caught the small defined shadows of a metal art sculpture which hung in our dining room just across from where I was sitting. The sculpture was aptly named "The Journey." Native American people dressed in simple clothes appeared to be trudging along a barren road. Small babies were strapped to their backs and it looked as if all of their earthly belongings had been stuffed into bags tied with ropes and secured to a horse-led caravan. They looked like they knew exactly where they were going in life. Their countenance revealed a peaceful determination as they persevered.

That morning I was reminded of my own purpose and destination. A Christian singer, Steven Curtis Chapman, sang the song "I'm Not Home Yet." How true! There were many times when Justin's cursing words or slamming hand brought me back to the truth behind that sculpture. I studied the iron people and imagined the plight of their lives. "I want to go home, Lord. This is too hard," I often muttered in the middle of the chaos. Jim heard me utter those words one day. "Don't pray for something unless you mean it, Pam. Do you want to go home now?" Jim made me analyze what seemed to be a good idea at the time. Well, yes, I certainly *did* want to be with the Lord, but honestly I wanted to still live one more day on this earth. Really what I wanted was a break from the chains we lived with day after day. I just wanted to be free from it all, a moment of reprieve from all the pain. Justin constantly struck at my heart with vile words and hateful behavior. I cried almost all the time, until that final day when I had no more tears to cry.

It was early one morning while I sat on my Jacuzzi tub prayer stoop that I heard a voice in my heart praising the Lord while I held a separate conversation with Him. I told Him about the nagging ache in my heart. An unexpected prayer "duet" happened. Two voices spoke at the same time. I enjoyed the backdrop of praise without understanding the significance.

It had been such a long night and in the approaching dawn I was pleading with the Lord to show me His hand in that moment. My body collapsed forward while I beseeched God to please answer my prayer. "Where are you Lord?" I managed to say aloud. Out of the deepest part of my being came this response.

"Pam, do you not know what is going on? I am allowing you to eavesdrop on the conversation between the Spirit and the Father." I was completely stilled. The familiar voice of the One praising the Lord was the voice of the Holy Spirit. It was a prayer time I would never forget.

It was hot in Arizona the middle of that August. Of course it was a dry heat as they say. I sat in the pool trying to cool down, even though the water felt like it had just been drawn for a warm bath. The phone rang, but I couldn't get to it before the answering machine picked up. Karen had called. Her voice was excited and frantic all at the same time. "Call me right away," were her only words. I stood and dripped all over the tiled floor while returning her call. She was relieved to hear my voice.

"Pam, I just heard about this place called the "Wilderness Treatment Center." I know it is for Justin." I grabbed a piece of paper and scribbled down the name of the program director along with the phone number. The center was in a small town called Marion, in the unfamiliar state of Montana. Karen was not a pushy person, but she felt so strongly about this place that my call to them was a matter of great urgency. We prayed before we hung up and said our usual "I love you's."

I strained to read my terrible penmanship while punching the numbers into the phone. What had I written? Was that a 9 or a 7? Maybe it was a 5 or a 6? My sloppy writing was so annoying. After two tries I finally got the right sequence of numbers. The phone rang and the director of the Wilderness Treatment Center was at the other end. She had a pleasant voice and tried to assess the seriousness of the situation by asking me a list of questions. It was when I began to describe Justin and our family life that she interrupted with "Mrs. Cox, Justin sounds like one of our boys. He's in trouble and needs help." Yes, I knew he needed help. Could it be possible that finally someone had something to offer to us? It seemed too good to be true. I replayed our short conversation over and over in my mind. Justin sounded like "one of her boys." There were other families with a son like ours? We were *not* alone? That reality stunned me.

Kay promised to send a video of "The Wilderness Treatment Center" so we could "get a feel for their program." The first thing that came to my mind was its location. It was in Montana and we lived in Arizona. How was that going to work? In parting were the reassuring words, "He'll get through this and so will you." Boy I wanted to believe her even though I wasn't convinced. I quickly called Karen back to report all the details of my conversation. She was so relieved to hear I had made contact with the center. It amazed her at how compelled she was to give me that information. She felt such a sense of urgency that she was unable to keep her mind on little else until my phone call. This would be a good thing we agreed. I borrowed Kay's words and reminded her "We'd all get through this." It was certainly easier said than believed.

Each day held both good and bad. We kept our emotional "scale" handy, always ready to drop the crisis on it to see how heavy it had gotten overnight. On the lighter days, we laughed more and tried to believe things were changing for the better. The heavy days were the impossible days. Those times were so difficult it took every bit of my energy to shower and find clean socks to put on. Justin's hate was very powerful. When he spewed his wrath, it soaked us like toxic venom making us all sick. I kept hoping the video would arrive soon. It had been over a week since my conversation with the Wilderness Treatment Center. Maybe she had forgotten to send the tape, or like me, maybe she couldn't read her own scratching with our address.

A part of me wanted to call Kay again, but a bigger part of me said to wait a little while longer. The thought of sending Justin to Montana for treatment was not appealing. We wouldn't be able to visit him with any regularity as it was so far away. There were so many pros and cons to be considered. The biggest and most important consideration was Justin, always Justin. He needed help.

In reality, we all needed help. Things had been pretty quiet for a couple of days. Maybe the trip to Montana would not be necessary after all. I wanted those less hostile days to signal Justin's life was somehow back on track. In other words, I wanted to believe he was "fixed." The truth was very different. The screaming sessions were such a common part of the day that I had come to accept them as part of a "quiet day." Both his bedroom door and the bathroom door had been punched so hard the hinges broke off the door frames. The huge bathroom mirror had been cracked for a second time. The medicine cabinet mirror was broken. He had driven his fists into the bedroom wall on two occasions leaving huge gaping holes. This was insanity. We needed help and there was no way I could escape that reality. My prayer became a redundant question, "Is the Wilderness Treatment Center something You want to use in Justin's life, Lord, and in ours?"

It was August 22, around 9 P.M., when the phone rang. My friend Linda was on the line in tears. She knew in her spirit Justin was in the midst of something awful. Her own sons were using drugs and she feared for them all. We prayed and wept. "Pam, I have to ask you to do something. Check and see if you find a bottle of Ritalin in Justin's pants pocket." Her son had been diagnosed ADHD too, and she, like us, wanted to do whatever she could to help him succeed. I hung up the phone. Jim and I sat up on the bed stunned by what we had just heard. I volunteered to be the one to check the pants, as I knew exactly what he had worn that day. All the way to Justin's room I prayed "Lord, don't let me find that bottle."

Justin was sound asleep on his bed, the light still on. I carefully picked up the jeans that were bunched in a pile on the floor beside his bed. Both back pockets were empty. I could feel myself getting a bit excited with a hope that maybe things were all right and Justin had not stolen the Ritalin. I pushed my hand into his front left pocket and…there it was. The bottle slightly rattled as I removed it from his possession. I looked at Justin while he slept. His breathing was calm and steady. The tiled hallway felt cold on my bare feet as I made my way back to our bedroom.

Jim was now sitting on the edge of the bed ready for the news. "Here they are, Jim." He unscrewed the cap and dumped them out on the bed. There were 15 pills left. It was a prescription our friend had just filled two days before the theft. The bottle said it contained "30" pills. Was it possible Justin had taken at least 12 of those pills?

Jim ran to Justin's room fearful we needed to call 911. I followed and watched him put his head down on Justin's chest. Jim even took his pulse. It was all regular, nothing abnormal about it. Jim whispered "Maybe he sold the pills?" His question made me feel as if I had been slammed into another wall? Not only was our son using drugs, he might also be selling them? The scope of the problem felt far greater than we had ever really comprehended it to be. We were walking in such unfamiliar territory. We still lacked a reasonable understanding of drug use, and now we were faced with the possibility that he sold drugs too. Throughout the night we took turns putting our ear to Justin's chest while taking his pulse, as he slept. The light never went out in our room that night.

CHAPTER 11

The Decision

The morning of August 23, was one we would never forget. Ashley came out of her room full of her usual good humor. We sat at the kitchen table, me with a cup of coffee and Jim with tea. Ashley sipped juice in between bites of jam-smothered toast. She was concerned about something and her furrowed brow quickly gave it away. A girl in her class was being "mean" to her. What should she do? I reminded her of the girl in another school in Dallas who also had been mean. Ashley completely remembered that whole situation and filled in every missing detail while I struggled to get part of it right. We had prayed about that girl and Ashley knew the strategy we used in Dallas would probably be the best one in Arizona. She would be so very kind to this new girl that she would see Ashley's heart. It was not my strategy, it was God's. It had worked before, certainly it would work again. The words of Jim's mom's caregiver welled up in my heart again. "I would love her even more," she had said. "Who can resist that?"

My coffee was cooling off just a bit, the way I liked to drink it. I sipped on it while Ashley and Jim talked about the upcoming science project. We really hated those things and became convinced over the years that those projects were designed to get back at the parents. Jim looked at his watch "Time to go, Dolly," he said. We both kissed her and off she went to catch the bus. Right after she left, we lingered in the quiet, me with my perfect coffee and Jim thumbing through the business section of the newspaper. After I finished the last drop of morning blend, Jim refolded the paper and laid it on the table. We looked at each other. "Jim, we need to pray. This is going to be difficult."

I knew when we confronted Justin with the bottle an explosion would erupt unlike anything we had experienced to date. "Lord," I prayed "Help us stand firm in You. Keep us focused on the fact that You are doing a work in Justin's life." I quickly added one more thing, "Thank you, Lord, for what You are doing in *our* lives too!" The edges of Jim's lips turned up slightly. I wouldn't say he smiled, but it was close enough. Jim got up from the table with the half-empty pill bottle in his hand. I heard Jim's low voice as he spoke to Justin. It was hard to hear exactly what words were used. Then there was silence.

I wondered if Justin was even awake and decided it seemed safe for me to tiptoe closer to Justin's room when an explosive rage threw me back as if I had been hit by shrapnel from a blast. Justin screamed curses as he headed toward me into the kitchen. Jim followed closely behind, still holding the pill bottle. I continued to back up until I stood safely behind the kitchen island. He slammed his hands down on the counter in front of me and glared at me with utter contempt and hate. He didn't know how that pill bottle got into his pants. Someone planted it there so he would get the blame. Justin dissolved into tears while he yelled about how we had betrayed him with our accusations. We wanted to believe him, but that would have been an exercise in absurdity. Justin had stolen the pills and we were all facing a serious problem.

Jim collected himself long enough to choke out Justin's four choices. He could go to the Wilderness Treatment Center, Teen Challenge, a Christ-centered program in Phoenix, or live with his friends. Our home was clearly not in the line-up of choices. Justin slurred his words when he asked, "What is that wilderness place?" Jim looked at me as I stood dumbfounded by the list of options. We hardly knew anything about either place and I hated the thought of going to the "drug house" ever again. It took me a minute, but after I cleared my throat, I told Justin what Karen had told me about the Wilderness Treatment Center. I threw in that "Auntie Karen believes it is the right place for you." The program was for two months. It was AA based and located in Montana. That was all the information I could get my brain to deliver in the moment.

Justin seemed to be contemplating what I had just regurgitated. My mind raced to all the questions I had about that treatment center myself. We still didn't know very many important details. How much would it cost? Was there even a bed available? What were there expectations from the family? Jim kept his eyes on Justin as if readying himself for the next series of blasts. Justin just stood still with his head hung over the countertop. There were no words spoken.

The sound of someone banging on our front door changed the direction of our attention. My raised eyebrow was Jim's cue that I would not be the one answering the door. Jim unlocked and opened the front door to the pleasant voice of a delivery man asking for a signature. Jim took the small package. I rolled my eyes as I thought about the miserable timing for a delivery. Who would be sending us something anyway? Jim read the place on top of the package indicating where it had originated. It came from the Wilderness Treatment Center, Marion, Montana. What perfect timing. The three of us walked into the bedroom while Jim continued to rip the last of the brown paper wrapping off the video tape. He popped it into the VCR player.

The Wilderness Treatment Center was quite a place. The tape brought us into the small log cabins where the resident's rooms were furnished with rough cut, wooden bunk beds and matching dressers. Rows of long red plaid cloths covered what appeared to be the dining room tables. Huge twisted wicker baskets filled with fresh fruit were used for decoration. The smiling faces and laughter of the boys in the film brought comfort to us as we watched.

Justin looked away from the video long enough to tell us his decision. He would go to this place in Montana. Without another word, he left our room seemingly disinterested in the rest of the tape. Jim and I were glued to every scene.

We looked at each other anticipating the obvious questions. Did they have room for him? How much was this program? I rifled through the enclosed paperwork to find the answers to at least one of the questions. My finger sped across the pages trying to get to the bottom line. I found it, yes it was *enormously* expensive. I handed Jim the sheet with my finger pressed to the line he wanted to see first. The program was thousands and thousands of dollars. It was for 60 days.

Jim sat on the couch in our room absorbed in thought. I knew exactly what he was doing. He was mentally putting the pencil to the enormous cost to our family. I put the video back into its box. My ears strained to hear what Justin was doing on the other side of the house. The only sound I heard was "quiet" and that was never comforting, unless Justin was asleep. Jim was still writing numbers down on a piece of paper obviously unaware of the unusual silence.

My ears led me down the hall following the unexplained stillness. Finally I heard the sound of someone snoring. It was Justin. Relieved, I went back to our room where Jim was adding a long list of digits he had put together. It was important for him to try to figure out a way to finance this drug treatment center without taking it out of our savings. I paged through our benefits packet to see if any of it was covered by our insurance. I found my answer far too quickly. Nothing was covered. We were definitely going to have to finance this decision ourselves.

At least an hour went by before he put his pencil down and began to tell me why he was having so much difficulty with this decision. It was not that we didn't have the money, because Jim had found it somewhere. Jim blurted out the hard truth. "Pam, it is hard for me to give more money to a boy who has continually robbed us. I resent it!"

I went over and laid my hands over his. Jim was a frugal man. We always had more than enough money, never overspending by one dime. It disturbed him to the bone that he would have to fund the boy who had stolen all the jewelry he had so painstakingly researched and purchased for me. More than the actual dollar loss, it was the absolute violation that we both still felt. Jim continued to jot numbers down on his paper and cross out others while I excused myself and sat on the now familiar "prayer Jacuzzi tub."

"Oh Lord," I spoke in a soft voice, "Help me encourage Jim about this decision and the money."

In an instant a voice spoke to my heart, "I am the One who provided the money for you in the first place. Are you willing to lay everything you have at *my* feet? This center will *not* fix Justin."

I got up from the ledge and broke into Jim's world of numbers. "Jim, the Lord provided us with all the money we have didn't He?"

"Of course," said Jim, without even a thought.

"Are you willing to lay down all of it at the feet of the Lord?" Jim put down his pencil and looked up at me. He seemed speechless.

I continued, "Well then, let's take all the money that this program will cost and lay it down at the feet of the Lord. This money will *not* fix Justin. We have to know with complete confidence that God is at work in this."

Jim continued staring at me, not even blinking an eye. "Yes, all of the money does belong to the Lord. I wish you hadn't put it like that, Pam." We sat staring at each other for what felt like forever. Jim began tapping the chewed eraser tip of his pencil on the paper. We had nothing more to say to each other.

"Pam, let's do it…for the Lord." His answer encouraged my heart. I picked up the paperwork from the bed and looked for the phone number to call the center. We still didn't have all the answers to our questions. Would they have room? Was there some waiting period not discussed in the literature? What did it take to become officially admitted into the program?

I began pushing the center's digits into the phone. I handed it to Jim as he wanted to have a personal contact with this place himself. The man who answered marveled at the uncanny timing. Usually there was a long waiting list and oftentimes the wait was as long as several months. That day the story was different. They had one bed open which meant Justin needed to be on an airplane headed to Montana soon.

The expression on Jim's face told me things were moving at an astronomically fast pace. With most of Jim's questions answered, he hung up the phone and went over to his flight bag and dug out the Southwest flight schedule. The earliest flight we could arrange was for Saturday morning. We had to get through one more day. I watched Jim's tender heart as he wept his way through all the necessary arrangements that had to be made so very quickly.

This was very hard on Jim. I rushed around the house digging through forgotten winter clothes and big heavy boots. I wondered why I was not feeling the same stinging pain in my heart. The words of my sister came back to me. "God is preparing you for something." Yes, when I had cried my last tear for Justin, I hadn't understood what was happening in my heart. Was I turning cold toward my own son? No, this moment revealed the purpose. I *was* being prepared to help Jim through his most difficult time. I smiled at the greatness of our Lord. Over the next hours I did everything from sorting to packing, to loading it all into our car. Jim watched amazed. I knew God was at work. It was my appointed hour to walk without tears this time, while Jim wept.

Saturday morning showed up far too soon. Jim had begun to have some doubts about our decision to send Justin to Montana. First of all Justin would have to change planes in Seattle, Washington. What if he got off the airplane and didn't get on the next flight? It was so far away. We lived in Arizona and it would be impractical to say we would visit often. I stopped all the questions by praying them to the Lord. Jim chimed in with a list of more obstacles that might make this trip a failure. I pressed Jim to stay with the plan unless he had become convicted in his heart not to send Justin. There was no contrary conviction. The decision was made. Justin would go to the "Wilderness Treatment Center" for the 60-day program.

Jim shaved while I made breakfast. Justin was already up, poking through the last few things at the bottom of his closet. Jim entered Justin's room and offered help and conversation filled with kind, encouraging words. Everything Jim said to Justin amplified the love he had for his son. He spoke openly about his own reservations and asked Justin if he shared any of those same concerns. Justin did not have much to say and really I don't think he could have said anything that would have altered the decision. I pretended to be focused on scrambling eggs. I continued pushing them around in the frying pan on the stove, while straining to listen to their conversation.

Jim's kindness toward Justin spoke to me about the Lord. For years and years Justin had stolen from us, lied to us, and robbed us of a peaceful home. When Jim could have unleashed all the hurt he had stored in his heart for all those years, he didn't. I saw a father who loved his son. Love being poured out to the unlovely…the violator.

"Oh Lord," my heart cried out, "help me to always remember this moment. You have loved me…the unlovely…the violator." Jim and Justin emerged from the bedroom carrying the remainder of the bags and a jacket. Ashley was still asleep. We sat at the table eating the overcooked scrambled eggs and talking about our great hope for Justin. Bottom line, it was and always would be about Jesus.

Justin asked what caused us to want to send him so far away. Jim's voice was choked with tears, "Son, we aren't sending you away from us. We are sending you there so you will be able to come back to us. Our hope is that this program will help you do one thing and only one thing…stay alive." Those words deeply moved Justin. I added that we had no deep expectations, no hidden agenda. It was simple. We just wanted Justin to *live*. The overwhelming influences in Arizona seemed to make it more and more difficult for him to find a clean place away from all the connections he had made in the drug world. He didn't know anyone in Montana.

Justin nodded in agreement while he pushed his chair in and grabbed one of the bags from Jim. I cleared the table, scraped the plates, and loaded the dishwasher with all the memories of that morning's meal. I looked up to see Justin casually wandering down to Ashley's room to say "good-bye." I expected there to be some type of emotional exchange, but there was nothing but a hollow "good luck" sent in both directions. It always surprised me how apathetic Justin was when he faced serious things. His demeanor would have fooled the unsuspecting to believe he was on his way to basketball camp and looking forward to all the fun. He hurled one final "good-bye" to Ashley and Hayden as he exited the house. Ashley chose not to go to the airport with us. She had nothing more to say. "Good-bye." seemed enough. Hayden stood in the doorway hoping for a treat or at least one last pat before we left. Jim, Justin, and I headed for the airport.

We drove in silence, each of us completely captivated by what was running through our own private thoughts. It was a nice surprise to find a convenient parking spot in Terminal Four, a rarity most days. Jim and Justin pulled all the suitcases out and started for the Terminal. I walked between them. We squeezed into an elevator with three other people loaded with more bags. As we neared the gate, a reservation person and gate agent approached Jim. They knew him from work and seemed interested in meeting his family. We smiled and shook hands and even tried to carry on upbeat small talk, all the while drowning in pain we were desperately trying to hide. I excused myself and walked with Justin to the far end of the gate area where there were plenty of empty seats. Jim shook the gate agent's hand again before he turned and started walking toward us. His smile faded with each step he took. We all sat together in silence.

The time came for Justin to board the airplane. I stood up and on my tiptoes hugged his scruffy neck. Void of any visible emotion, I repeated the same words of hope and encouragement he had heard throughout his life. I let go of Justin to watch him face Jim. All Jim could do was grab Justin up in his arms and sob. He didn't want to let go. The last boarding group was called and Justin picked up the can of soda he had rested on the chair next to him along with his coat and boarding pass and said a final "good-bye." It was time to leave. Justin walked into the jetway and disappeared down the long tunnel. We stood in silence as the jet taxied down the runway and took flight. He was gone, again.

CHAPTER 12

Family Week

One month passed before we heard a word from Justin. It was only through the staff that we learned Justin had arrived safely at the center. They said he was busy "working the program." In those 30 days we had almost forgotten how miserable mornings had been for us for so many years. Now I loved mornings. The smell of the freshly-brewed coffee, coupled with the desert sounds of daylight breaking outside our window, filled my senses with a newly discovered delight. Ashley enjoyed having the bathroom all to herself. The counter top of her once shared space was now loaded with her favorite fruit smelling lotions and carefully assembled collection of hair accessories. Rollers got smashed into the not very accommodating cupboards. Getting ready for school had become an event complete with loud music and sweet scents that escaped from the bathroom as she walked into the hallway. The difference we all felt in our home was made evident in Ashley's glowing smile. These were great mornings.

One afternoon while I was vacuuming the same spot over and over, hoping to suck up a stain, the phone rang. I was so engrossed in what I was doing that I didn't hear the phone until it clicked into the answering machine. I picked up. It was the voice of Justin's counselor encouraging us to attend "Family Week" at the center. My first knee-jerk reaction was to ask if we had to go. I held my tongue and waited until he gave all the details before I hit him with my question. He said it was an important week for Justin in recovery. His last words were direct. We needed to be there.

I resented being told we "needed" to do something outside of live in our new found world of peace. Certainly, Ashley, Jim, and I didn't "need" this. I told the counselor I would check with Jim to see if it would be a possibility. Jim got home and I skirted around the "Family Week" subject even though I gave an otherwise full accounting of my conversation with the counselor. It wasn't long before I half-heartedly threw in the part of the conversation where the counselor said "We needed to be at the upcoming Family Week."

I stood ready to defend my irritation about the whole thing. I didn't want to go; that was obvious. Jim listened carefully and reluctantly agreed with the counselor. We should go to "Family Week." I shook my head feeling an uncomfortable conviction about my whole attitude. "OK, Lord," I said to myself, "my attitude stinks and only You can get me past it." I took a deep breath in hope the fresh air would provide a new outlook. I thought about the note that had to be written to Ashley's teachers.

The note got written and sent. All the arrangements were made to pick up her class work for the week she would be missing school. Jim and I changed our schedules so we would have that time free. The last person in our house to consider was our dog. My good friend Sue took him into her home and promised to give him lots of love. We bought our airline tickets, booked rooms at a B&B recommended by the center, and reserved a car. Everything was packed and ready for the trip. I couldn't shake the dread I felt in my heart. It was a trip I just didn't want to take.

Super Shuttle loaded our bags into their van early on September 27, 1997. We were on our way to a place we knew nothing about, a little town called Marion in the equally unfamiliar state of Montana. We had decided to fly to Seattle, Washington, and drive a rental car the rest of the way. It was fall and we expected the scenery there would be spectacular. The flight went without any problems. Jim directed us to baggage claim where we stood for a short time waiting for our bags to make their appearance on the moving carousel. Ashley grabbed her bag first. She had her bulging backpack already on her back and suitcase handle pulled up ready to go. Jim lifted my bag and then his. It was all going according to plan. The only thing left was the rental car.

We stood in line at the car rental place chatting about the change in weather we felt penetrating our already inadequate jackets. Jim and I both went up to the counter together. Ashley followed closely behind. Jim handed the girl behind the counter his license while Ashley finished telling me a story. Jim's awkward fumbling motion and strange tone of voice told me something was wrong. The weirdest thing had happened. Jim's driver's license had expired, so he would not be able to rent the car. Not a problem, I thought, as I dug into my purse and found my license. I handed it over to the girl and she couldn't believe what she saw. My license would expire on my birthday. My birthday was September 27, that very day. Jim and I couldn't believe we had *both* let our licenses expire. The girl was as shocked as we were, but knew there was nothing she could do about our untimely oversight. Jim backed away from the counter while Ashley and I stood for a minute longer, obviously bewildered.

Slowly Ashley and I walked toward Jim who was standing between the baggage claim and the car rental reservation desk. Several silent moments passed with only the sound of people rushing by us. Ashley mustered up the courage to ask Jim to come up with a plan "B" because he had never failed to have one in the past. We examined every option we could imagine from calling a pilot Jim knew who lived in Seattle, to getting a hotel for the night in an attempt to get our licensed renewed, to the most absurd plan of all… we would take a cab all the way to Marion, Montana. None of the plans worked even though we tried mentally to put each one of them into motion.

Ashley's wrinkled brow indicated she was very worried, and Jim's sighs said that he was becoming increasingly more and more upset. We stood close together in a small desperate huddle not having one idea about what to do next. I closed my eyes for a split second and remembered the fact that we *did* know Someone who lived in Seattle. He would help us! It was the Lord. We needed a God-sized miracle right there on the spot. We began to pray. Jim, Ashley, and I held hands as we lifted up the impossible situation to the Lord. Our prayers were very specific. Jim prayed to God to give us a way to get to Marion, Montana. I prayed we would see the very hand of God move in this unfortunate disappointment. Ashley prayed God would give us the rental car.

Just as we all resounded in "Amen," the girl behind the counter motioned for us to come back to her. She said she saw us praying and it moved her so much she got on the phone and called her supervisor who called his supervisor. We made cursory introductions. There was a way to get us to Marion, Montana. My license was still valid for that day so she would rent us a vehicle for one day and write on the contract the special circumstances, extending the rental for the entire week. As she filled out the extra paperwork and began to write the lengthy explanation, we looked at each other knowing the Lord had heard our cry *and* answered each of our prayers.

I signed all the papers, agreeing to pay for all the extra insurance and gas. I would be the driver on this trip, an unfamiliar duty for me. Our reservation had been for a compact-sized car, nothing fancy. The reservation agent tapped on the counter with the tip of her pen while studying her computer screen.

"Well," she said smugly, "I don't have any small cars to rent to you" She looked up at me and smiled. "You will have to take a luxury car, at the same rate, of course." I looked at Ashley and she could barely contain her enthusiasm. This was so much better than we had planned. The attendant handed us the keys to a Crown Victoria. The extra space and plush velvet-like seats were going to make the trip far more comfortable than we had ever anticipated. The first thing we did, after we were all buckled into our seat belts, was to thank the Lord for blessing us with this car. We felt like we were driving *His* car. What a way to start the week.

Marion, Montana, is a very small town. How small is it, you might ask? It was so small that as soon as you reached the "Welcome to Marion" sign, you were heading out of town. That's right! I'm talking *small*! We crept along on a dirt road until we came to a marker on the road that had been given by the hosts of the B&B as the indicator we were close to the Inn. Jim thought he would be able to guide me through the winding directions, but soon realized the lack of street lights made his expectation far too optimistic. We called our hosts and they were quick to tell us to "Stay put." Someone would be there in a pick-up truck in less than five minutes to direct us to our new home.

While we sat in the darkness waiting for our escort, I prayed. "Lord," I said in the quiet of my heart "Please, make this a beautiful place for Ashley." I peered at her dim reflection in the rearview mirror. She was completely still, gazing out the window into the pitch black night. I wondered what she was thinking. I watched her and thought how much I admired her willingness to make the trip even though she was the one who had to sacrifice the most.

When we told her the trip would mean a full week out of school, she never complained even though I knew she didn't like the idea of missing just one day. She liked school. All of her teachers had prepared packets of homework she would need to complete sometime during the week. Ashley was prepared to do all the work. She brought an enormous selection of pens, pencils, erasers, and paper. Certainly her stash was greater than her need—but that was Ashley, always completely prepared.

My attention shifted from Ashley to the sound of a pickup barreling down the dirt-packed road in front of us. A puff of dust rose up from the darkness and sprayed on our windows just before the truck came to a complete stop beside the driver's window. I rolled the window down and choked as the billowing dust burst into our car.

"Follow me," the faceless voice said. I saw his hand motioning us to drive behind him. It was a challenge for me to navigate the unlit path through the thick veil of fine dirt that was constantly being sprayed across our windshield by the truck in front of us. I followed closely behind.

Then out of nowhere, lights blazed from between the tall evergreens. The vision was so inviting. We were directed by a hand signal, to park in the designated lot close to the house. The man from the pickup jumped out of the truck, and with one hand he extended a warm handshake while he reached for our bags with the other. Ashley was distracted by the two big dogs that nosed at her leg trying to get her attention. A lovely woman came out into the shadow of the dark parking lot to welcome us into her home. She ushered us up the stairs of the white wooden porch and into the brightly-lit living room. It took a moment for my eyes to get adjusted to the illuminated surroundings. The sound of crackling and sputtering logs came from the handmade fieldstone fireplace across the room. Fragrant bunches of vibrant, fresh cut flowers filled rust-colored clay pots and jewel-toned glass vases everywhere. The man and woman instructed us to stand by the fire while they finished hauling our luggage inside. We stood with our hands directly over the flame while the logs popped and spit ash below. It felt so good to our cold bones. Before we knew it, our hosts had all of the bags lined up in a row ready to be dispensed to the bedrooms we would be assigned for the nights. The woman, Nikki, broke the ice by asking us about our trip. I couldn't help but tell her every detail of the "car rental" story and how God took care of the crisis.

She listened intently and together with her husband Larry, announced they had prayed for us every day since the time we made the reservation. They were Christians. This house was another gift from the Lord. His presence was clearly visible at every turn. A verse of Scripture came to my heart as we pulled our bags into our bedrooms. "When he has brought out all his own, he goes on ahead of them, and his sheep follow him because they know his voice" (John 10:4). *Life is such a journey,* I thought as I dug into my suitcase to find my pajamas. The Lord already had come to Marion, Montana. He had prepared the way for us.

The first day of "Family Week" at the Wilderness Treatment Center was interesting. My family laughed when I used the expression "interesting." They felt what I really thought was it was weird. No, it wasn't weird, it was just as I described…interesting. The road from the B&B to the center was not well marked and we thought we had taken the wrong turn several times. It was such a relief when Ashley pointed out the small unfinished wood sign etched with the words "Wilderness Treatment Center." I carefully turned down the road beside the sign. Every 10 feet there were posted speed signs, "5 miles an hour."

In the distance we finally saw another car, framed in a cloud of dirt generated by tires traveling far faster than the legal limit. I commented how anxious those parents must be to start "Family Week." Ashley laughed. At the end of the road was a newly-mowed field which served as the parking lot, obviously in anticipation of many rental cars (after all who cares where you park a rental). There were only a few cars in the lot when we arrived, but by the time we parked and got out of the car that had all changed. Ashley asked Jim if he had any idea where we were supposed to go to start this thing called "Family Week?" Jim and I answered in unison. "We'll just walk in the same direction all the other people are walking." She followed a step or two behind us, not having much confidence in our directions.

The brisk air caused everyone to look as though they were breathing through pockets of vapor, centered squarely in the middle of their face. Pine trees and thick green grass acted as lush background for the two rows of mini-log cabins that lined the driveway. It looked just like the video. All the activity seemed to be centered around what appeared to be the main building on the campus. It reminded me of what we called the "mess hall" in my girl scout camping days. As we approached the entrance we saw the window sills lined with steamy Styrofoam cups of coffee. Cigarette smoke drifted in from the outside. I was annoyed that "smoking" was allowed. Hadn't we all read somewhere cigarettes contained nicotine, a drug?

Ashley thought I was making my comments a bit too loudly. I assured her I'd be quiet, but couldn't help but shake my head while I tried to avoid standing in one of the cigarette-generated clouds of haze. Why would they let these boys smoke? It baffled me. Weren't these people supposed to be professionals? Jim noticed the angst expression on my face.

"Are you OK?" he asked. Of course I was OK. I was just completely irritated that's all. If it was true that first impressions are lasting impressions, then I'd say the program had dropped from about a five (mid-expectations) to less than zero.

We entered the narrow smoky hallway that led us into a big "meeting room" of sorts. Chatter filled the room as families appeared to be reconnecting after the days of separation. The dynamic among the various families was not the kind found at a family reunion. There was a guarded civility. If you didn't know it was "Family Week" you would have thought you were looking at a collection of strangers forced to stand together and engage in meaningless conversation. Smiles floated across the room as people tried to find someone with whom they identified. Several people looked my way. I smiled back and cynically thought, "Yes, buddy we're all in this stinking boat together."

One man gathered up the courage to intrude on the little huddle Jim, Ashley, and I formed while waiting for Justin to make his entrance. He put his hand out to me in an attempt to get acquainted and asked where we lived. I politely said, "Arizona," and contemplated speaking what I really felt…"in hell, sir. Isn't that the state we are all living in?" I was relieved that he didn't seem to catch my subtle disdain about being there. I kept smiling and nodding while I examined his fake tan and ill-fitting toupee. I couldn't help but wonder if he really thought it looked good? I discreetly looked down at my hand, just curious to see if it had turned orange during introductions.

Justin marched right up to us with an entourage of his new "best" friends. He proceeded to make us all laugh with his "right on" impersonations of staff and residents. It was all in good fun, nothing like the tasteless stuff I was thinking. Jim, Ashley, and I became the audience to those clowns. There was no hug, no questions about how we were doing, or answers to our question of how he was doing? It was an uneasy beginning. We immediately identified the director of the program, not by the nametag he had stuck on his shirt, but rather by his unusual gait. Justin had completely nailed it just moments before.

He invited us all to find a seat on one of the hard metal chairs stacked by the wall on the opposite side of the room. Sheets of paper were passed out with the bold heading "Schedule for Family Week." All the chairs had found people to fill them and the director began the introductions and expectations for the days to come. I knew I was already bugged by the smoking, but I grew even more agitated when he said, at least 10 times, these boys all had a *disease*. What a hopeless word. This "disease" he contended had no cure and there was no evidence anywhere that they would ever find one—such a completely dismal life assigned to these young men. The director had lots more to say that day, but I never heard another word.

With regularity I found myself "people watching" before each session began, trying to figure out which person was doing the best "acting" and which person was most "real." There was a boy who sat next to his dad, the one with the toupee and the bottled tan. They rarely spoke to each other or to anyone else. I wondered about their lives. Another boy who sat across from me caught my attention. His parents were obviously divorced, though they both were present and determined to maintain a degree of politeness. After watching them for a short time, it became easy to recognize this boy's tactics as he "worked" them. There was an arrogance he exhibited as he went from one parent to the other purposefully annihilating each one with a well-aimed curt word.

I stopped watching them as I couldn't add their pain to the load I was already carrying myself. Then there was one mother named, Ann. Her strong New York accent and penchant for questioning the validity of every single word uttered by the director or staff, created an atmosphere that boarded on comical. She was the one parent who shot down the dirt road at record speeds each morning, completely ignoring all the posted "5 mile an hour" signs in an effort to be on time for a session. At least 30 minutes late every day, we'd all watch the cloud of dust settle as she slammed her car door shut. Daily the staff reprimanded her for disregarding the clearly visible speed signs and for disrupting the sessions with her tardiness. She always responded by shaking her head as if to beat it into submission. Jim and I often looked at our watches and came to almost pick the minute we'd see her barreling down the road. I wanted desperately to laugh out loud, but never quite felt it would have been appreciated by the discussion leader. Levity didn't have a place at the center at that time.

Every morning we broke up into assigned groups. The purpose of the small group meeting was to give a safe forum for the residents to expose the pain that had "caused" them to spiral into the depths of heavy drug use. The notion that the addiction had been triggered by just "one" thing seemed far too simple to me. I listened to all the theories without saying a word…at first. Then I heard two boys in particular share their hearts. Their stories touched me deeply.

There was the boy from California. Everything about him made me sad. His mom had left his dad when he was very young. He remembered with amazing clarity every detail of his parents split. In a quiet voice he relived everything about that day. The group listened.

He recalled the smells coming from the oven that morning. The kitchen table had old cigar boxes filled with crayons and markers next to a thick stack of used paper. A small boy, just five years old, he had sat at the table diligently working on a self-assigned coloring project. He remembered how he labored over the best way to connect the string of the brightly colored balloons to the hand of his stick figure person. His mom entered the kitchen and brushed his hair with her hand while commenting on the excellent art work. He kept his eyes fixated on his nearly completed picture. The dad was now in the kitchen too. There was something going on between his parents and he felt it. Finally, his mom announced that she was…leaving.

The once-little boy recaptured every sensation he experienced in that moment, and even though he was almost a man, it still broke his heart. His clean-shaven face gave up its macho-mask and became the face of that small child. He looked at his mom, who sat beside him, and asked her why she felt she needed to leave…him. He reminded her of the pictures he had been working on at the kitchen table so long ago. Yes, she remembered them. He wept and sat crunched down into his seat, obviously still hurting deeply. "Mom," he said "I colored that picture for you, but you never took it."

The director of the session stopped the meeting for a time. We all remained still while he waited for that wave of pain to subside. The boy's mom tried to console him by putting her arm on top of his big manly shoulders. He looked up at her and continued pouring out his heart. "Mom,

Dad never packed my lunch box right. You knew exactly how to do it. I missed you everyday." The mom put her head down on his shoulder and whispered something into his ear. He nodded his head and tried to push back the tears.

Later that day, after two more sessions, we had our scheduled lunch break. Jim and Ashley were being entertained by Justin and his buddies while I wandered off toward the table where the boy from California sat alone. He watched me and when I got within earshot, he asked me to sit down with him. I looked at him as I ate my ham sandwich and marveled to myself how much of that five-year-old face peeked out of the 18-year-old frame. His life spilled out all around me as he told one story after another.

My heart throbbed as he spoke. I was compelled to touch him in some small way, so I pushed the tray with the pile of uneaten food to the side and put my hand on his arm. "Oh, dear one," I said, "It is going to be OK." He looked into my eyes with a deeply rooted skepticism. "Oh Lord," I said silently "please help this one." In that moment, he was not just some boy with a troubled family. He was *my* boy. I got up from the table, wrapped my arms around him and together we wept.

Lunch never seemed to be very long, but according to the schedule we always had our allotted 30 minutes. The theme of the session that afternoon was "feelings." We were all surprised when the young man from California began the meeting by blurting out that he had lost true emotions. He was convinced drugs had taken them all away leaving him with nothing more than hollowness. We all listened intently to every word he said, hoping to gain insight into our own lives. He kept his focus directed toward me. I uncomfortably moved back and forth in my seat looking at Jim hoping he'd rescue me from this unwanted attention.

Something was going on and it was something very important for this young man. I resettled in my chair having regained my composure while he recounted every detail of our conversation over lunch. Several members of the group began to stare at me. I became more and more uneasy. It wasn't that I felt our conversation was extremely personal, it was just that I hadn't planned to have it reviewed by the 30 families and staff members. I was amazed by all he had gotten out of our simple little exchange. It somehow had reached a part of his heart he thought was dead.

His eyes surveyed the group when he asked "When I cry is it a reaction to pain, like an involuntary response, or is it something coming out of my heart? Do I have any feelings left?" The discussion leader redirected the question in an attempt to take the group away from answering him. His concern was never addressed.

I waited until I thought the leader had finished her offhanded shift in the track and raised my hand. She granted me permission to speak to the group. I first looked at Ashley to make sure she wasn't embarrassed by my request. She smiled and put her hand on my back. I took a deep breath and looked around the room. It was absolutely still. It felt as if everyone had held their breath to keep the room in such a state of hush. The California boy kept his eyes fixed on mine.

I began, "The answer to your question is…yes. You are experiencing real feelings when you laugh and when you cry. They haven't died." His eyes filled with water. I knew every family in that room had asked themselves the same thing. His question belonged to all of us. The answer was freeing. The sound of tissue being ripped from the teeth of cardboard boxes broke the silence. There were a lot of tears. It was as if some were celebrating the life of the "feelings" long ago given up for dead while others mourned their loss. It was a very emotional day.

There was one other boy I would never forget. He was older than the rest of them. In one of the sessions he spoke of his life in a way that conflicted with the boy we all saw in front of us. He was pressed by a staff member to bridge the gap between what he said and what we saw. Finally, he exposed his real life to us, like thunder announcing the long-awaited storm. The voice from the once-gentle face articulated great anger. He stomped his foot and cried out in anguish as he spoke about a father we would never meet. His dad was an alcoholic, not pleased by anything or anyone… especially this son. In his young years, feedback from his dad took the form of criticism. He had never been able to do things in a way considered "acceptable" by his dad. It seemed impossible for him to do anything "right." The destructive words of his dad stripped him of any reason for trying. No matter what this boy did, it never seemed to be the right or best thing. Even when there was an accomplishment to celebrate, it was always received by his dad with "disappointment." In a quiet, broken voice, this young man revealed the greatest pain in his memory. He had been "disowned" by his own dad.

With those words, I quickly joined him in that same storm. My heart started to beat faster, an invisible cold wind blew over me and I couldn't prevent tears from forming in my eyes. I stared blankly up at the ceiling begging God to rescue me from this unbearable moment. I tried everything imaginable not to internalize the story that had broken open in front of me.

My wedding ring became a good distraction. I counted the stones and even rubbed the wide gold band on my sleeve, commenting to myself how much better my ring looked after it was polished by the jeweler. It slipped back on my finger easily. The ease of its return to my finger made me ask myself if maybe I had lost weight in my finger. What a ridiculous thought. I searched for any distraction to keep my attention away from the boy whose voice was all I could hear.

None of the diversions or private questions could tune out even one syllable of this boy's life. He continued for some time talking about the hurt he endured by the words of a drunken dad. The pain he carried made life hard to live. The story was finished and the room was absolutely stilled by his life's story. The only thing that could be heard among the sounds of people clearing their throats or an occasional cough was the steady sobbing of one person. It was me.

This young man in the tan turtleneck sweater had described my life, and it was the first time I had ever heard anyone say it out loud. Every word he said mimicked the very things I had never assigned words to describe. The woman in front of me leaned back toward me. Her red tear-stained eyes told their own story. She handed me the box of tissues she had stuck under her chair. Jim put his arm around me and Ashley moved her chair so she could snuggle close too.

The counselor allowed the moment to linger for some time before he acknowledged the hand of a man who was sitting way in the back of the room by the windows. The man bent forward in his seat and asked if he could address this young man. The counselor cocked his head to one side and nodded his approval. The young man faced the stranger, moving to the front of his seat to get a clear visual of the voice from the back of the room.

"Forget him," was the advice the man had waited so patiently to deliver. "You don't need him. Look how far you've come without him. Forget him. It is the best thing for your life." The man ended his statement to a round of applause and loud "yes's" from other parents and residents. My eyes stayed on the face of the group leader awaiting this "professional" to jump into the conversation. Moments dragged by, but there was no response from the counselor who stood with crossed arms propped up against the wall. If my eyes had any power, they would certainly have pulled words out of his mouth. I kept thinking *say something....Certainly you aren't going to let this destructive advice stand?*

I looked over at the man who had just dished out his words of wisdom and thought what a "stupid bozo" he was for offering such poor counsel. The group leader didn't move from his position. He just stood there not speaking. Finally, he stepped away from the wall and said, "Well, that was pretty powerful stuff." He smiled at the young man and continued, "I'm glad you said all that you said. You are very courageous." He finished by adding a thank you to the man in the back row for sharing his thoughts.

What? My insides went ballistic. Did I really hear the counselor (an obvious dud) thank the bozo for *that* advice? Jim looked over at me and knew I wouldn't be able to contain myself for one more minute. My hand flew up in the air, Ashley whispered, "Oh, no" as the room turned and gave me their complete attention.

The counselor said, "Justin's mom, please take the floor." In the seconds before I spoke, I asked the Lord to forgive me for virtually calling the counselor a moron, but I just couldn't ask for forgiveness regarding my thoughts about the man in the back of the room. He was a total bozo.

"Please, Lord," I continued to pray, "give me the right words to begin a healing in the heart of a broken boy." I cleared my throat and began by saying how important it was to speak life into each other. We need to speak words that build up our lives. I looked directly into the wounded eyes of this boy, almost a man, and said, " I know your life. Everything you said came out of the chapters of my *own*. I know your ache. There *is* a way to heal from this deep hurt and it is *not* to forget about your dad. The answer to all the hurt and pain is simple…it is forgiveness." Healing would come when he understood the power of forgiveness in his life.

The boy looked awestruck by this new thinking. "You did that?" he asked in a hesitant voice.

I smiled and continued, "For years I prayed that the Lord would help me do the impossible… forgive… my dad. I continued to visit him and even tried to help him when he needed it, but I had not at that time, come to the place of true forgiveness. Then one day, when I didn't expect it, the Lord answered my prayer. I forgave my dad. The hurt I had from him was replaced by an overwhelming love for him. It is a love I carry to this day." The young man's sobbing face fell into his hands. The parents and boys sat soundless as if someone had pushed an imaginary mute button. The director of the group propped his arm against the chair next to him while he watched everyone. Ashley began gently rubbing my back. The room remained quiet while my mind took me back to that day, the day I forgave my dad. I will never forget it.

My dad had suffered a small stroke and was recuperating in a nursing home. Karen was good about keeping me well-informed regarding his health. I lived in another state and was certainly not able to visit him as often as I would have liked. It was time for me personally to check on dad. I jumped on a plane and headed for Rhode Island. Karen picked me up at the airport and we drove to the facility. When we arrived, the dinner trays were making their rounds. The smell of over-cooked meat and baked potatoes drifted across the waiting room helping to disguise other less pleasant odors.

I will never forget the scene. Karen and Dad entered the room, her arm carefully tucked under his. I went up to him and kissed his cheek. He sat down on an old scratched, wooden chair that had obviously been through many visits before ours. We chatted. Karen's contagious laughter rang out all around the room. Occasionally, I would insert a thought or a funny story, though I felt something serious going on inside me.

I had every reason to be angry with my dad. He had spent most of my life pointing out my flaws. I was loaded with them. For years I believed dad hated me. After all, at one point he had even disowned me. His words persistently stung my heart, though they had been delivered decades earlier. I watched the dynamic between Karen and Dad while the Lord spoke to my heart. "Pam, I forgave you. Give *my* forgiveness to him."

The moment caught me completely off guard. The hurt I had felt from my dad from all the years suddenly disappeared. In one unexplainable moment it was gone. I looked at this man, my dad, and longed to be close to him. I loved him. The late afternoon shadows broke through the window announcing the end of the day. A nurse came up to us and with a smile said, "Your dad is needed in the dining room." He pushed himself up out of the chair while she folded her hand gently around his arm. I went right up to his face, those piercing blue eyes looking right into my heart.

"Dad," I could barely squeak out a word with the boulder-sized lump I felt lodged in my throat, "I love you."

His face crumbled into tears as he sobbed "I love you too, Pammy." Karen and I both quietly whimpered as he slowly ambled with the nurse toward the sweet smell of apple pie. When Karen and I got into the car, she put her hand on mine and said with great tenderness, "Pam, you have forgiven Dad." Yes I had, and that forgiveness birthed in me a type of love I had never known before. It was forgiveness that restored my life. That was the story I told the assembled group.

The counselor cleared his throat in an attempt to break the silence and get everyone's attention. Jim handed me a small paper cup filled with ice water. I took a deep breath and slowly sipped on the water. From the back of the room came a question, "How do you forgive someone who doesn't care about you?" The Lord pushed me to address him in kindness. My voice cracked while I said, "Forgiveness is not about the other person. Forgiveness is about you. It is the one thing that allows you to …move… on."

The man continued to aggravate me with his questions. "Mrs. Cox, maybe you didn't have it as rough as this kid. You certainly don't look like you had his type of life."

Now I wanted to walk down to that *bozo* and throttle him. My mind went into overdrive as I silently relived my life at the hand of my father—such as the many times my Dad called me on the phone just to curse me. No, I hadn't said a word about all the nights my distraught mother stood at the front window waiting for my drunken father to show up. No, I failed to mention how I just never quite lived up to my potential. Though it was true, I hadn't shared the intimacies of my life in front of the group. I knew the depth of the despair those details had brought to me.

I shook my head while my mind silently reviewed the uncanny parallel between my life and the life of this young man. The group continued to look at me as if waiting for me to respond to the assault from the back of the room. I looked up at the leader, and even he appeared to be anticipating my response. I gulped the last swallow of water from my small cup and placed it at my feet and said, "I… have…lived… this young man's life. I understand his pain. What I look like now has nothing to do with what has happened in my life. There is nothing more powerful in life than forgiveness. It turns bitterness into blessing. When Jesus Christ is your Lord, He transforms the troubled heart into the triumphant heart. If you trust God to take the hate for your Dad out of your heart, He will. You will live in a new place of freedom."

There was no answer from the back of the room. The young man nodded as if he were taking it all in, expecting to sort it all out later. My eyes caught Justin's as he raised his eyebrow to let me know he knew that the answer was forgiveness. I was surprised the counselor didn't cut me off long before I got to the end. I had thrown the schedule way off. No one complained.

Each counseling session began with one of the fundamental components of AA. It was hard for me to relate to a lot of the "counseling" especially when we were talking about people with a terminal "disease." The AA approach really rubbed me the wrong way when a staff member told the group to remember "anything" can be your higher power. During one of the "higher power" discussions, I had to ask the question. "Can every higher power heal you?" That proved to be a great discussion question. The group leader chided me with the words "Pam, not everyone here believes in your God." *My God?* I thought. That was the problem. We were talking about trusting a god that was… manufactured…used and owned by people. The only One who could help any of us get through this drug-induced nightmare was God, the one and only true God. I didn't say another word about it. I just listened and prayed.

There were many tears shed during the first few days of the sessions. Ashley cried as much as Jim and I. One day after a full day of listening to stories about the lives of so many devastated families including our own, I asked the Lord to please provide Ashley with some wonderful surprise. I prayed the Lord would bless her in a very special, personal way. I couldn't imagine what it would be, but I knew the Lord was very creative. When we pulled into the driveway of our B&B, our hosts ran out to greet us. They were very excited. It seemed that through the various conversations they'd had with Ashley over the past days they had learned how much she loved to ride horses. They had a very special surprise for Ashley.

"Ashley," said Larry, "How would you like to ride one of our prize Arabians?" Her mouth dropped open. She could hardly believe what she was hearing. Jim immediately said how incredible it was they had thought of her. Their horses were show horse—not trail horses. Nikki assured Jim that Ashley would have the ride of her life. "Well, Ashley, are you up for this?"

"Absolutely!" was Ashley's instant reply. We all walked toward the barn not knowing what to expect. Larry handed Ashley a pair of boots and hoisted her on top of this giant, elegant steed. His name was "Lightning." The dappled hair of his mane danced as he pranced before us. We watched the performance of a lifetime. He trotted to the side, curtsied, and bowed his head with aristocratic grace. It was clear he knew we were watching and he was ready to put on a masterful show. Ashley giggled with delight as we praised her for getting the horse to perform such difficult maneuvers, perfectly. Ashley's face gleamed as she clutched the saddle's horn and moved into the next part of his act. Never in her life had she come close to touching such a magnificent creature. Now she was fixed in its saddle.

Jim and I stood star struck. Lightning was quite a showman. For over an hour they paraded around the barn, both so proud to have come to know the other. Ashley hadn't smiled that much in days. The tears from earlier had all dried up and all that was left of that day was the sparkle in her eyes. What a wonderful surprise. As I watched Ashley on Lightning, I whispered an audible prayer to the Lord, thanking Him for His goodness. Another answered prayer.

It was when we came home from the fourth day of the program I noticed the "markers" we had used to direct us back to the B&B. One clump of bright red trees stood right next to the narrow, winding dirt road. I was reminded of the place in the Old Testament where the Lord made a provision for the Israelites to keep them on the right road as they walked in the wilderness. In so many ways I felt like we were in the wilderness too. God provided a pillar of clouds by day and a pillar of fire by night for them. That cluster of trees clothed in fire red and sun-kissed yellow became my "pillar." It always led me home.

Our time in Montana was difficult. We had all thought that we had cried every last tear we could possibly squeeze out, only to find a flood waiting in the wings ready to be released. Jim and I stayed up late into the night replaying all the events of each day resolved to find something positive. We were drained.

On our last day, we were asked to meet with Justin's counselor in private. The purpose of the meeting was to discuss the next step, called "placement." The day was so beautiful the staff decided to hold the meetings outside. Small circles of folding chairs were positioned across the grassy area between the buildings. The deep emerald green color of the pine trees shimmered in the light of the sun. Jim, Ashley, and I found our places quickly. Most people squinted as they walked past us, trying to see through the blinding daylight, while looking to identify their appointed places.

Justin's counselor, Susan, sat with us completing our small circle. She began by telling us what observations she had made after interacting with Justin on a personal level for several weeks. She strongly believed his drug-using days were over. The next step, of great importance, was to send Justin to a halfway house for at least nine months if not longer. Jim interjected we would need help finding a halfway house in Arizona, as we were totally unfamiliar with them.

She nodded, but believed Justin would do better out of state completely. I could see by Jim's expression he was thinking about the money again. If I had a penny for every time I read that man right, we'd have been millionaires. Jim asked her what would something like that cost? Bingo…I knew it! She said that it depended on where we sent him and it ranged anywhere from $1,000 to $1,500 per month. Jim's eyes grew so wide I could see part of the white over the frames of his glasses.

Ashley leaned over to me and whispered "Mom, do we have that much money?" I patted her little arm and assured her that God would help us find it. Susan continued to talk about the two houses she thought might work best for Justin. One house, the cheaper one, was in Michigan. The other was in Louisiana. Susan asked us if we were disappointed by her recommendation not to send Justin home after the program. I quickly responded with "definitely not." Jim concurred along with Ashley. We had come to love the quiet safety of our home. It was imperative we keep it that way as long as possible. Susan motioned to another staff member to bring Justin to our meeting. He plopped down on the chair beside her. Jim and I knew immediately things were all… wrong. The clues were everywhere.

First, Justin wore the sunglasses he had purchased with the money he had stolen from us. Jim and I called those his "drug glasses." Justin always had a belligerent attitude the moment he put on those shades. The antagonistic body language was back. What was it about those glasses, we often asked ourselves? I was distracted by the fact his eyes were hidden by the deep gray color of the tinted lens. It was nearly impossible for me to keep my attention on Susan when what I really wanted to do was rip those blasted glasses right off his face.

There was another clue something was wrong. Justin sat in his seat like the "old" days, one arm flung over the back of the chair while the other hand tapped out a beat on his pant leg. He had tuned us out…completely.

The third and most disturbing clue was Justin's unwillingness to rationally consider any halfway house except the one in Louisiana. He stood indignantly firm on his decision to go to that one, and that was the end of any discussion. Oddly enough, Susan stood in support of him. I was disgusted with them both. Had he been able to con *them* too? Didn't she see all the red flags being waved right in front of her?

Jim shifted back and forth in his seat sighing as he mentally put the pencil to what this would mean financially. "Do we have to make that decision right here on the spot?" Jim managed to ask.

"Well, Mr. Cox, whichever house you choose, it will take lots of coordinating and planning before it will happen. I was hoping we would have this all hammered out before you left today."

Justin took his "drug glasses" off and rested them on his knee. I stared at them while Jim probed Susan for more information regarding the differences between the halfway houses. It took all of my energy not to lean over and grab those glasses so that I could have the supreme pleasure of smashing them under my foot. I thought about how I was gracefully going to nab those specks throughout the whole discussion on the pros and cons of each house.

Justin had made up his mind and it appeared Susan had made up her mind too. I hated that. I felt like we were really at "Family Week" to get us prepared for the next step, the real agenda, a halfway house and an immediate financial commitment. Susan saw how turned off I had become, and tried to get me back on board by saying that she and Justin had come to that decision independently.

What? I thought. *Was that supposed to make it our decision too? What business did she have making any part of this decision? It had nothing to do with her.*

Jim took a deep breath and said "OK. We want to do the right thing for Justin, and you believe this house is the right thing for him. We will send him to the one in Louisiana. I guess we should be glad you're in agreement, Justin."

The "drug glasses" clung to Justin's leg tightly as he jiggled his leg up and down. Ashley recognized the glasses and cupped her hand to the side of her mouth to ensure no one heard the words she whispered to me. "Mom, those are the sunglasses Justin bought with the money he stole from you, aren't they?" I half-smiled a "yes" trying not to give my contempt away to anyone else in the circle.

I was furious. Susan asked Jim to sign the paperwork for the transfer while assuring me we had made the right decision. While Susan reviewed the papers, Jim tapped my shoulder. He had heard Ashley's question. He glanced at the "drug glasses" now resting safely on top of Justin's leg. Jim was mad too. Susan tucked the paperwork back in her binder and voiced what a pleasure it had been to work with Justin. He was going to succeed; she had no doubts about it.

I couldn't believe what I was hearing. She had such enormous confidence in something she apparently had little understanding about. All the signs for impending doom were staring her in the face. Justin was going to use drugs soon. Jim, Ashley, and I knew this had not been a good "Family Week." It was finally time to wrap things up and say good-bye. Susan extended a handshake along with "have a safe trip home." Justin slowly got up from his chair, barely catching the glasses that were on their way to the ground. He hugged each of us with stiff arms and air kisses. A counselor interrupted our moment by announcing to us that Justin had finished the second part of the program and would begin the final phase the next week. He would be on an 18-day trek into the wilderness. Justin nodded his head up and down and gave a "two thumbs up" to two of his buddies while he ran ahead of us as we walked to the car. It was obvious he was more interested in saying good-bye to the families of those he hardly knew.

We got into our car and yelled out a final farewell, but he barely seemed to notice. Ashley got irritated with me for not rolling up my window and leaving without another word. She couldn't stand the way Justin acted toward us. I started the car and Justin came running up to Jim's side of the car to tell him how glad he was we made the trip. While I backed up, he waved and mouthed "thank you" to Ashley. He sprinted back to rejoin the group of buddies he left assembled in the parking lot. As we traveled down the road in the middle of the caravan, we knew things had not changed. Jim muttered his contempt toward Justin for "daring" to wear those sunglasses in front of us. We all agreed his audacity was hard to handle. The pelts of tiny rocks hidden in the blasts of sand pounded the sides of the car. We were anxious to be off those roads and back on the solid feel of the blacktop. It was time to head home.

CHAPTER 13

The Halfway House

Everything at home was just as we had left it. No surprises. The anger I had felt toward Justin slowly subsided. Three weeks went by before a staff member called. It was the counselor who had just completed the "18-day trek" with Justin. He wanted to tell us about an event on that journey. On the fourth day, Justin went to him and commented on how he appeared to be different from the other counselors. "What made him different?" Tim was quick to respond. "Justin," he told him, "the difference in my life is Jesus." Each morning, thereafter, when the breakfast had been cleared and the heavy packs settled into the muscles of each one's back, Justin and Tim prayed as they hiked together. It made the trail easier as they spoke to the Lord aloud with each footstep that sunk deep into the snow-packed trail. I loved hearing all of that. What hope it brought me. And once again, I was reminded that Justin had not slipped through the Lord's fingers. God could reach Justin anywhere, even on the frozen trek of an isolated trail.

Jeremiah 32:27 spoke to my heart; "I am the LORD, the God of all mankind. Is anything too hard for me?" Nothing was too hard for God. I knew that was the truth.

It wasn't long after my conversation with Tim that Justin called. At first he was very excited and wanted to share all the details of his difficult long journey into the woods. Then for some reason his mood changed and the discussion centered on his next living place. I told him we thought the decision to send him to Louisiana was a done deal. It was my understanding the center had agreed to get things rolling on their end. I had even followed up with them regarding the plan and was assured everything was set up for him in Louisiana. Justin became more and more agitated. Things had changed.

For some reason the center decided, without any warning, not to make any arrangements for the "students" and relinquished that job to the parents. It was certainly possible that other parents had resisted the pressure of making a snap decision regarding the financial commitment of a halfway house while at "Family Week." Oddly enough, though, no one ever called to tell us about our new responsibility. This lack of communication would cause a real problem as Justin would be released in four days and didn't have a place to go. I told him not to panic because God was bigger than this mess up. It would somehow all work out. The tone in Justin's voice lowered making it evident he had calmed down a bit and was even somewhat excited about "getting on with his life." I made all the arrangements.

The day Justin arrived in Gonzales, Louisiana, he called us. The flight had gone smoothly with only one connection. Already he found things about the place he didn't like: a weird director, strange spicy food, and the thick almost unintelligible Louisiana accent. He shared his impressions of the unusual Cajun speech which made for a good laugh. The telephone he was using was located outside amid intense humidity and threatening rain clouds making our conversation less than enjoyable. Most of the boys in the house were from different programs across the country and only a couple had come with him from Montana.

He rattled off a list of things he "needed." The list never changed over the years. It was always the same things…socks and underwear. It occurred to me while I was jotting down the list that we must have bought Justin at least 100 pairs of underwear and even more socks over the years. His final request was for a bike so he could get a job. I knew Jim would agree to that, so I told him to find a bike and call us back with the price. He had all the information about it right at his finger tips. It was $200.

What! I thought I had just heard the boy who does not have one single dime to his name, ask his parents for a bike that would cost *them* $200.

"Mom," he said "it is perfect for this area. I promise I will take care of it and lock it up at work." I must have had a meltdown because for some stupid reason, I agreed. He gave me the phone number for the bike place and in the minutes remaining before he hung up, asked about Jim and Ashley wondering when we would visit him. The conversation always seemed to end up the same way. I told him we loved him and prayed into the phone right before we hung up.

When Jim got home, I did take a little heat for approving the "absurd" bike. Jim spoke to the owner of the little bike store and was assured the bike was ideal for Justin's needs. I watched Jim dig out his master card and slowly read the numbers to the man on the other end. Jim didn't want to buy Justin that bike. The expectation irritated him.

The conversation we had after Jim put away his credit card was one I knew was coming, yet dreaded. "Pam, it's always about *money*," Jim said in great despair. Yes, it seemed to be the case. It had been years since we had had a contact with Justin that didn't include something he needed us to buy for him. It was a double-edged sword. On one hand we wanted to encourage him any way that we could, and if it meant underwear and socks, that's what we bought. On the other hand, we were disgusted by the constant demands. This time it was a bike. It was always something.

Gonzales, Louisiana, was a typical southern town. Thick, heavy air surrounded us as we made our way to "Power House" for our first visit. We pulled into the small parking lot of what appeared to be a motel. The rooms were all facing the outside and a long porch encircled the entire structure.

Several boys were playing basketball while three others raked wet piles of dead grass and withered leaves. Jim got out of the car and knocked on one of the doors. A boy in his mid-teens poked his head out and volunteered to get Justin. Ashley and I sat in the car watching the boys push the metal rakes around the yard. They certainly didn't work hard at their job and spent more time joking and playing than collecting the remnants of fall. Nearly empty dark green garbage bags were stationed all over the grounds. Ashley and I wondered how any of them would ever get filled. We waited patiently in the car while Jim stood in the doorway of Justin's room, waiting too.

It had been three months since we had seen Justin and we all expected he would be anxiously anticipating our arrival. Instead, we realized someone had to wake him from a nap. I was so disappointed. We had just been on a long flight, from Arizona to New Orleans, Louisiana. We had rented a car and driven several hours to get to his town. He wasn't sitting somewhere all dressed, ready for our long-awaited visit. I felt as if we were treated like an inconvenience.

Finally, Justin appeared, gave Jim a hug, said a few words, and together they walked toward the car. I rolled down my window and smiled a big hello trying to hide my feelings. He stuck his head into the car and yawned in between a few vague sleepy words of welcome. The cold weather didn't seem to awaken him much, even though he stood bare-footed wearing only a T-shirt and jeans. I was frozen just looking at him. Where was his jacket? All weekend I asked the same question over and over, "Where's your jacket?" (It was a mom thing.)

We spent a little bit of time in his room. It was more like a two bedroom apartment complete with a living room, kitchen, and laundry facilities. We sat on an old, hard couch while Justin told stories about past roommates, new roommates, the director, and the AA meetings. I tried to act interested, but really none of it interested me… at all. I wanted to know the important stuff. Where was the Lord in all of this? Did Justin see Him? Was there a good church close by? I couldn't hold my tongue any longer. "Justin, what about Jesus, where is He in all of this?" I was stunned by his response,

"Mom, the director and staff here frown on me talking about Jesus."

What? I had spoken to the director myself and she had led me to believe the underpinnings of their approach to AA were Jesus. She had even gone so far as to assure me other Christians were in the program and would be there to help him along the way. I was disgusted. Jim saw the revolted look that took over my face.

"Son," Jim asked, "have you found a good church?" Justin nodded and said he had been going every week to a Baptist church which wasn't too far from his house. A man from the church picked him up each Sunday. He had become friends with the youth pastor and felt the church had become his home away from home. "I can't wait for you to meet my new church family. You will love them!" Jim and I hung onto the sweetness of those words.

After a full day of eating out, walking around the mall, a new haircut, and lots of laughter, it was time to get him back to his house for the nightly meeting. We kissed each other goodbye and promised to be back to pick him up first thing in the morning for church.

A gray Sunday morning arrived without dampening our excitement about picking up Justin for church. It took me by surprise to find him all cleaned up, ready to go. He climbed into the back seat with Ashley while quizzing her about her first impressions of Gonzales. She was quick to say she thought it was a dirty, damp town with not much to offer. Her honest assessment made him laugh. We pulled into the parking lot and joined other families who were making their way to the front door of the little church. We found a place to sit in a section to the left of the middle of the worship center. The congregation began to file in and warmed us with welcoming hugs and information packets. The preacher wasn't the best orator I had ever heard, but it was the best time with the Lord I had ever experienced. The teaching was solid and we were surrounded by loving people. It was exactly what I thought worship should be.

In the middle of the message, the pastor invited people to come forward and pray for each other in the front of the church. It was obvious this was a common practice, as many people rushed to the altar. I hadn't planned on participating until a woman came up to me. I had just met and spoken to her briefly. She took my hand and led me to the front with her. Ordinarily I would have felt strange making that move, but in that moment it felt like it was exactly what I should be doing.

We stood holding hands in the front of the church surrounded by many people doing the same thing. She told me she understood the difficulties we had had with Justin for so many years. It was her heartfelt resolve to be his "Louisiana mom" in my absence. I closed my eyes while she prayed out loud. A familiar scenario came to my mind. It was one I had imagined in my dreams many times before, but this time I was awake. In the vision I was running in a race holding a baton in front of me. The force of the wind made it difficult for me to hold onto the stick, but it was important I only release it when I felt it grasped by the faceless woman way off in the distance. The hand of the woman was always outstretched toward me, but she was too far away to reach it. It was as if I was watching someone in slow motion coming toward me but really not moving at all. It was my crazy dream that erupted into what was meant to be prayer time.

The sound of murmured voices continued to fill the air while I quieted my mind once again and thought about details of the dream. The woman was actually running toward me at warp speed. My hand shook as I held the small piece of wood against the unrelenting blasts of air. The woman blew by me so fast I barely got a glimpse of her face. It was when she wrenched the baton out of my grip that I recognized her. It was this woman. My heart pounded loudly in my chest while my whole body grew clammy. I opened my eyes to more closely examine the woman who had become the face of the once blank image. She continued to pray with her eyes tightly shut as if she hadn't noticed my uneven breathing or sweaty palms. I closed my eyes and returned to the strange dream I had left behind. What did it mean?

The Lord spoke to my heart, "Pam, you are my child and you need rest. I am putting my child, Justin, into the care of this woman, for a time." I cried. I had been given the privilege of bringing Justin into the world and now it was as if I had to give him up. As difficult as the journey had been, I didn't know if I was ready to release him into someone else's care. It wasn't really about letting go of Justin into the care of this "new" mom that troubled me. It was something more overwhelming than that. The time had come for me to give Justin over to the Lord…completely.

I sensed the warmth of the Lord's love around me, as I let go of the woman's hands and fell to my knees. It *was* time for me to finally rest. I thought of Hannah in the Bible. She was an Old Testament woman who had promised God if He gave her a son she would give him back to the Lord. How impossible that moment must have been for Hannah when she stood at the temple holding the small hand of her son, waiting to place him into the care of the High Priest. And so it was with me. I awkwardly climbed back to my feet and hugged the woman while we both wept. Slowly I moved down the aisle and returned to my seat beside Justin, squeezing past Ashley and Jim as I moved into my place.

The congregation burst into singing "Amazing Grace." I could only listen to the words as my mouth wasn't able to retrieve any voice. Justin raised his arms high and joined in the harmonious praises to the Holy One. I gently wrapped my arm around his waist while whispering to the Lord. "Your grace *is* amazing Lord. Justin is yours, completely."

The calendar said it was early December, but my spirit told me it was Christmas. I pondered over the words I had heard in my heart while I stood beside Justin. The voice had called Justin His child. "Oh Lord," I continued to pray, "I believe Justin *is* your son. Help him know You more and…help me keep letting go."

We went back to Louisiana several more times. The routine became easier with each trip. Ashley and I got louder and louder as we sang to the tunes on the radio all the way from New Orleans to Gonzales. Justin had his ups and downs. One of his roommates had relapsed and tried to commit suicide. Another boy had been killed in a tragic motorcycle accident close to the house. Other boys ran away while new boys with bad attitudes started the program. Justin stuck it out. He complained constantly about the AA approach to life. He knew the answer, and His name was Jesus. His faith was tested often by the staff and the other boys in the house, but he stayed firm. Often he'd call us to unload feelings that he was losing his footing. In the course of our conversation we would always end up at the same place, the feet of the Lord. Psalm 50:15, became very important in those days. "Call upon me in the day of trouble; I will deliver you, and you will honor me." I often repeated that verse and the ones below late into the night, believing they would give him rest.

"For the eyes of the Lord are on the righteous and his ears are attentive to their prayer, but the face of the Lord is against those who do evil" (1 Pet. 3:12).

"The angel of the LORD encamps around those who fear him, and he delivers them (Psa. 34:7).

"Planted in the house of the LORD, they will flourish in the courts of our God" (Psa. 92:13).

Justin thrived in his new arsenal of comfort.

Months went by and gradually Justin began to back away from church. He always had a million reasons why he hadn't been able to go. His attendance at a family's home Bible study became sporadic, and after a time we rarely heard about the youth pastor who had once been considered his lifeline. Even the "new mom" had fallen by the wayside. I constantly reminded Justin how dangerous it was to step back from the Lord and other believers. He was in a battle and it was raging all around him. It was no time to move away, it was time to press in like never before.

With each word I spoke, I imagined in my own mind what that might look like. Holy angels in full armor posted at their stations in front of every door and window. A battalion of unholy angels dashed at every turn, their efforts hopelessly thwarted by a holy multitude. I trusted the Lord for the victory. God's plan of attack was always on my mind. "Keep your armor on, Pam!" It was the mantra that played over and over in my head. Many times during the day I got into my best fighting position...on my knees. The Bible was filled with victory "The weapons we fight with are not the weapons of the world. On the contrary, they have divine power to demolish strongholds" (2 Cor.10:4).

Night after night I begged the Lord to keep Justin secure in Him. I prayed these words over Justin each night, even though we were thousands of miles apart.

> He will cover you with his feathers,
> and under his wings you will find refuge;
> his faithfulness will be your shield and rampart.
>
> You will not fear the terror of night,
> nor the arrow that flies by day,
> nor the pestilence that stalks in the darkness,
> nor the plague that destroys at midday.
>
> A thousand may fall at your side,
> ten thousand at your right hand,
> but it will not come near you.
>
> You will only observe with your eyes
> and see the punishment of the wicked.
>
> If you make the Most High your dwelling—
> even the LORD, who is my refuge
> then no harm will befall you,
> no disaster will come near your tent.
>
> For he will command his angels concerning you
> to guard you in all your ways.
>
> —Psalm 91:4-11

It never failed, however, when all the lights were turned out and my last prayer uttered, fear gripped me. What if Justin continued down this path, isolated from Christians? Would he no longer see God's hand in his life? Would the world crowd in so much he would forget about the Lord altogether? Maybe. Inevitably, the Lord calmed my heart with His Word: "For the LORD your God is a merciful God; he will not abandon or destroy you or forget the covenant with your forefathers, which he confirmed to them by oath" (Deut. 4:31). Yes, God would not forsake Justin, nor would He forsake me!

The halfway house experience in Louisiana had come to an end. Justin had been there for 10 months. He was offered a job driving a truck for a window company in a neighboring town. One of the residents of the halfway house moved into an apartment and offered Justin one of the bedrooms. It all sounded so positive. We were excited for him. Jim, Ashley, and I even flew out to help him get set up in his first apartment. The local Target store provided all the stuff he would need to live on his own. Our arms were loaded down with all the necessities of daily life. Jim laughed at me, as I coordinated everything from the shower curtain to the coffee cups. Justin appreciated how nice it looked when it was all hung up and put away.

CHAPTER 14

The Mistake

In three months it all collapsed. Justin wanted to come home. He had a bad roommate, the guy who lived next door was a druggie, and he wasn't making enough money to pay all his bills. It sounded reasonable, but the idea of having Justin home stirred up all the old fears we had promised ourselves we would never taste again. Our home was the calm environment we had always wanted it to be. Ashley blossomed in the pleasantness of her newfound peace. She believed she would never have to worry about an outburst from Justin again. I never wanted to disturb what had taken us so long to acquire. On the other hand, Justin *was* our son. He needed a place to live, and what better place than…home.

The idea of his return haunted me. Jim and I sat up until late into the night praying and sorting out our reasons, fears, and motives. Did we want Justin home because it cost so much to finance an apartment for him? (That was a question I directed at Jim.) Or was it because he was our son and we felt trapped by a sense of responsibility? (That one was from me.) What if having Justin home was as bad as it was before? What if things got even worse? I wrestled with the predominant question, the truth that lurked far below anything I verbalized. Was I ready to risk everything…again?

It appeared Justin had stopped using drugs, so maybe the time was right for him to come home. We prayed and asked counsel from some of our close family members and friends. It was a difficult decision. Ashley thought we were of our minds to even consider letting him back into our house.

"He doesn't care about us, Mom. He only cares about himself. Don't let him come back home." Ashley couldn't hide her feelings. Jim and I didn't share Ashley's deep anger toward Justin. Sure, we were upset and disappointed and all of that, but mostly we were hurt and concerned…for him. What would be the best thing for Justin? I prayed for direction.

The thought of bringing Justin home, upset me to the core. The thought of *not* bringing him home didn't bring any peace either. After a few days of going back and forth, Jim and I agreed to bring Justin home because we just didn't want any regrets. We discussed with Ashley why we felt it was the right thing to do. She couldn't believe we would be willing to take more abuse from him. No, we were not willing to take *any* abuse. We were willing, however, to help him stay on track…drug free.

The whole atmosphere in our home changed. No one talked about it, but we felt it. It was as if we were already missing the peace we had enjoyed for so many months. Ashley tried to pretend everything was the same, but her efforts didn't hide the fact she just didn't laugh and hardly spoke when she ate breakfast. She started relocating her hair supplies from the bathroom to her bedroom to make room for the intruder. Rows of lotions and sprays had already been moved from the cabinet underneath her sink to big plastic tubs set on the floor of her closet. Dread was in the air. We all knew the feeling and it had begun to take hold of our lives and choke us.

The day we wished would never come, arrived. Jim grabbed his small aluminum suitcase, kissed Ashley and me goodbye, and headed for the airport. It was time for Jim to help Justin get moved out of his Louisiana life. When all the loose ends got tied up, they would drive back to Arizona together.

It was early in the evening when Jim called to check in with me. His voice was clearly agitated. He was appalled at the condition of the apartment and furious with Justin for allowing it to have become such a disgusting pit. Initially, we thought Justin would be packed with just a few last minute things to finish. That was not what happened. Nothing was done and that completely incensed Jim. Not only that, Justin owed his roommate money and the rent had to be paid. Another check had to be written to clear the debt with a promise from Justin that he would "pay it all back." Everything got packed and paid off and they started on their journey home. Ashley and I went into our own private mourning as we said goodbye to the quiet comfort of a joy-filled house. There was no peace in our decision. Was it the right one?

Jim called with news he expected they'd be home by nightfall. Ashley spent the morning busily moving the last of her creams, lotions, and nail polish. She had quite a collection and it had not taken her long to completely fill up every inch of space in the bathroom with her stuff. Justin would be home soon, so she needed to make room for him, somehow. I laughed when I checked in on her and found her methodically lining up her favorite fruit-smelling possessions in perfect little rows under her sink. She was doing a great job of organizing, but couldn't understand why all her efforts didn't produce more elbow room. We both laughed when we counted 20 bottles of raspberry lotion. Finally, some concessions were made and begrudgingly an area for Justin's things appeared.

An unfamiliar car door slammed outside, Ashley and I ran to the window. They were home long before we expected them. A small bright orange U-haul truck was parked in front of the house. Chains and hooks kept Justin's deep blue Honda Prelude attached to the back of the truck.

The car reminded me of the day Jim bought it. The bike just didn't cut it. We expected that would happen. It couldn't get him to his new job in another city. It was just too far. Jim found the Honda on one of the trips to Louisiana when Ashley and I stayed home. It was used, but in good enough shape to get Justin to and from work safely. I forgot we would need to find space for this car too. I watched while Jim unfastened the chain that released the Honda from the truck. Justin slowly walked to the front entrance.

Ashley opened the door and Hayden ran outside to be the official greeter. Justin bent down and began petting the ball of fluff while saying a mildly interested hello to both Ashley and me. Jim walked into the house trying not to step on Hayden. He gave me a very concerned look while kissing me on the cheek. Ashley was standing close beside me when Jim leaned down and gave her a big hug.

"Pam," Jim said, "we need to talk." His words startled me, as they had not even been home for a few minutes. I followed Jim into our bedroom. He sat on the edge of the bed, dirty and sweaty from the long drive. His face became increasingly more serious as the crease in his brow deepened. He took one deep breath and while sighing announced, "This is a mistake." I could hardly believe my ears. I grabbed the bedpost as if I needed something to hold onto while I processed what I had just been told, yet had known from the beginning.

Questions flooded my brain. Why was Jim telling me *now*, when Justin was already moved here? I had prayed the Lord to *reaffirm* our decision, but not this! What happened? How did Jim come to the place where he was now so very, very sure it was a mistake? A million questions exploded in my head. My eyes studied the fibers of the rug under my feet while I tried to deep breathe and assemble my questions. Jim put his hand on my arm and said, "Pam, the old Justin is back."

I hated those words. Tears of disappointment uncontrollably drenched my face. "Jim, what happened?" Panic made it nearly impossible for me to even form the question.

"Things were far worse in Louisiana than we could have ever imagined. His apartment was a wreck. He owed his roommate quite a bit of money and honestly the drive home was a nightmare. The drug attitude is back."

Jim could tell by looking at me his words had taken my small drop of hope and trampled it into despair. I cleared the knot in my throat and was about to speak when Jim interrupted me. "Pam, Justin is not interested in making a new life here. He wants to get back with his old buddies again." We had dealt with his "buddies" for years, and none of it was good. Jim stood up and walked over to me. He put his arms around me and we both cried.

Ashley was the first one to come into our room. She knew something was up. Jim was wiping the tears out of his glasses while I was blowing my nose. It was obvious we were both devastated. She ran over to Jim and hugged him while grabbing my hand into hers. The nightmare had begun.

It was a school night and Ashley had some homework to do. Jim walked her to her bedroom while I worked in the kitchen putting the last of the plates into the dishwasher. Justin was stretched out on the living room floor playing with Hayden. I couldn't help but smile as I passed them. Hayden had missed Justin as much as Justin had missed Hayden. Questions crowded my mind. What was life going to be like?

The night was quiet. Justin had fallen asleep on the floor. Ashley had finished all her homework and was ready for the routine of kisses and prayers before bed. Jim went into her room and they talked for some time before I was asked to come in for prayer time. I knew Jim was sick about the attitude we had brought back into our home. He felt Ashley needed to know we would never let our home become unsafe again. We would always take care of her. His last words were always so precious to Ashley "Goodnight, Dolly."

We closed her bedroom door and moved down the hallway to the family room. It was still so quiet. I wondered if somehow Jim had gotten the wrong reading. Maybe Justin was all right? Maybe he did want to start a better life? I prayed all the way to the couch that Jim had read Justin all wrong or that Justin had a miraculous change of heart. Jim went to put on the tea water when Justin finally got up from his nap.

"Where's the phone?" was his first question. Justin knew where the phone was, so we knew the question was not about the phone. It was really a statement about his next step. He was going to call his old drug buddies.

"Justin, it's late," I managed to say. "You don't need to call anybody tonight."

Jim stood at the stove nodding his head in agreement with me while squeezing the last drops of orange pekoe out of his tea bag. "Not tonight, Son," Jim added.

Justin became irate. "I am not going to be a prisoner here," he said. I looked at Jim while he carefully sipped the hot tea. "Justin, it is late. We had a long day and we are all tired. Get some sleep and we'll talk about your friends tomorrow."

Justin slammed himself down on the couch and began searching for the television remote we kept on the coffee table in front of him. If I had not known differently I would have thought Justin had just spent the day getting high with his druggie friends. I kept asking myself if it was in the slightest realm of possibility for Justin to have found a way to use drugs on the trip with Jim from Louisiana to Arizona. I whispered my concern into Jim's ear. His face told me, he had wondered the same thing.

"Justin," I asked, "have you used anything?" Immediately Justin went into an indignant AA pat response. He delivered all the clever catch phrases we had heard from him so many times before. The reason he failed was because we expected him to fail. I resented those words. It got worse when he added that our inability to trust him made it impossible for him to stay drug free. Those words enraged me. The accusations continued. His glare was directed at me when he said, "Mom, you just can't quit living in the past, can you?"

What? I thought. Didn't it matter to him at all we had just sacrificed the calm we had come to enjoy…for this? If we were so stuck in the past we would have *never* have let him come home. I didn't say a word. Jim didn't say a word either. Justin took our silence as an "I told you so." He smugly looked at us as if he had just won a round in a boxing match.

"Do you know the worst thing about coming back here?" his words broke into the uncomfortable silence. "You knew before I stepped foot into this house, that I wouldn't be able to live by your rules. You planned for me to fail!" With those words he charged to his room and slammed the door.

Jim and I stood stunned. This entire scene had taken only a few minutes, as Jim still had hot tea in his cup. We revisited the so-called "impossible rules" we had placed on Justin. Life had boiled down to three rules. Rule 1: He would be respectful to his family. Rule 2: He would go to school full-time or work full-time. Rule 3: He would tell us where he was going to be at all times. These couldn't possibly be the "rules we planned for Justin to be unable to follow." What was Justin talking about? And what was all that about "living in the past?" The plain and simple fact was we didn't trust him. Oddly enough our lack of trust didn't entirely stem from what he had done in the past. His behavior was untrustworthy in the present! The fact that we continued to try to rebuild our lives didn't seem to matter to him. It always appeared to be about his "perception" of our motives. He couldn't stand our demand for accountability. It caused him to go into a tirade about trust. It was true, however, to some extent, the underlying agenda behind every question we asked, was to detect if Justin was still using drugs. What were we supposed to do? Fall into the deadly trap of belief that his strange behavior didn't signal trouble for all of us? We couldn't take that chance with our family...ever again.

The night was getting close to morning and it was time to go to bed. Jim took the dog out one last time, while I poked my head into Ashley's room just long enough to kiss her on her sleeping head and tell her how much I loved her. I carefully opened Justin's door and found him sound asleep too. I tiptoed into his room and leaned over and kissed his forehead. I touched his soft brown hair while I prayed for the Lord to protect Justin and our family. This was a difficult battle. I begged the Lord to help me stay at my post—at the feet of Jesus. I whispered the words "I love you," while quietly closing the bedroom door behind me. The door squeaked when it latched shut. I stopped immediately and prayed the sound hadn't disturbed Justin's sleep. I shook my head as I walked down the hallway toward the kitchen realizing my old patterns were resurfacing too. What a first day home!

Sunday was reminiscent of the past. The day started out with church and was followed by lunch at a nearby restaurant. While we all sat with long rectangular plastic menus in front of our faces, Justin spoke about all the "friends" in Arizona he looked forward to seeing again.

Those words were disturbing and they needed to be addressed. Jim reminded Justin about our concern regarding his so-called "friends." It was obvious Justin resented the comments and fired back by saying it all boiled down to one thing. It was always the same accusation. We didn't trust him. Jim and I didn't respond, but Ashley did. Every time Justin spewed hostility at us, Ashley struck back. She called his friends "losers."

Right after the waitress had taken our orders, Ashley asked Justin to name the people who had stood by him throughout all of his bad drug days. The food arrived right in the middle of her question. It didn't stop her. "Justin, name one person," she pressed. Justin stacked the tomato and lettuce on top of his burger as if she had never even addressed him. Ashley didn't let it go. She recounted the fact that his so-called friends never even tried to contact him when he was in any of the rehabs. Disgustedly, she threw her napkin on top of her plate signaling she was done with lunch. "Justin," she said in a low very serious tone, "the only people who care anything about you are Mom and Dad. There is *no one* else who cares. Do you get it?"

My hands crumpled up the napkin that rested in my lap. I looked up at Ashley who seemed unmoved by the substance of the words she had just blurted out. Her attention was turned from Justin to something else...a chocolate brownie ala mode. I watched her as she fingered the desert description, wondering if she had purposely left her own name off the list of people who cared for Justin. Both Ashley and Justin ate dessert.

I thought about what Ashley had said about his "friends." Oddly enough, it was true that none of them had ever gone to visit him even one time at any of the rehabs. Yet those were the people he treated with great importance. How very sad.

It was still dark that Monday morning when Jim closed his packed flight bag. He tucked his shirt into his pants and adjusted his belt before he grabbed his uniform coat. He would be gone for three days and dreaded it. I knew why he felt that way. It was obvious we were only days away from the storm we saw brewing in Justin. Jim hated the fact I would have to face it alone and frankly, so did I. Justin had only been home two days and already the tension in the air was as thick and smothering as it had been for so many years in the past. The volcano was going to erupt. We just didn't know when.

Justin and Ashley were both asleep when Jim made his quiet rounds of whispered good-byes and soundless kisses. We smiled at each other and nodded a final good-bye completely aware of the tremendously difficult days ahead of us. Honestly, I was convinced that I was about to face the toughest days of my life. Jim smiled one last time as he opened the laundry room door and punched the button to activate the garage door. I walked out into the garage with him and watched while he methodically slid his suitcase and flight bag into the trunk of his car. The shadow cast by the trunk light revealed old leaves that had blown into the garage. It was so early in the morning the night had not yet given way to a new day. Jim backed out of the garage and vanished into the blackness.

I walked back into the house, picked up Hayden, and began scratching his ear while I slowly strolled back into the bedroom. I sat down on the bed, too worried to go back to sleep. The whirl of the wind whipping the fall leaves around the back patio was the perfect background for the thoughts swirling around in my head. I began to pray. I needed the Lord to keep me focused. The battle in the unseen world was raging all around us. "Stick to the plan, Pam." I said to myself. "Victory will come. I just need to: Put on the full armor of God. Stand firm. Take up the shield of faith. Take the helmet of salvation and the sword of the Spirit. Be still. Pray and be on the alert." I was ready.

The daily bedlam I had come to enjoy with Ashley as she got ready for school was absent. She now kept her bedroom door closed while she curled her hair and listened to her music. I missed the sweet chaos I had watched the mornings before Justin came home. It seemed beyond my own imagination that we would put ourselves back into the hell we had just barely survived. The sound of Ashley's bedroom door opening pulled me out of my thoughts.

"Mom," she asked, "can I have some lunch money?" I found my purse and dug around in it and handed her a bunch of change. She smiled, and while adjusting her backpack, told me she loved me and walked toward the door.

"Ashley," I protested, "where's my kiss?" She giggled and planted a surprisingly big smooch on my cheek. We both laughed. I prayed silently as I walked with Ashley to the front door. She hugged me while I grabbed one more kiss.

"Mom," she said in an authoritative way, "it will be OK." The big wood front doors shook as they came together behind her. She was already down the front walkway and about to cross the street before I caught a glimpse of her through the slats of the shutters in the guest room. My eyes filled with tears. I wanted to believe I would have the strength to get through the nightmare one more time.

The house was still quiet. I sat in the family room and read Ephesians in the Bible, knowing it was the only way to build the faith I needed. I asked the Lord to protect and direct us. I sighed while I thought about how I had prayed for the Lord's direction concerning Justin's return home. At the time I thought it was the better decision to bring Justin back, even though I knew it wouldn't be easy. I hid my fears under the heading "the right thing." But now I knew in my gut, we had made a mistake.

"Oh Lord," I begged, "please keep me on track with you." I closed my eyes and spent a few minutes in quiet at the feet of the Lord. It would be OK. I was ready. I got up from the couch and looked at the time on the microwave. There was still not a sound coming from Justin's room. My mind began to reflect on one of our impromptu conversations. Justin had agreed to finish high school. I had heard about "Gateway Community College" and through research on the internet learned that Justin would be able to finish his high school degree and even start college there. I got up and began sorting through old papers I found stored in a metal file cabinet. It didn't take me long to get all the information organized and stacked in a neat pile on the kitchen counter, ready to take to registration. I felt a strange sense of accomplishment, even though nothing had really been done at all.

Justin woke up and found everyone gone but me. Breakfast didn't appeal to him that morning, even though I offered to make him whatever hit his spot. It concerned me that he didn't want to eat. It reminded me of the past. He plopped down on the couch, flipped on the television, and began to channel surf. I told him I was going to get dressed because registration for school had only a small window of time left. He leaned back on the couch as if he was getting ready to take a nap.

I couldn't help but notice one strange habit of Justin's. He always wore one sock to bed. It was the foot with the only sock he started shaking as if he had an uncontrollable twitch. "Justin, we need to get going so you can get registered for classes," I managed to force out of my mouth.

"I am not going right now, maybe later," he said as he stretched and dangled both feet over the side of the couch.

Oh Lord, I thought, *help me to be strong and yet kind.*

"Justin, we need to go this morning."

"OK," he responded indignantly. "Just give me 10 minutes."

I conceded and walked to my room to take a shower and get ready myself. I decided not to take a shower. I didn't have a good feeling about leaving Justin alone on the other side of the house. Clean clothes and a "sponge bath" would have to do for now. After a few short minutes, I walked toward the family room while asking Justin if he was ready to go. His answer surprised me because I was ready for a fight. "Yeah," he said. "Let's get it over with."

Registration went relatively easily. I had all the materials needed to keep it a smooth, painless process. I felt we were quite the sight, Justin seated beside me slouched back in his chair looking bored, while I sat attentively shuffling and retrieving all the right paperwork.

They accepted Justin into the program and told him that he would need only two classes to get his high school diploma. I was definitely the one more excited about the news. He raised his eyebrows and nodded an unemotional affirmation while I patted his back, hardly able to hold back my enthusiasm. The idea of Justin finishing high school completely delighted me. It was a great thing for him. I barely had all the school material gathered up into my arms before Justin grabbed the car keys out of my hands and ran to the car. By the time I got there, he was searching the radio stations trying to find the music he loved the most…rap.

We finally agreed on the one radio station I was able to tolerate. Justin used his fingers as drumsticks on the dashboard as we drove into the traffic of the busy highway. It was hard to talk over the loud noise that crowded into us in the car. The song was over, so I quickly turned the volume down to allow for some semblance of conversation.

"Justin," I asked with some emotion in my voice, "are you excited about finishing school?" He yawned and asked me if we could stop at Taco Bell on our way home. "Justin," I pressed the question, "doesn't finishing high school mean anything to you?" He flipped the radio back on and adjusted the volume control knob. I knew none of it mattered to him. The staccato ear-piercing scream of the radio needed my attention. I shut it off.

When Jim called that night he was pleasantly surprised to hear how uneventful the day had been. I knew, though, that I couldn't let down my guard and rest in what appeared to be a "good" day. It was important to stay focused on what was really going on. Justin was in the middle of the fight of his life. My mind rested in the promises of the Lord.

"Gateway Community College" started. Every day I drove Justin to the school and later picked him up as his car seemed to spend more time at the repair shop than at our house. When he got home, I would physically sit down at the computer and almost beg for him to let me help him. He always blew me off. It didn't take long for me to accept the fact that he had no intention of doing any of the work because school meant nothing to him. Why didn't it matter to him? And why did it matter so much to me? The answers never came. I continued to drag him to school and badger him until he worked on his assignments. He resented it. I resented it too.

CHAPTER 15

The Hurt

It was Christmas morning, 1998. The stillness of what had been a quiet Christmas Eve spilled into the new day. Jim and I got up long before Ashley and Justin. We laughed while recalling past Christmas mornings. We were the ones trying to grab a few extra winks back in those days. How things had changed. Now we were the ones up and ready, waiting for the children to finally drag themselves out of bed. Jim made the tea while I finished putting the turkey into the oven. It felt like Christmas. I plugged in all the lights and turned on the sweet carols that played on the radio. The Christmas tree glowed against the darkness of early morning.

Jim flipped through the worn pages of his Bible as he looked for the passage to begin his customary reading. It had been our tradition to read the Scripture about the birth of Jesus on Christmas morning. Jim and I sipped our tea while we discussed Justin's final two weeks of school. I couldn't bring myself to tell Jim what I was really thinking. In my heart of hearts I didn't really believe Justin was going to finish school. There was something about Jim's line of questioning that led me to believe, he had his doubts too. Christmas morning didn't seem to be the time to talk about my skepticism. I covered up my doubts by talking about the assignments Justin had to finish during the short Christmas break. We smiled and laughed and thanked God for His mercy and goodness, while basking in the "false" peace I chose to embrace.

Ashley was the first to wake up. She rubbed her eyes while she walked to the beige tweed chair in the living room. I put my tea mug down and got up to get the gifts ready to pass out. I always played Santa in our house. I am not sure if I took the job as Santa or if it was given to me. It seemed I was the natural choice for the job. After all, I was the one who purchased, wrapped, and hid the gifts until it was time to crowd them under the tree.

Jim was fine with that and enjoyed watching my excitement as I lined things up under the tree in a particular order.

Just as I finished getting all the presents perfectly positioned for distribution, Justin arrived. He was barely awake and sank into the other soft fabric chair across from Ashley. My tea had one more sip left. I picked up the mug to enjoy the last drop and watched Justin start to doze off while we waited for Jim to locate the beginning of the passage he wanted to read in Luke.

Jim cleared his throat and began to read about the first Christmas morning, the birth of Jesus. It always moved us when we read the humble beginnings of our precious Savior. Both children listened to the Scripture while I sat quietly and prayed they both were hearing the words. When Jim finished the reading, he closed the Bible and placed it in the middle of the stone coffee table, in front of him. We both spoke about salvation and its relationship to the birth and death of Christ. How incredible to consider that the God of the universe sent His only Son to carry our sin and save us from eternal death. It took His death to do that. Justin mumbled a few words about God. It was hard to make out exactly what he was saying. Ashley rolled her eyes while he spoke as if to say, "Don't you see he's trying to scam you with the Bible too?" Jim nodded, affirming Justin's thoughts while Ashley sighed and shook her head.

"Please, Lord," I prayed silently "Be real to Justin and Ashley. And thank you for being so real to me."

It was time for Santa to start the festivities. I loved it. After we refilled our tea cups, I brought out the Egg Nog. It was Ashley's favorite. I handed a gift to Ashley and then Justin, one present at a time. Jim and I smiled at each other while we watched them rip through the paper. Justin opened his things and hardly had any reaction. I watched Ashley while Justin tore open the carefully wrapped "baseball cap" she had purchased for him with her babysitting money. Justin had very little to say to Ashley. He just looked at the hat and put it on top of the pile of his other new things. Ashley watched intently to see if he even liked it. Justin had nothing to say. My stomach went into knots as I witnessed his complete disinterest.

He is so unappreciative. I said to myself. I couldn't stand it any longer so I jumped in and tried to rescue Ashley's heart. "Justin you love hats!" I quickly reminded him. It was as if I was trying to kick-start an attitude of thankfulness that had gone dormant or was just not there at all. Nothing worked. It didn't matter to him in the slightest what I said.

Finally, Justin passed out a cursory "thank you" to each of us. I saw the hurt on Ashley's face and knew there was nothing I could do about that. It hurt me too. The attention quickly shifted to me. Ashley proudly watched me open the meticulously wrapped gift she had bought especially for me. Jim opened his gift too. We smiled and gushed over the thoughtful presents. Justin sat completely expressionless. He had nothing to give. *How sad for him,* I thought. He didn't understand the great pleasure of giving. Ashley ran to the kitchen pantry to retrieve a large garbage sack. We stuffed it full of all the brightly colored Christmas wrappings. She contemplated keeping many of the bows but ended up discarding them with the rest of the crumpled paper and ripped boxes. After hours of enjoying the festivities, we all disappeared into our bedrooms. It was time to get ready for our family, Christmas dinner.

CHAPTER 16

The Real Focus

Three days later at 2 A.M., the front door opened and slammed shut. It had become Justin's habit to come into our room to say goodnight when he got home from work. Justin had just started a job working as a valet, so it was always long into the night before I heard the click of the front door. This night was different. I listened for him to come into our bedroom, but only heard the banging of dresser drawers on the other side of the house. I jumped out of bed to investigate.

Justin had a pile of clothes heaped on his bed. He was packing. Jim appeared behind me and we both stood in the hallway in front of Justin's room, watching him in disbelief. What had happened? Justin muttered his reason for moving out. He hated all the rules. We had made it impossible for him to live in our house because he felt as if he were living in a prison. What was he talking about? We had reduced the rules to the bare bones minimum. If there was anyone in our home who felt imprisoned, it wasn't Justin! Jim looked at me bewildered while I reviewed the rules in my mind. Rule #1: I said to myself, "Be respectful to all family members." That couldn't be the rule that was throwing him into this state. OK, I thought what about Rule #2: "Either school, or a job fulltime?" How was that the problem? He only took two classes and worked part-time. Jim and I had not complained to him about any of it. The problem couldn't possibly be that rule. Rule #3 was simple: He had to let us know where he was at all times. Oh, I thought, was that the *impossible* rule? Strangely enough, that rule seemed the simplest to me.

Jim stood completely silent, while I began to probe Justin with a few questions. "Justin," I said, "which rule is the impossible one?"

"I'm an adult," he fired back with hostility. "I shouldn't have to live by any of your rules. I can make my own decisions."

I didn't have anything to say to him. Living in our home meant following our rules. Jim spoke sternly when he told Justin the rules were not going away.

"I am moving out now," was all Justin managed to say. I knew it really wasn't about the rules. Justin had another agenda. Jim and I both found ourselves moving into Justin's room. Jim sat on the bed while I leaned up against the wall. For some odd reason Jim started to fold shirts and neatly place them into the old army green canvas bag positioned in the middle of the soft comforter that draped over the bed. It almost made me laugh to watch Jim, as I knew Justin had no appreciation for the well-placed creases folded into his shirts. I appreciated it though.

I went over to the top drawer of his dresser and grabbed bunches of socks and underwear and tried to find a new spot for them in the crowded bag. There was no talking. Occasionally, I looked up at Justin and Jim both entrenched in their tasks. It was ironic to watch Justin rip price tags from his new clothes only to mash the clothes into the small available space near the top of the suitcase. I ran into the kitchen and dug baggies out of the pantry. After I carefully screwed the cap on the toothpaste and wiped the old smeared toothpaste off the flattened bristles of his toothbrush, I dropped them into the zip lock bag and jammed them into the little compartment on the side of the suitcase. He was ready to go.

Justin didn't bother to close the bag before he hoisted it under his arm and headed for the front door. I simply couldn't believe what I was witnessing, and by Jim's expression, neither could he. Justin said goodbye to Jim with a hug and gave me a peck on the cheek.

"Good-bye. I'll call you," were the last words we heard from him before he and his Honda evaporated into the night.

Jim and I turned and looked stunned as we tried to conjure up a few words to say to each other. "What just happened?" was really the only thing we found ourselves repeating over and over. A faint, almost inaudible sound, came from down the hallway. I wondered if Hayden had gotten stuck under a bed and we were hearing his plea for help. No, it wasn't Hayden. I followed my ears to Ashley's room and opened her door. She was sobbing.

"Mom, why did you make Justin leave?" Her little voice cracked as she spoke. I bent down and wiped the tears that had dripped all the way down her chin. Jim stood in the doorway behind me.

"Dolly," he quickly replied, "we never told Justin to leave. He left because he decided he didn't want to live with our family rules anymore."

I curled up on her bed and rubbed her head while she cried from the deepest part of her heart. I knew it wasn't really about the rules. There was something else going on. Finally, she mumbled a few words "We are his family. Where is he going to go?" Neither Jim nor I had an answer for her. We all cried together.

Days went by and not one word from Justin. January 6th, his birthday, came and went without his presence. Karen had made the trip from Rhode Island to surprise him for his special 21st birthday. There was no celebration.

The phone rang in the middle of the day on January 15th. My heart raced when I heard Justin's voice. He asked if he could stop by for a visit. His casual demeanor amazed me. It was as if he had been away at summer camp and was now anxious to come home and tell me all about it. My sinus headache pounded while we chatted on the phone. I held an icepack to one side of my face while the phone pressed on the other side. He didn't ask one question about Ashley, Jim, or me. The only thing he wanted to know was when he could stop in for a "visit." It seemed important that the day and time be settled before he hung up. Even though I felt as if my head was ready to explode, I invited him to come over whenever it suited him...even that day. He accepted the invite without hesitation and said he would be right over. We hung up.

There must be some underlying reason for Justin's impromptu visit, I thought. His voice told me he needed to come home soon. I kept wondering what he really wanted. Certainly he did not want to chit-chat with me. I settled back down on the couch and prayed the Lord would relieve my throbbing headache. More importantly, though, I asked the Lord to reveal the real purpose of Justin's visit. I fell asleep.

Hayden's bark woke me up. I walked to the door still in my pajama's holding the icepack up against my now cold cheek. It was Justin. He came right in and immediately rolled around on the floor with Hayden. I loved hearing Hayden's happy growls as he tumbled and played with Justin. I sat on the soft, leather living room couch waiting for Justin to join me. Finally he sat down right beside me.

"So Justin how are you?" I asked in a quiet voice.

"I'm fine. Mom, I need the title to my car," he quickly threw in. I shook my head while I processed his request. So that was why he wanted to come home. It wasn't for any other reason than to get something from us. That always seemed to be the case. I looked at him in disbelief. *What gall,* I thought while I mentally reviewed the agreement Jim and I had regarding Justin's car. We had bought Justin the car. It was his car. I got up from the comfort of the couch and walked barefoot on the cold tile of the hallway until I reached the soft warmth of the carpeted bedroom.

The ice pack stayed in my left hand while I shuffled through an old metal file cabinet with the other. I found it. It didn't take me long to stuff the disrupted stack of papers back into place. The ice pack was hard to keep propped in one place on my face while I sorted through all the paperwork, so I laid it on a shelf in front of a huge mirror. I caught a glimpse of myself in the reflection of the glass. What a horrible sight! My face was ghost white and my eyes were almost swollen shut. Knowing how bad I looked made me feel even worse. I shook my head and pushed the ice pack into my face to help reduce the sinus pressure while walking back to the living room.

Justin was pacing back and forth. I handed him the title to the car. He wrinkled it while trying to fit it into his back pocket. We stood in the hallway beside the front door and hugged for a brief moment. "I'm going to be OK Mom, don't worry," he said with a strange new confidence. My headache pounded harder as tears rushed to my bulging red eyes. He opened the front door and almost ran to his car without saying another word. I watched him screech out of the driveway and peel down the street.

Oh Lord, I whispered in my head *Do you see what is happening? Please help him!* The words of Hosea 14:4, spoke up in my heart "I will heal their waywardness and love them freely, for my anger has turned away from them."

"OK, Lord," I said to myself. "I am going to hold you to your Word." I nodded my head up and down while I replayed the Scripture over and over in my mind. There was nothing I could do for Justin. Actually there wasn't anything anyone could do. The only One who had the power to change Justin's heart was God. Even though my head ached, my heart ached even more and it was time to press into the Lord. I prayed.

The days became weeks and quickly turned into a month. No word from Justin. I begged the Lord to keep me focused on the plan. Often I found myself standing so far down in a pit of pain that all I could see was the blackness of despair. Questions ran through my mind all the time, as if an endless ticker tape were posted at the bottom of my brain. I had no answers. The nagging questions never ended. "Where is *your* peace Lord?" I cried. "Is he OK? Please, keep me focused on you Lord. This is too big for me." I cried a lot.

Early one morning the words of the Lord sprang up in my heart. The words came from Philippians 4:8, "Finally, brothers, whatever is true, whatever is noble, whatever is right, whatever is pure, whatever is lovely, whatever is admirable—if anything is excellent or praiseworthy—think about such things."

Yes, I needed to focus on what was honorable, right, pure, lovely, and of good repute. I regularly searched my mind for those things. I loved the ocean, so I pushed my mind to visualize the crashing waves of the sea. I envisioned trying to walk on the sand while my feet sank deep into the soft wet mud. The smell of salt and seaweed filled my senses. Yes, I assured myself, these are the thoughts that would bring peace to me. I breathed deeply and enjoyed the images. It wasn't long before the thoughts of the ocean were crowded out by the dark familiar pit of hopelessness. How could I keep my mind from wandering to that place? What was wrong with me? I resented my inability to follow the Scripture. I wondered why it was impossible for me to stop thinking about Justin. Where was he? I thought of a million reasons why I wasn't able to stay focused on the beauty of the ocean. I just wasn't able to sustain peace in my heart.

One day something unexpected happened while I prayed. It wasn't anything weird like a vision. I didn't hear the Lord speaking to me with an audible voice, but I did hear that small voice speaking to my heart.

"Pam, stop trying to focus on what *you* think is honorable, right, pure, lovely, and of good repute. You will fail every time you try to do that yourself. Focus on Me…Jesus."

I ran back to the Scripture to read it again. Yes, the answer was not the ocean, although I had enjoyed imagining the sound of the ocean grabbing the beach sand and carrying it back into the unseen depths of the sea. Those thoughts would never be able to bring me peace. The answer for real comfort came from another place. I went to the throne of grace and mercy and stood in awe as I pondered…Jesus.

CHAPTER 17

The Look of Death

Another sunny day had come and gone and still no sign of Justin. It was evening and the shadows of light streaked the wall through the holes on the ceramic fixture in front of the house. Someone was at the front door. I looked through the peep hole. It was my son. My heart wanted me to fling open the door and grab him up into my arms and tell him everything would be OK...but my head gave me different directions. I knew I had to be careful. A person on drugs would do anything to get what they wanted...*anything!*

The door felt harder to pull open that night. Justin stood silently in front of me. His flip-flops exposed filthy black toes. In one hand he held a see-through "Target" shopping bag. It was stuffed with something that looked like a sweatshirt, a pair of tennis shoes, and one sock.

"Mom, I'm hungry and I need a shower. Can I come in?"

My skeptical expression gave way to an uncontrolled broad smile followed by a warm hug. He would always be able to get food and a shower in our home. I had remembered saying that to him a long time ago. While he walked out of the shadows and into the light of the house, I saw that his face, arms, and legs were so completely covered in red oozing sores that I couldn't tell if he had just been in an accident or if the horrific bleeding holes were from the drugs. Justin had some difficulty negotiating the step into the house, so I braced his arm as he walked by me.

"Oh Lord," I said to myself, "please hold back the tears." I brushed away the water that had already escaped down my cheeks. I tried to act as if my allergies were getting the best of me. He didn't seem to notice. I ran to the refrigerator and pulled out the miracle whip, tomatoes and "good" bread to make his favorite sandwich.

Justin's skinny pitted arms seemed to have difficulty pulling the wrought iron chair out from under the island. He sat still while his leg shook at a warp speed. I excused myself for a moment to find a wash cloth and medicine for all the open sores. He didn't move or make a sound while I bathed each leg in soapy water. The bleeding holes were everywhere. I didn't speak either, I just prayed and wept.

Justin finally stopped the arduous task of chewing long enough to say, "Thanks." He stood up very slowly causing the iron chair to make a screeching sound as it scraped along the tile floor. He walked toward the bathroom barely able to determine the direction. Tears kept rushing down my cheeks. It wasn't long before the sound of the shower disappeared in the sound of my own long sobs. I took a deep breath and reminded myself to get refocused. I thanked the Lord for keeping Justin alive. I stared at the bathroom door.

The sound of the water as it splashed against the shower stall gave me a moment to collect my thoughts. I knew Jim would not be happy with me for letting Justin in the house in his absence. Jim knew it wasn't safe and scolded me often when I did things in an effort to help Justin while seemingly putting myself in jeopardy. I rationalized that Justin had come home this time for food and a shower. These things I had said were always available to him.

Jim wasn't home, so I had to do what I thought was best. In that moment, it seemed best to do what I was doing…help Justin. I even nodded to myself a silent affirmation as I pushed the last of his food into the garbage disposal. It would be OK. I went to Justin's room to look for some clean clothes that might have been left behind from one of his many moves. A T-shirt, shorts, and underwear were all neatly accessible in one of his drawers. I was so glad to be able to give him clean clothes…somehow I felt better.

The shower went on for 30 minutes, then 40 minutes and then 50 minutes. Even after I knocked on the door a few times, his "be right out" never materialized. The very long shower was just one more piece of evidence forcing me to reevaluate my notion that things would be "OK."

I pulled out the chair Justin had just occupied and sat on it. Small crumbs of bread on the counter in front of me kept my hands busy while my mind raced. "Oh Lord," I found myself saying out loud "What can I do to help this boy?" I stopped playing with the crumbs and put my head in my hands and cried. The ongoing sound of the water beating on the shower curtain brought me back to the realness of the moment. For one split second I considered the scary possibility that having Justin in the house might be unsafe. Fear gripped me. What was I going to do? The small voice of the Lord spoke to my heart.

"Pam," I heard, "there is nothing you can do for him. I will do it all. Your job is to believe, just believe."

I rubbed my eyes while I searched my brain to uncover that verse in the Bible. Yes, it was "Then they asked him, 'What must we do to do the works God requires?' Jesus answered, 'The work of God is this: to believe in the one he has sent.'"

The bathroom door handle clicked open and I turned around to see Justin as he stood in the hallway with a towel wrapped around his waist. The dirt infested wounds looked bright red to me in the halo of the bathroom's bright light. His bony arms had great difficulty manipulating the towel completely around his malnourished frame.

"Hey Mom," he said as if we saw each other all the time. "Do I have any clothes still here?" I smiled and nodded while pointing to his room. The sight of Justin's gaunt body struck at my heart like a knife. I had to keep telling myself to breathe while I choked back tears.

"Wow, this is great," were the words I heard echoing down the hallway. It wasn't long before Justin emerged from his old room. Even though I could see that he was now wearing clean clothes, and I knew he had taken a shower (for 50 minutes to be exact), he still looked dirty. The drug scars looked like pockmarks that appeared to be very deep into his flesh. They could not possibly heal without leaving permanent holes in his skin.

He began to pace back and forth on the tiled kitchen floor as if his body was being pulled by some unseen force. I watched him and wondered what was going to come next. He leaned up against the wall and glared at me while saying, "Something wrong, Mom?" That was the question that would end all questions, I thought. Is there something wrong? *What?* It took all my energy not to scream out the answer from the place of anguish it generated. *Are you kidding?* I thought to myself. *Is there something wrong?* No…there is not *something* wrong, *everything* is wrong!

Justin kept his eyes on me, waiting for an answer. I cleared my throat. "Justin, you need help. Do you understand that you need help?"

His fingers started picking his arm while he said, "Yes, I know I need help."

I continued, "Do you understand that this drug life will only end in your death? There are no happy endings for people who use drugs. Do you really get that?" The old scab was now fresh with new blood. "Justin your heart is not going to be able to take those drugs much longer. One day it is going to quit and you will die."

Small droplets of blood ran down his arm as he looked at me while digging at another encrusted place. He didn't have anything to say, but I prodded as if my concern would cause him to become alarmed at the seriousness of the situation. All of my questions gave rise to hardly any reaction. He moved toward me and finally sat down on the tooled leather chair beside me.

I put my hand on his ghost-like body and began to pray out loud. "Oh, merciful wonderful God, we come to you now…powerless in ourselves and needing your intervention. Please hear our plea and know that we cannot continue another minute without your help. Oh, holy sovereign God of the universe, we thank you, in the name of Jesus we pray. Amen."

In days past, Justin would have bent his head and even closed his eyes. This time he didn't move. He continued to stare straight ahead as if he was in some far distant place, waiting for the "amen" to signal his return. After the prayer, I began to rub his back. I felt every rib spaced by a deep empty indentation between his bones. Justin didn't look at me.

"Mom, I don't believe that God can help me. I don't think I believe anything anymore!" My hand dropped to the counter in front of me.

"Son, why don't you think God can help you?"

"Well," Justin spoke very deliberately, trying to disguise the fact that he sounded as if he had a mouthful of marbles, "I have prayed and prayed that God would get me out of this drug world…but He hasn't…and I am stuck in it. I don't want to be stuck Mom. I hate this!" He bent over and put his head into his hands and sobbed. In that moment I saw the little boy I remembered from so many years ago. My fingers touched each strand of his damp brown waves with tenderness.

"Justin, I love you. I have loved you from the minute I knew we were going to have you…long before you were even born. I have never given up on you. You are my boy, my son, and I will love you always."

Justin turned his head and looked into my eyes. His once sparkling blue eyes were dull and lifeless. I smiled and silently prayed he could see the love of the Lord in my eyes. "If I love you that much, Justin, then imagine how much God loves you! He knew about you before time. After all He created you! He knew about your drug use and yet He continues to walk with you through this pain. He loves you. Justin, God has an incredible purpose and plan for your life…and He is going to walk you all the way to that end."

There was silence mixed with the sound of sniffling. Soon he picked up the leftover napkin from lunch and began to roll it into a little ball. That was something left from the "old" Justin. In days gone by, he would stick the used wad of paper into his jeans and it would end up in a million small wet pieces stuck to the rest of the laundry. A special smile came over my face from that memory. I watched him as he squished the napkin into a misshapen mass. He hardly seemed to be present.

"Why isn't God getting me out of drugs?" His words were strong and sincere. The moment slipped into minutes of quiet.

"Justin, do you really want to know what I think?" He nodded and began shredding what was left of his napkin. My mind scanned all the truths I knew. I began, "Well, I know that when we trust the Lord, His promises are real to us. The Bible is full of the only truth there is in this world. The Word teaches there is no temptation that can overtake us. The Lord will always give us a way out."

Justin's somber expression told me he just wasn't buying it. "You don't understand what this is like. Mom, you will never understand it."

Boy, that statement was filled with the absolute truth. I didn't understand how someone could want drugs more than life? It was a bewildering thought to me. He was right, I would never understand it. My eyes traced the features on his face. He was hardly the same boy I had held in my arms not too many years ago. Justin kept his eyes fixed on me. Finally, I said "You are right, Justin, I don't understand nor will I ever understand drug use. But there is something I do understand…and that is sin. You lust after drugs…it is everything to you. It gives you a false sense of who you are…a sense of power. The worst of it though…is that it glorifies the enemy."

Justin's eyes widened. The dark circles made the red lines in the white of eyes even more obvious. "You make it sound as if I *like* taking drugs. I hate it. I hate it!" One hand pounded the counter in front of him as he spoke each word.

"I know you hate it…but you don't hate it enough to stop, Justin. Honestly, I believe God is at work in your life. The first step is for you to hate the sin. With God's help you can hate it enough to give it up." I had to say what I knew was the right thing, even if it meant Justin would become angry. I waited for his response.

"Mom, I hope you are right." His once-fisted hand was now relaxed and in his lap. Once again I patted Justin on the rib cage that stuck out from the back of his t-shirt. The numbers on the microwave reminded me of how much time had passed. It was almost 11:30 P.M. Jim would not be home that night and Ashley was safely tucked away at her friend's for a sleepover. It was time to get to bed. "Justin, why don't you stay here tonight?" I said those words as if Justin had other options available to him. He grabbed up the tiny remaining piece of his napkin and stuffed it into his front pocket. Slowly he got up from the chair and together we walked to what use to be "his" bedroom. I sat at the bottom of the bed and begged God to breathe hope into Justin's life. Before I could say goodnight…Justin was in soundless sleep.

It was a long night for me. Actually, it was a long night for both of us. Justin slept for a short time. Then I heard his feet slap against the tile as he walked from one end of the house to the other. I got up twice to see exactly what he was doing. It appeared harmless to me. He paced the halls all night while I listened to the sound of his feet on the tile. Sleep didn't happen for either one of us. But at least for that night I knew he was safe…and *he* knew he was safe. For some odd reason it gave the sleeplessness some good purpose.

The early morning sun pushed through the partially opened slats of the shutters. The house seemed quiet. Maybe Justin was asleep again. It was no wonder, as he had confessed to being awake for four days straight. He must be beyond tired! I pulled the covers back into place, threw the decorative pillows on the bed, and headed for the kitchen. Justin was not asleep. He was just sitting up like a statue on the family room couch. His gaze was fixed on the blank screen of the television in front of him. I opened the refrigerator and said, "Good Morning, Justin."

It shocked me when he responded with the quick wit of a straight thinking person. "Mom, did you ever learn Dad's 'cheesy egg" recipe?' " I laughed. Jim was not someone you found hanging out in the kitchen developing new egg recipes. Occasionally he made breakfast and that *always* included his rendition of scrambled eggs with cheese…later called "cheesy eggs."

"Yes, Justin, I have uncovered Dad's recipe for cheesy eggs. Would you like some?" He chuckled. I made eggs and toast and even cut up some fresh fruit. His plate looked pretty, filled with a colorful array of appetizing items. In between bites of egg he told me he needed to go to the drug rehab program called "Teen Challenge." It was the Christ-centered program we had offered to him once before. My fingers worked their way down the small print of the pages until I came across the contact number for that rehab. I always felt like I was Justin's personal secretary. It seemed, no matter where he was I had a phone number that he needed and could not find. That always amazed me when I considered the fact that he had his drug dealer's numbers permanently etched into his brain. Justin took the phone and punched in the sequence of numbers. Yes, Teen Challenge would take him. The only hitch was that they only did admissions on Tuesday, and it was Saturday. It was hard for me to believe that his cry for help could last for four whole days. Would he stay in our house until then? I had Ashley's safety to think about. Maybe I needed to call a shelter? What a disturbing thought. What should I do?

I glanced down at my watch and saw that it was almost 10 A.M. Jim should be home very soon. My thoughts were interrupted by Hayden's bark as he raced to the laundry room door. He was the official welcoming committee. I ran to the door right behind Hayden. Jim stood holding his hat in one hand and flight bag in the other wearing his usual big smile. "Hi, Hun!" was all he said as he gave me a hug and bent down to give Hayden some badly-needed attention. My forced smile and worn out appearance made it obvious something was going on.

"Pam, have you heard from Justin?" Yes, I had heard from Justin. He was sitting in our kitchen sopping up the last bit of eggs with his toast. What are we going to do? I followed Jim into our room and sat on the edge of the bathtub. While he hung up his uniform, I told him about Justin. The smile he had when he entered the house was gone. Jim led the way from our room to the kitchen. His gasp made it evident he saw the same desperately thin boy I had seen the night before. Justin sat crossed-legged on the kitchen chair seemingly unaware of the intensity with which he was shaking his foot.

"Son, Mom says you are ready to get some help. Is that true?"

Justin turned to face Jim and mustered up the strength to say, "Dad, if I don't get help…I'm going to die. I am going to go to Teen Challenge. He spoke as if this would finally be his answer.

"That's great, Son! If you really want this help, then we will let you stay here until Tuesday."

Justin looked down at the counter as if distracted by some fascinating message inscribed in its surface. After a few moments he looked up at Jim again and faintly whispered, "Thanks."

Jim was quick to list the new "rules" Justin needed to follow while in our home. Ashley and I needed to feel safe. First, Justin would have to stay in our bedroom. He would sleep on the couch in there. He would have to be with one of us at all times, unless he was on that couch. There would be no phone calls or visits from old buddies.

Justin nodded in agreement and asked if he could go to bed. He was exhausted. Maybe he would finally sleep. I ran to the linen closet to find fresh sheets and a blanket. I retrieved a pillow stored in the laundry room. Justin propped himself up against our dresser while he waited for me to finish making up his new bed. The bedding smelled so good. It felt like I was finally doing something to help him. Before I could even gather up the discarded throw pillows from the couch, Justin was sound asleep.

I tiptoed out of the room to find Jim making tea in the kitchen. I took Jim's hands and asked if he would mind if we prayed. He readily agreed and I began to pray that we would keep our focus on Jesus. I had learned that victory in crisis would never be found in the circumstance. It was only found in the face of Jesus.

Prayer was an important part of my life. It had changed over the years as I grew more dependent on the Lord. During the first years of Justin's drug use, I prayed for the Lord to keep Justin off drugs. Then I prayed for the Lord to keep Justin away from his druggie friends. Other prayers ranged from keeping Justin safe on the streets to asking the Lord to help Justin become repulsed by drugs. Over time my prayers ran the gamut. Then one day, my prayer life changed dramatically. I no longer prayed for Justin in the same way. I prayed that God would speak into Justin's heart—that he would see the Truth—and I prayed constantly for the Lord to keep my focus on Him. I prayed for the ability to walk in obedience regardless of what it looked like to me. I didn't want to get in the way of what God was doing in Justin's life, even when it looked desperately bad to me. I also prayed for the Lord to show me how to love Justin the way He loved him.

Those prayers might have appeared vague, but they were piercingly specific to me. I learned many truths through those prayer times. First, God had allowed Justin to use drugs for some reason. He would use that experience in Justin's life for His purpose. Secondly, God had chosen me to be the mother of this son. I knew this was no mistake! For some reason, something I would never fully fathom, God had appointed me to the task. God was Sovereign and I completely and totally believed that fact. I didn't have to worry about the future. God had all that figured out. He knew it all.

It felt like it took years to get to the Tuesday when Justin would be admitted into "Teen Challenge." Justin had spent most of his time in our home sleeping and the rest of the time eating. I monitored every minute and frankly was exhausted emotionally and physically.

Justin packed two suitcases he uncovered from a pile of Christmas ornaments stored in the laundry room. Jim started the car after he pushed Justin's two overstuffed bags into the trunk. I got a quick hug and a promise he'd stick it out this time. I smiled and waved as the garage door came to a thump on the cement floor.

Yes, I thought, *God was at work!* Not only was He at work in Justin, God was at work in me! "Thank you, Lord," became my mantra all that morning as I faced the arduous job of removing all the remnants of meals past, from the refrigerator. Two drawers of shriveled fruit and vegetables waited in line to be cleaned or thrown away. The timing was perfect. I hated cleaning the refrigerator even when it was in such need of being cleaned. Yet today, everything felt different. My grateful heart gave me a new zest. I joyfully scrubbed for hours.

CHAPTER 18

Teen Challenge

Teen Challenge was a one-year rehab program. Though there was a one time nominal admittance fee, it was primarily funded by donations. The total thrust of the program was Jesus. Bible study and prayer time made up most of the typical day of a student in the first months of the program. Little did we know this would be the first of at least three more times he would go to Teen Challenge.

Justin seemed to thrive spiritually in that environment. He always had so much to tell us about what he had learned through his Bible study. We visited regularly on Sundays and I packed a lunch for Jim, Justin, and me with plenty left to share with boys who didn't have family to visit with them. Ashley never wanted to go with us. On those rare occasions when Jim flew, Ashley went as my "protector."

Teen Challenge was about a 20-minute drive from our house, depending on the traffic. We always filled our plastic cooler with loads of sandwiches, fruit, and cold soda. It had become our weekend ritual. Justin almost always greeted us with a big smile and a new "best friend." We would follow him into their dining room where we maneuvered all of the lunch goodies between the crowded rows of secondhand round tables. The poor acoustics made an average conversation sound more like a shouting match. Jim and Justin would separate three metal chairs from the pile of seats stacked up against the wall while I found and claimed a table. Our conversations were dominated by shallow summaries of daily life and vague discussions about the future. Our table was always filled with guys looking for an extra sandwich or can of soda. For months I enjoyed the routine.

One Sunday while Jim emptied the overcrowded cooler onto a badly-scarred old table, I caught the eye of another mother. She sat at the table right beside us. I guessed her to be quite a bit older than I. At first my eyes were drawn to her brightly-colored blouse fastened at the top by one large safety pin. Her sad eyes drew me into the scene in front of her. The table was stocked with several kinds of soda, huge bags of chips, and neat rows of cardboard boxes filled with crème-filled cupcakes. I couldn't help but keep my eyes on her while she focused on her son.

He was one of the guys Justin brought into our conversation on many occasions. His laughter resonated in the room while he handed out the small cellophane wrapped cakes to anyone who would take one. Justin noticed my preoccupation with the other table and noted how nice it was of that kid to "bless" so many people by giving away his little desserts. I didn't think it was nice at all. This boy was "blessing" everyone with something he had no right to give in the first place. Those treats belonged to his mother. They were gifts that had come with great personal sacrifice. She had carefully put together that "care package" as her way of saying "I love you." I recognized those words in her eyes when the blue of mine met the brown of hers. It infuriated me when I heard the son's callous dismissal of any conversation initiated by his mother. He preferred the pointless chatter of strangers to the heartfelt words of the gentle woman patiently seated beside him. She had provided all the treats and not one word was spoken to her about them.

The son tossed one of the last small packages of cupcakes to Justin. I grabbed the dessert out of Justin's hands before he had a chance to tear open the wrapper to indulge in its sweetness. Justin said "Mom, what are you doing?" My glare made it clear he wasn't going to get any response from me until he moved his chair and positioned it right beside mine. Reluctantly he dragged the metal chair around the table until he found a space very close to me. "OK, Mom, what is the matter?"

A part of me felt incensed that I had to explain myself to him. "Justin, those cupcakes were bought by that boy's mother. Why is he giving them out as if they are things he paid for with his own money?" Justin tried to keep a serious face, but soon after I asked the question, broke into a smile.

"Mom, those are his. His mom brought that food for him. Look, she hasn't had any of it." It was obvious that Justin hadn't understood my feelings.

"Justin, that food is *not* his!! It belongs to his mother." The sternness in my voice made it apparent that I did not find any humor in the situation. I continued, "I find it hard to believe that boy could just give away all that food without asking his mother. What if she planned on packing up what was left-over and bringing it back next week? That stuff is expensive!"

Justin nodded and volunteered to go over to that table and thank the mother for the treat he was about to enjoy. The legs of the chair made an awful noise as he pushed away from the table, picked up the snack, and leaned over the rest of the treats that sat on the table beside us. The mother held a white lacy handkerchief in one hand, and a worn out leather brown purse in the other. She gave Justin her complete attention.

"I just wanted to come over and thank you for bringing these snacks. We never get to eat this stuff during the week, so we go a little crazy when we get it on the week-end. I really appreciate it. Thank you so much." Justin slapped the back of her son, in his usual playful manner and looked up at the mom when she motioned to him with the hand that held the wrinkled white cloth. For the first time she appeared delighted. She had brought just the right thing for so many to enjoy. Her broken English and deliberate search for the right words made it apparent to me how touched she was by Justin's thanks and appreciation. She turned her head and smiled and nodded at me. I couldn't help but return the smile and nod…one mother to another.

Weeks went by. We heard the same "right" words from Justin as we had heard so many times before. He bubbled with enthusiasm as he explained what "neat" things he saw God doing in his life. It thrilled me to know God certainly was at work. I continued to beg God to keep my eyes on Him and not on Justin.

Every Wednesday night was parent's night in the chapel of the Teen Challenge campus. Often times I would go alone as Jim would be gone on a trip. One time in particular moved my heart. It was a time I would never forget.

The chapel was a small brick and cement-faced structure attached to the far end of the main building. It was exactly like walking into a miniature church. The simple pews and altar looked as "holy" as the ones you'd find in any gold embossed, lavishly adorned cathedral. I usually sat in the fifth row from the front, close enough to the altar without feeling too obvious. My seat offered the perfect vantage point to watch all the boys and men in the program. They filed into the chapel dressed in their Sunday best. At first I didn't pay much attention to anyone in the program, but oddly enough, Justin changed all that. Every time I interacted with him, he would drag over a new "friend" and it wasn't long before I knew most of their names, family situation, long list of bad decisions and prayer requests. I became committed to pray for all the families involved with the program. Certain people made a permanent mark on my heart.

One young man brought his freckled-faced wife and four small children to meet me. The little blond heads bounced all around as they hugged and nestled up against their beloved dad. The mother let the little ones run unrestrained while she interacted with her husband. Their marriage was not safe. The stress from the lack of finances and forced daily separation was obvious when they snapped at each other. They were both struggling to survive. I wondered to myself who had the greater difficulty? Was it the boy comfortably pressed and well fed and in the program or was it the mom, who had the greater struggle—the one with the hungry babies and lack of time or energy to do anything about all the sticky fingers and torn, wrinkled clothes? The answer was never clear to me.

There was another person in the program who unexpectedly touched my heart. He was a rough looking older guy who often spoke of the "good old days" when he was a professional boxer. Drugs took him down and killed every relationship he ever had. They nearly killed him too. This guy loved Jim. Every time I saw him at the chapel he would make sure to tell me to give Jim "his best." Nearly every Wednesday night this man spent most of the time at the foot of the altar where he sobbed uncontrollably. Person after person tried to offer consolation, yet nothing was able to reach the root of his pain. I knew the Lord would be the only One who could soothe the ache of this tortured man. I thought of him often when I prayed.

So many broken lives collected into one small space. I always looked forward to the distraction of the singing. It was the time when all the despair in life melted into a magnificent hope-filled melody. The funny thing about that time of singing was that most of the guys in the program weren't gifted in the area of music. The truth was most of the guys could barely carry a tune. But when that group of 50 or so boys and men got together and sang to the glory of God, let me tell you there wasn't a dry eye in the room. It felt as though I had become invisible while they entered into their own very private worship.

Justin often led the group. His crystal clear voice added such sweetness to their songs. Family and friends were always encouraged to sing along. We all clumsily followed along while desperately trying to find the tune in the unfamiliar songs. As strange as this may sound, even though it appeared worship was happening for most of the people in the chapel, it was not a time of worship for me. Yes, there was always such great music and an even better message, but there was something missing in it for me and I could never really but my finger on it. On one of those nights in the chapel, when everyone was singing, I found myself distracted by a sound. The whimper of a muffled cry drew my attention to the back of the room. I discreetly turned around to uncover the source of the sound.

There was a woman completely bent over in pain. She sat on the hard wood bench in the back of the room. Her seat creaked as she rocked back and forth sobbing. I understood her pain. I turned back around to face forward, all the time wishing I could run to her and sit beside her. My fingers dug into the pew in front of me while I pretended to sing. I wanted to throw my arms around that woman and tell her about the power of God in our lives. He had not forgotten her. I impatiently waited for the message and music to be finished before I made my way to the back of the chapel.

There were few people over the years that I respected as much as Pastor John and his wife Maurie. They invested their hearts and souls into the lives of the boys and men in Teen Challenge. Every Wednesday evening, families of the residents were invited to hear a message from Pastor John or Maurie. They spoke words of life and hope into the damaged lives of those in the program. Their commitment to the Lord brought light into all of our lives. They offered the truth. The real answer was always…Jesus. I simply loved them.

The people chattering in the front of the chapel didn't distract me from the constant sobbing I had heard throughout the evening. Justin and I pushed our way through the group of people waiting in line to talk to the pastor and his wife. I spotted the woman I wanted to meet. As we approached her seat, I spoke in a hushed voice to Justin that I wanted to spend a few minutes with her. He didn't seem to mind, just as long as I found enough change at the bottom of my purse to buy him a Coke out of the machine. I had gotten accustomed to his request for money for the soda machine. My fingers collected the loose change at the bottom of my purse. He was excited when he realized there was enough for an extra soda for his new "best friend."

Justin disappeared into the exiting crowd. I squeezed past a woman and man while approaching the soft sob that still echoed from the back of the church. I sat down beside her and put my hand on her back. Her profound sorrow brought me to tears.

After a few minutes she lifted her head and looked me straight in the eyes. The anguished expression on her face asked me if I really understood the depth of her pain. I didn't say anything. I just wiped the tears away from my eyes and continued to gently pat her back. She cried through every carefully spoken word she said. Her detailed story spanned the course of the last five years. I shook as she revealed all the sordid details of her husband's affairs. His cruelty went so far as to parade each new conquest in front of her. He had spent all the money she had worked so hard to collect at her minimum wage job. Even the little bit of money she had managed to save from years of yard sales was gone. The rent hadn't been paid in months and there were two small children. The car had been repossessed and he had stolen and pawned everything but a few pieces of furniture.

She wondered if I had ever met him. I searched through my mental
Teen Challenge photo album. I just couldn't get his face to come up on the
page. I did remember hearing Justin and several others talking about the
two guys who had just left the program. Her husband was one of them. In
between deep shaky breaths, she asked me an important question. "Is there
any hope for me and my husband?"

Wow! What a question! "Oh yes," I said with deep conviction, "We do
have hope!" She took the tissue I offered and stopped the rocking motion
to listen to me. "Your hope cannot be in your husband. He will fail you.
Your hope needs to be in Jesus Christ. He will never fail you." I wiped my
own eyes. She nodded while she stared at the used tissue she had wrapped
around one of her fingers. Her life continued to unfold before me.

She had loved God when she was a child. Things were different now,
she explained, as if that bit of information was something she thought I
needed to know. Her circumstances had stolen her focus away from God.
She had even forgotten what it felt like to think about God.

Justin came back into the chapel holding his newly acquired can of
soda. He smiled at the woman while he leaned over and whispered that he
would be waiting outside for me. I nodded and told him I'd be a few more
minutes. The woman asked me if Justin was my son. She said she saw the
resemblance in our eyes. I smiled, but thought how often I was told Justin
looked like Jim. The break in our serious conversation gave her a chance
to catch her breath and ask me some questions.

"Is life hard for you?" She asked with a new intensity. I looked at the
cross in the front of the empty chapel for a moment then looked right into
her eyes.

"Yes, it has been hard to watch Justin's drug use. It has been going
on for many years. Yes, there are were many difficulties in life. But life is
good. God has always been faithful to me. He has never let me down." I
feared my words were too simple. I didn't want her to think I'd given her
some kind of pat answer I had picked up in a meeting. This really was the
truth I lived by.

She put her hands on top of my hands without letting go of any of the
bunched tissue lodged between her fingers. "Do you believe God can help
me? I want to believe that."

I smiled while I squeezed her hands in mine. "Oh yes, yes…" I spoke
with great assurance. I not only knew for absolute certainty that God could
help her; I knew she could live a victorious life…in the middle of her worst,
most painful, seemingly impossible, circumstance.

We continued to speak for a few minutes before she sat straight up in her seat and said "My goodness, I have kept you here, away from your son for such a long time. Please forgive me."

Justin had always been very sensitive about the needs of hurting people in the past so I assured her he wouldn't mind a bit. We exchanged phone numbers. I hugged her and whispered into her ear one more time, "Remember, God hasn't forgotten you or your husband." Her tear drenched face broke into a smile. There was hope.

Justin stood outside the front door of the chapel. His body language made it clear he had been waiting far too long. I told him I was sorry it took so much time, but I felt I needed to speak to that woman. I tucked my Bible under my arm and threw my purse over my shoulder as we walked toward the car. Justin was still clearly annoyed with me. It was written all over him. While we briskly approached the car, I wondered why it had bothered Justin so much. That woman needed encouragement and it hadn't crossed my mind for one minute that he would have a problem with that!

Our shoes made a crunching sound as we walked on the blacktop's loose gravel. Finally we stopped right in front of the car. I plopped my purse and Bible down on the hood with the intention of uncovering the root of his "attitude." But before I had a chance to say anything, Justin asked me if I had enough money for him to get one more soda. I shoved my hand into my purse and fished around the bottom hoping to find a quarter or two. It seemed easier to empty my purse onto the hood of the car than to keep up my endless hand search.

Several coins rolled out of my purse. Justin eagerly took them and ran to the soda machine. The ping of the quarters being plugged into a machine drew the attention of several guys. The Coke can clunked and landed with a thud at the bottom of the dispenser. The dimly lit area in front of the machine made it hard for me to tell who was standing beside him. There must have been a few others because all the laughter and talk belonged to more than Justin and one other person.

I watched Justin's silhouette as he raised his long arm holding the Coke can, high in the air. His audience exploded into laughter. I probably should have been happy Justin was having such a great time, but I wasn't happy at all! Actually, I was miffed! Week after week I had come to the Wednesday night function, and week after week it was the same thing. The most important part of the entire time we spent together was the Coke time. He would always ask for Coke money, and I would always find it somewhere. This week it irritated me more than usual. I felt for the first time that all Justin really wanted out of me was the lousy change I managed to scrape out of the bottom of my bag. If it really upset him that I was spending time with that mother and not him, then why was he standing on the other end of the parking lot every week while I stood alone in front of the car?

The laughter continued. It appeared the other guys added to his story as unfamiliar voices took some of the attention. Over the loudspeaker a booming voice called the evening to a close. The unseen speaker thanked each family for spending another Wednesday evening at the center. I propped myself up against the car while watching family after family kiss and hug their son or husband goodnight. Finally, after many of the cars had left the parking lot, Justin hustled over to me to make his cordial goodbyes. I didn't want to appear too sensitive about the whole soda thing. Maybe I was making a bigger deal out of it, than it actually was. I decided in the last few seconds of conversation to ignore my irritation and say goodnight. The last words I heard out of Justin's mouth were the same week after week, "Mom I love you. Am I going to see you on Sunday?" I nodded a yes while I said "goodbye and I love you too." I climbed into the front seat of the car right before all the lights around Teen Challenge were turned off for the night. Justin disappeared up the stairs to his room. I drove out of the parking lot, the gate locked behind me.

All the way home I reviewed the evening. The blessing of the night for me was the conversation with the mother. She needed encouragement and the Lord gave me the words to point her toward Him. That conversation made everything worthwhile. How odd it seemed to me that I would find the sad woman in the back row, the highlight of the evening. It was as if the praise music, God directed message, and sobbing boys at the altar, had little meaning. What was it that made me feel that way? I took the night apart piece by piece.

Yes, the singing was great and many were moved to tears, but it didn't ever feel like "worship" to me. I always felt like a spectator watching a theater production. I guess that was it! It felt like a performance. Every Wednesday I'd watch the guys throw themselves down at the base of the altar and wail. Each hymn we sang brought almost every hand into the air declaring the awesomeness of God. There was something about all of it though, that lacked genuineness. *Yes*, I thought, *I saw lots of tears, but were they tears of repentance?* Repentance was something very different. Was it possible to repent and not shed a single tear? Of course! Repentance was not triggered by emotion. It would be generated by a changed heart. The guys who stood outside the chapel, after we sang and heard the godly message from Pastor John, appeared to be the same old guys. Conversations were easily overheard, though efforts were made by parents to "keep it down."

For the most part, what I saw every week was the same unflattering behavior. They were rude, disrespectful, and even used language that made my hair curl. Justin fit right in with the rest of the group. When he led the singing he spent the entire rest of our visit talking about how badly it all went on the "stage." Those were the worst visits. Often times I promised myself I wouldn't go back if Justin was going to lead the music. Most of the guys behaved just like Justin. Yes they had on a clean, pressed shirt but that is as far as the cleaning went. Underneath it seemed as if they were all the same dirty guys looking for someone to con. I laughed as I thought about all the quarters I had donated to the Coke machine over the weeks. Did any of them, including Justin, ever ask me or anyone around me for that matter, how we were? No. Never! The only thing that seemed to matter was the free soda and cheap laughs that followed the service.

What a cynical person I had become, and that certainly was not anything that made me proud. I shook my head and tried to redirect my thoughts before I pulled into our driveway.

Months went by and the first part of the Teen Challenge program was over. The daily personal devotion time, group prayer, wonderful choir practices led by Maurie, and deep truth-based teachings of Pastor John had come to an end. With a bit of sadness and a great deal of anticipation, Justin was moved to the second part of the program called "The Ranch."

The Ranch had a halfway house flavor to it. When the guys got to the ranch, they had all just come from an atmosphere of intense daily Bible studies, regular morning prayer time, church twice a week, fund-raising during the week, and scheduled choir practice along with the sharing the tasks of daily living. They brought with them a great hope about what God was doing in their lives, and about what God would do in their lives as they faced the future.

It didn't take long to see all that disappear after only a short time at The Ranch. Most of the days were centered on chores, which took very little time. The bulk of the time was used for door-to-door fundraising. They were all bunched together in a small white van and dropped off in the "better" neighborhoods in search of donations. There were no organized Bible studies, no organized prayer, and hardly any church.

It was so disappointing, and yet I continued to remind myself that God was still in charge. He would call Justin to read His word, pray, and find a way to get to church…if his walk was real. The seven months at the ranch ended up being a downhill slide for most of the guys. Justin wanted to come home. He had seen many of the guys he had lived with for so long drop out of the program. He believed he could stay sober and live at home. This time would be different from all the other times.

Even though Jim and I felt worn down by the years of promises and disappointments, we just couldn't help but agree to help him again. Maybe this time would be different. Maybe he would be able, with the Lord's help, to stay straight. We carried his things to the car and brought him home.

CHAPTER 19

Me, a Chaplain?

Jim was gone a lot. He carried a regular flight schedule and would pick up a trip or two if the money made it worth his while. I didn't mind and often encouraged him to take the extra trip knowing it would be less time for him to have to face life with Justin. We thought it might be challenging. We didn't know it would become almost impossible.

The first thing Justin did when he got back home was to inspect his old bedroom. I had changed it quit a bit while he was gone. The bed was moved from one side of the room to the other. Everything in the room was new to him. The paint, bedding, and wall hangings were all clean and fresh. He examined all the changes carefully and seemed genuinely pleased. I smiled too, as he had no idea how much scrubbing I had done to get the smell of the past out of that space. I had hoped to erase all the bad memories out of the room. The hard work seemed to pay off. Justin said he felt the "fresh start" the room offered to him. Life felt good...for a minute.

It was never hard for Justin to find work. He could walk into a place, flash his smile, and get hired even though the work history section of the application was hardly ever filled out. The only thing he had to do to get started was to take a drug test. Other parents probably don't even give that requirement a second thought, but let me tell you, I held my breath every time I dropped him off to get tested. My guess was there were times when I had taken him to be tested that he never actually went into the lab at all. Those were the job opportunities that mysteriously went away. At times he crafted intricate stories that loosely explained why they had not called him back. Other times, he completely ignored a prospective job in hopes we wouldn't notice how everything seemed to fall apart right around "drug testing" time. Justin was always quick to deny he was using drugs. I knew, even though I wanted to believe differently, Justin was still using drugs. The old days were back. Maybe they had never left.

Finally, Justin got a job. He started working nights. He assured us it would be easier for him to stay clean if he slept all day. If you can believe it, I actually bought it! OK, I thought it made some sense. All of his friends, or so-called friends, worked during the day. In the past, the drugs happened at night. The new job would keep Justin working at night. Obviously it would be harder for him to keep in contact with his drug buddies. I thought if Justin were away from the people who used drugs, he'd stay clean. My logic didn't pan out the way I had expected.

Things were tolerable, at first. Most days I stayed home just to make sure everything was OK. The pressure of that task day after day drove me to feel more and more like both a warden and a prisoner. I was always on guard and I felt trapped in my own home.

One morning, Justin came home from the long night at the gas station, outraged. He slammed doors until they splintered. The bathroom mirror cracked under the pressure of an angry fist. The walls in his bedroom blistered at the hand of his devastating rage.

I stood in the kitchen clutching the sink and praying for the Lord to intercede. It was clear I was vulnerable. Justin would be able to overpower me very easily. The safest place for me, I thought, was braced up against the white-washed kitchen cabinets at the far end of the house. Maybe this storm would pass quickly. I wondered if I needed to call 911. I waited and waited for the calm to come, while Justin's thunderous screams drove terror into every part of my being. Hayden stood crammed behind my legs while my eyes clung to the brightly lit minutes on the microwave. Time went by one fear-bound minute to the next. I was too afraid to cry or breathe. All of a sudden, it was quiet. I found myself guardedly taking a deep breath. The storm had passed. I calculated that this tumultuous event had lasted for only 20 minutes. It felt like it went on for hours. Hayden was still buried behind my legs and not interested in giving up his safe haven. I leaned down to pet his shaggy head as a way of letting him know the tirade had past. I stroked his neck while the warmth of my tears bounced off my hand and fell unto the kitchen floor. I knew living was hard for Justin. Living was hard for me too.

The stillness from Justin's room lasted for hours that day. When I felt it was safe, I picked up the phone to call my sister. Even though she lived thousands of miles away, the phone lines brought us right together. I didn't feel so alone. She listened while I wept about the trauma that had just broken loose in our home. It was the same story over and over, just a new day.

Karen always listened and reminded me to keep my eyes on the Lord. Yes, I thought as I listened to her, "God would use this in my life someday."

I crumbled into tears again as I grappled with the reality of my life. Serving God had always been important to me. My life felt as if it was out of control. Clearly, I was useless to God. How could He use me? I was barely functioning as it was. My walk with the Lord felt as if it couldn't possibly glorify Him. After all I wasn't much of a soldier in the battle I was committed to fight in my own home. With one ear on the receiver while I spoke to Karen, I kept the other ear attentive to any sound that might come out of Justin's room. I intentionally lowered my voice so as not to disturb the sleeping lion. Karen heard my heart and reminded me about all the people I had come to talk to and point to Jesus through this excruciating journey. Yes, I nodded into the phone; there were all the parents at Teen Challenge I had come to know through the support group I had started. And there were those faceless voices I had spent countless hours listening to on the telephone while they wept about horrific drug stories. That was nothing to me. I blew my nose and kept right on believing that I brought very little joy to the Lord.

Our conversation went for nearly half an hour when the phone beeped. I had just come to understand what the signal for "call waiting" sounded like. Even though I was in the habit of ignoring the beep, that day I felt compelled to switch over and take the call. Karen held on while I attended to the person on the other line. I blew my nose one last time and took a deep breath before I said hello.

A pleasant man's voice identified himself as a chaplain from Marketplace Ministry in Dallas, Texas. He went on to tell me several people had given him my name as someone he needed to consider hiring for a "chaplain" position he was looking to fill. I couldn't believe my ears. I wiped my nose and excused myself for a moment while I clicked over to my sister to tell her the unbelievable thing that was happening on the other line. We agreed to continue our conversation later that day.

I patted my eyes and even tried to rub off some of the almost dried mascara that had made black tracks down the sides of my face. Dan Truitt was still on the line. He asked if it would be all right to come by to meet me and drop off some information. There was one small glitch, however, he only had a short time before he would have to head back to Dallas. It seemed out of the question to suggest we arrange another time for the meeting. The time was now.

I hung up the phone in complete amazement. It was only a few hours earlier that I had cowered in the kitchen while praying for the storm to cease. Was it possible for the Lord to use someone who spent most days hiding from her son? What kind of testimony was I?

Karen's words echoed in my head, "Pam, God has a special purpose and a plan for your life. What you are going through is not without usefulness to the Lord." Maybe Karen was right. Maybe God would be able to use me, even when I believed I had only disappointment to offer to Him. I ran to the mirror to wash the last of the hopelessness off my face. I brushed my teeth and tiptoed to Justin's room, just to make sure he was still asleep. The house was at complete rest. I waited for the doorbell to ring.

Dan showed up at the door, arms loaded down with material from Marketplace Ministry. We sat in the living room as far away as possible from Justin's room. I listened intently. It was exciting to hear about the type of job he thought I should prayerfully consider. He asked me to think about becoming a "lay chaplain" to women in the Phoenix area. The job entailed traveling to different parts of the Phoenix area several times a week. Marketplace Ministry was hired by companies to provide a "caring" service for all employees. I was intrigued. Specifically, I would be a listener and through growing relationships with the employees point them to Jesus Christ. It must have been obvious to Dan how completely foreign a "chaplain" job was to me. I nodded, asked very few questions, and promised I'd certainly pray about it. He left to catch his flight to Dallas. I sat at the kitchen table surrounded by stacks of Marketplace Ministry material.

I had come to understand after much reading, the job of chaplain was in some ways like a church greeter. It involved making small talk with people I had never seen before. It certainly seemed feasible to assume I'd be shaking a lot of hands. I sat at the now-smudged glass kitchen table and laughed out loud, remembering my feelings about church greeters.

For years I prayed specifically for our church greeters. After all, I thought they had the worst job in the church. They were the ones who extended their hands each Sunday to welcome people they didn't know and possibly didn't really want to know. Often times I found their enthusiasm a bit overpowering and wondered if our church "guests" held the same view. The greeters stood outside of the church disregarding the weather. If the church was open, the greeters would be in their places ready to welcome you. For some peculiar reason I started praying that the Lord would *not* call me to be a greeter. It was neither a job I could do, nor did I want to do. Yet, oddly enough, I was attracted to the joy-filled smiling faces of our church greeters and continued to pray for them for years.

As I studied the long application in front of me, I thought about this strange situation. I had been feeling for some time that God couldn't use me. After all, I was having trouble wading through life myself. How was it possible for me to do anything like this for God? I shuddered over the inconsistent way I followed the battle plan God had designed for me to fight the enemy on Justin's behalf. I failed miserably. In discouragement, I put my hand down on the stack of papers and asked God to help me stand firm, take up, put on, stand still, pray, and be on the alert. It seemed so hard for me.

I picked up the article Dan had given to me about Marketplace Ministry that had appeared in the Dallas paper. The scope of the job was certainly far more than being a "greeter." It was about serving people. As I finished the last few lines of the article, something became very obvious to me. The success of Marketplace Ministry rested in the chaplain's complete dependence on God. It was not about what they could do, it was about what He would do through them. Certainly, I had forgotten the basic truth about Christian living. Life wasn't about what I could, would, or should do. Life was about the Lord. It wasn't about me. What an awakening! The truth was so clear to me. I would never get Christian living down cold. My life would always be filled with mess ups. Yet, God made me "useful" when He called me to enter into a personal relationship with Him. I don't have to prove myself to God. He knows all of it. As a matter of fact, He knew all of it before the beginning of time.

Yes, God knew about Justin's drug use and my inadequacies in the struggle, long before the dawn of the first day. I smiled to myself when I realized how difficult I had made the Christian walk. It really wasn't intended to be difficult. It was way beyond difficult. It was impossible…without Jesus. Once again I was reminded of the importance of staying centered on the One who would accomplish it all.

I picked up my pen and answered all the questions on the application, stuffed it into an envelope, and licked it shut. I collected the papers that were strewn all over the glass table and put them into a folder I labeled it "Marketplace Ministry." The house was still quiet. Obviously Justin was still in a sound sleep. I quickly grabbed my keys, gave Hayden an assuring pat on the head, and headed for the mailbox in our neighborhood. I chuckled one last time as I dropped the letter into the blue and red metal box. I was applying for a position as "chaplain"—me, the person who couldn't even imagine the job as "greeter" in the church—me, the one who couldn't possibly be of any use to the Lord. I was reminded of a simple Truth. God's ways are not our ways. I smiled and headed back to the house.

I got the job! I learned quickly about the heart of Marketplace Ministry. This was a ministry that had its roots in loving people in the workplace. Our job as "chaplains" was to listen, encourage, and point people to the Great Hope…Jesus. The businesses that hired us wanted to offer their workforce far more than a 1-800 "crisis" number. We were the face of hope and confidentiality to many who had no one to listen to them. Yes I shook a lot of hands and talked to a lot of people about the weather, but in the end it became a job about relationships. The interactions were always uncomfortable for me at first. Never did I feel it was something I could do without the Lord's help. Each time I pulled up to a business, I asked the Lord to walk into that business before me. And constantly in those prayer times I would ask the Lord if He was sure I was the right person for this important job. The last time I asked that question was the day I heard the Lord speak to my heart with these words: "Pam, I never asked you to accomplish this task. I called you to be a chaplain so you would have the privilege of watching *Me* do it." From that day on I kept on the alert to make certain I didn't miss His handiwork.

At one company, after weeks of small talk, a woman asked to speak with me in private. "Pam," she said "my nephew is living with me and I haven't told anyone, but he has been using drugs for some time. I am at my wit's end. I know you don't know anything about a kid on drugs, but I thought you might be able to point me to someone who has had this happen to them." She sobbed. I grabbed her up into my arms and sobbed with her. I understood…completely.

For weeks I met with this woman and listened to her story. She revealed her intensely deep despair. My eyes filled with tears as I relived some of my own desperate moments with Justin. Life can be hard, incredibly, impossibly hard. It was easy to identify with her pain but not with her hopelessness. There was hope even in this horrible situation…and the hope we had was in Jesus. Each time we got together she presented me with questions about God. It was clear she had really put a great deal of thought into each one. Finally one day she asked me why she felt like she was losing her mind. Was she losing it? Boy! That was a question I had asked the Lord several years before. The same Scripture that comforted me then, came back to me in that moment for her. "For God did not give us a spirit of timidity, but a spirit of power, of love and of self-discipline" (2 Tim. 1:7).

She asked me if she could borrow my Bible until we met again. I handed it to her with an apology for all the underlining and personal thoughts written in it. It was clear she was touched that I would entrust such a treasure into her care. I ended up giving that Bible to her and watched her make her own notes in the margin. God was at work and He was using my pain with Justin as a pillow for this woman to rest her head. I was completely humbled by the privilege.

CHAPTER 20

The Bible Study

The days rolled one into another. Justin worked all night and slept all day. I loved the sweet calm his nightshift brought into our home. Often I tiptoed to his room to whisper a prayer into the air he breathed. Drugs were a big part of his life and ours. His denials did not influence what I knew in my heart. "Oh Lord" I whispered, "help me help Justin."

I often sat in the family room on the turquoise and rust overstuffed couch…just thinking. It seemed the best thing to do some days. The time was right to drift high above this world when I knew Ashley was tucked safely away on the school bus and Jim had boarded the airplane for his flight while Justin slept. My mind left the mundane of this world and traveled to the heavenly places. Often times I contemplated the sovereignty of God. Have you ever done that? I mean to just check out of the moment and put your mind on spiritual things? I took great comfort from those times. Although I knew that the sovereignty of God was way over my head, I thought about the fact that whatever happened in life was allowed by God for His purpose. For some unexplained purpose God had allowed Justin to be a drug addict. I never thought God wanted this kind of life for Justin, nor had I ever considered that God caused Justin to want methamphetamines. What I truly believed was that God knew all about Justin and allowed him to be on the path he was on, for His reasons. The out-of-control life Justin led was completely within the grasp of God. Nothing escaped the notice or the attention of our precious Lord. Even the very breath Justin took was provided by God Himself. I pondered His magnificence. The incredible God of the universe and beyond had the power to march Justin into victory. I clung to my marching orders and basked in the glory of knowing such a wondrous Lord.

Typically, Justin's key to the front door announced he was home from work around 7 A.M. It was good timing for Ashley. By the time Justin got home each morning she was already hidden behind her bedroom door sitting cross-legged on the floor while she finished the final few curls on her head. I was either putting the last of the breakfast dishes into the dishwasher or scrambling around trying to find the money Ashley needed for lunch.

It was Tuesday morning and our routine was the same one we had practiced since the beginning of school. The only difference was Justin hadn't come home from work that morning. Ashley left for school smelling great and looking like the "dolly girl" Jim always liked to call her. Jim was home, and as was his practice spent his morning sipping tea while studying the stock market. He didn't say anything when 7 A.M. came and went. Ashley kissed us both goodbye and made me promise not to worry about Justin. I laughed realizing how well she knew me. Jim was really the worried one.

As soon as Ashley disappeared down the street with the neighbor, Jim closed the newspaper and put his teacup down. His big hand began rubbing his forehead while he said what we were both thinking. What happened to Justin? Was this a drug-related disappearance? Did something happen to him at work? What had *happened*? It didn't take long for us to agree that we had seen the familiar markers of drug behavior. We just didn't want to believe we were seeing them again! No doubt Justin had re-entered the life he professed so often that he hated.

Justin was gone for only a couple of weeks that time. As soon as he got home, slept, and ate, he picked up and left again. This happened time after time for years. He went from drug rehab program to drug rehab program; from halfway house to halfway house. When he got kicked out of one, he would find another. If nothing worked out, he slept on the street. We didn't know where he was most of time. The only thing—the one and *only* thing—I clung to was the sovereignty of God.

Good friends tried to offer encouragement by sending me information they had found on various drug rehab centers around the country. I accumulated a good-sized pile of possibilities. Justin had been involved in more rehab programs than I could count on both hands. Many people sent us information about one program in particular. It wasn't one I had ever heard of before that time. I kept that material on the top of my hopeful stack. The shiny brochure attracted me in some strange way. For days I fingered the glossy finished paper until I finally decided to share this new possibility of hope, with Jim.

Jim was tired of trying to figure out which program would be the best one for Justin. He reminded me that Justin denied he was still using drugs. So how in the world would we be able to convince him to get into another rehab? Jim was right. Every time I brought up my suspicions to Justin, he would go into a tirade. The house shook under the earthquake of his emotion. The best way to handle this would be through prayer.

Prayer was a dangerous thing. Often times it convicted me to be a part of things I'd never considered like leading a support group at Teen Challenge, or working as a chaplain in Marketplace Ministry. In those sweet conversations with the Holy One I would even find myself compelled to get involved in things I had never even wanted to consider before.

One afternoon after prayer, I picked up the phone and dialed the number listed at the bottom of the brochure that sat on top of a stack of so many. The name of the program in bold print above the phone number was "Second Chance." A sweet young voice answered the phone. She told me a little bit about the program. Out of the blue, I asked her if the group of parents met for regular Bible study. The silence on the other end of the phone made the answer obvious. "No, we don't have a Bible study right now," was her delayed response. Without giving it a thought, I immediately volunteered to teach the Bible study. I had not planned to volunteer or do anything for a group I didn't know anything about—let alone volunteer to teach a Bible study! Certainly prayer had something to do with it! She quickly gave me the date of the meeting and directions to the home of one of the parents. I marked the day on my calendar. For the next few days, I retraced the conversation with the young girl in an effort to understand how I had come to volunteer to teach a Bible study. I was both nervous and excited about this new challenge.

Tuesday night came much quicker than I had anticipated. Jim was at home relaxing on the couch in our bedroom while filing airport updates into a big plastic binder. He had a huge stack of work in front of him, so I knew he would be busy for hours. Ashley was across the street at the neighbors having "after homework" brownies. Justin was sprawled out on the couch in the family room dozing with a half-eaten sandwich in front of him waiting for it to be time for him to go to work.

I didn't invite Jim to come with me to the first Second Chance meeting as I really didn't know why I was drawn to this particular program myself. It seemed a better idea to check it out first, than ask him to go. However, I did invite Justin, but wasn't surprised when he said a flat "no."

It was nearing 7 P.M. I grabbed my Bible, said goodbye, and headed for the address I had scribbled on the back of the brochure. As I sat in my car in front of the house I had to laugh at the fact I had volunteered to teach a Bible study to a group of people I had never met who were involved in a drug rehab program I had never heard of. This all underscored something even more glaring than anything else. I really didn't know what they believed.

I collected the teaching material and my favorite Bible from the passenger seat of the car while fumbling to find my purse which had found its way from the seat to the floor. I looked in the rearview mirror and rubbed the lipstick off my teeth while thanking God for how He was going to use this in my life…somehow.

I was greeted at the door by a delightful woman who ushered me into the living room where four parents and a young girl were assembled in quiet conversation. I found a seat near the doorway in one of the two metal folding chairs. A pizza box was open on the coffee table in the middle of the room with most of the pizzas sitting on flimsy paper plates on the laps of the chatting parents. It was strange to me how comfortable I felt in that group. I didn't know any of them and yet I honestly felt connected to them.

It wasn't long before the focus was turned from the thick slabs of pepperoni pizza to me. I smiled nervously while the young girl introduced me as a parent with an "addict" son who had volunteered to teach a Bible study to the group. It was the first time I had heard a stranger refer to Justin as an "addict." Terms like "user," "druggie," and even "tweeker" didn't have the sting that "addict" had. The thought startled me a bit. I pushed myself quickly through the desire to stop all conversation and talk about why she called Justin an "addict." I hated that term. In that brief millisecond though, I accepted that truth. What a way to be introduced to the group. She said the one thing, the very thing that was the hardest to hear. My son was an "addict."

I took a deep breath and in my heart wrestled with the truth. Justin *was* a drug addict. It took me a minute to get refocused on the couples who sat in front of me. No one seemed to notice the spin my mind was just coming out of. They welcomed me with warm smiles and gentle loving eyes. A guarded joy underscored the group's enthusiasm as each parent verbalized how this program, Second Chance worked for their son. That discussion was interrupted abruptly by the young lady. "Pam," she said while looking down at her notes, "are you ready to start the Bible study?"

"Yes," was all I could get out in an equally hurried manner.

After brief introductions, I asked if anyone in the group had heard of the study "Experiencing God." I loved that study and knew even if not one other person in the room got anything out of it, I certainly would! Several of the parents nodded their heads while looking intently at the man whose house hosted the meeting. I directed my attention toward him as well. He was clearly going to act as the spokesperson for the group.

"Pam," he said with a practiced assuredness, "the kind of Bible study we need is one that is AA centered. Our children are getting that kind of teaching, so we feel it would help us stay on the same page as our child."

I listened carefully and was really taken aback by the request. It wasn't that I didn't like AA. It's just that it felt backwards. The tenets of AA should fall under the teaching of the Bible, not the other way around. I understood where these parents were coming from and I respected their desire to reinforce what their children were learning, but…and this was a big BUT for me… what if what they were learning was *not* in line with the Bible?

The man's comments came to a close and the other parents seemed to want to make certain that I understood his request was "right on" with the goals of the group. I prayed as I listened to their thoughts and was relieved when it became clear the depth of love these parents had for the Lord. I agreed to use the AA principles with the understanding God's Word came first. We agreed to meet faithfully for eight weeks, and then re-assess our direction. It was hard to believe it was already 9:30 P.M. and time to call it a night. I helped clean up the clutter from the pizza and folded the metal chairs. There was excitement in the air as we talked about the blessing of studying God's word together.

"Goodnight" was filled with handshakes and hugs. I even felt comfortable enough to ask for the name of the pizza place, as it had been really good. Bible in one hand and pizza information in the other, I juggled to push the right place on my keys to click the opener on my car as I walked down the narrow old cement walkway in front of the house. As I turned the key in the ignition I glanced back at the house and wondered what God was going to do in that study? I belonged with that collection of people for some reason. I smiled to myself as I pulled away from the house and headed home.

Our weekly gatherings were filled with deep heartfelt discussion. Everyone grappled with the possible underlying cause for their child's drug use. Lots of feelings were exposed. Week after week I listened as they explored their own guilt-based theories of why the drug use had begun. Blame-shackled parents sat in front of me Tuesday after Tuesday, clanging their chains of "should haves" or "should not haves" completely paralyzed in their circumstance.

As I listened, I was struck by the need of parents with "addict" kids to expose their own personal flaws as if our flaws "must be" the reason for our child's turmoil. I had gone through that personal flogging years ago. Was there an answer? Was the reason for the demise of our child our inadequacies as parents? Those were tough questions to face. Even at our church the annual family conference banner that got carefully strung up over the entrance read "How to Raise Kids Who Turn Out Right!" Could it be that we, the parents of "addicts," had missed some important aspect of parenting that caused our children *not* to turn out right? Was there a formula for successful parenting?

I shook my head every time I walked into church past the banner. Several parents would hunt for me after church as they glared up at the hopelessness of that conference title, asking me if it was even possible to "raise kids who turn out right?" Time after time I would point them to the Scripture. God was perfect, and yet he had Adam and Eve, who sinned. Then the flawed Adam and Eve had one son named Cain who murdered their other son Abel. And who could forget King David who had troubled children, and yet God called David, "a man after His own heart."

There was one real reason for the drug use of a child. It was sin. For years we have heard the Scripture about the sins of the father being passed down to the son. Yes, it was true that genetically we can pass on a predisposition for a certain sin, but what we don't pass down is the sin! Every person is responsible for his/her own choices. That teaching was eye-opening to these parents. Was it possible for them, and me, to believe that the decision of their child to use drugs had nothing to do with them? That was a stretch to get our emotions around, but it made sense to the mind. In the Bible, God addressed Israel when people were grumbling about the consequences they felt they were enduring because of the sins of their fathers. God addressed that notion in Ezekiel 18:1-18:

> The word of the LORD came to me: "What do you people mean by quoting this proverb about the land of Israel: 'The fathers eat sour grapes, and the children's teeth are set on edge'? As surely as I live, declares the Sovereign LORD, you will no longer quote this proverb in Israel. For every living soul belongs to me, the father as well as the son—both alike belong to me. The soul who sins is the one who will die. Suppose there is a righteous man who does what is just and right. He does not eat at the mountain shrines or look to the idols of the house of Israel. He does not defile his neighbor's wife or lie with a woman during her period. He does not oppress anyone, but returns what he took in pledge for a loan. He does not commit robbery but gives his food to the hungry and provides clothing for the naked. He does not lend at usury or take excessive interest. He withholds his hand from doing wrong and judges fairly between man and man. He follows my decrees and faithfully keeps my laws. That man is righteous; he will surely live, declares the Sovereign LORD. Suppose he has a violent son, who sheds blood or does any of these other things (though the father has done none of them): He eats at the mountain shrines. He defiles his neighbor's wife. He oppresses the poor and needy. He commits robbery. He does not return what he took in pledge. He looked to the idols. He does detestable things. He lends at usury and takes excessive interest. Will such a man live? He will not! Because he has done all these detestable things, he will surely

be put to death and his blood will be on his own head. But suppose this son has a son who sees all the sins his father commits, and though he sees them, he does not do such things: He does not eat at the mountain shrines or look to the idols of the house of Israel. He does not defile his neighbor's wife. He does not oppress anyone or require a pledge for a loan. He does not commit robbery but gives his food to the hungry and provides clothing for the naked. He withholds his hand from sin and takes no usury or excessive interest. He keeps my laws and follows my decrees. He will not die for his father's sin; he will surely live. But his father will die for his own sin, because he practiced extortion, robbed his brother and did what was wrong among his people."

So what did that mean to us, parents of "drug addicts?" It meant that each person is held accountable to God for his or her choices. It was a personal reckoning. We are all tempted to sin. But to actually commit the sin, was a personal choice. James 1:12-15 says:

Blessed is the man who perseveres under trial, because when he has stood the test, he will receive the crown of life that God has promised to those who love him. When tempted, no one should say, "God is tempting me." For God cannot be tempted by evil, nor does he tempt anyone; but each one is tempted when, by his own evil desire, he is dragged away and enticed. Then, after desire has conceived, it gives birth to sin; and sin, when it is full-grown, gives birth to death.

Those words spoke such truth in the case of drug addiction. The Lord held each of us accountable for our own lives. There was nothing a parent did that caused their son or daughter to use drugs. That was an enormous uncovering for each parent in the group. I kept pointing to the root of the sin—the presence of spiritual warfare! How painful to watch our tortured child and yet we also knew that God provided a way of escape. Again in James 4:7-8, the Scripture read:

Submit yourselves, then, to God. Resist the devil, and he will flee from you. Come near to God and he will come near to you. Wash your hands, you sinners, and purify your hearts, you double-minded.

It all started with submission to God. Could any of us say that our child had submitted to God? That would be the first step to healing. Honestly, I wondered if anyone in the group noticed how God's word held the perfect "AA" (power Already Available).

On one occasion, after we finished the meat of our Bible lesson, one parent could hardly contain her exuberance any longer and began to share her son's victory. He was off drugs, taking school more seriously, and pursuing a personal relationship with Jesus Christ. The small group ate up the victory and enjoyed it as a personal one for each of us. The encouraging report from one set of parents almost made it impossible for the other couple not to share how their son was doing in the program. I sat in anticipation of equally great news from them. The mom sat quietly for a moment, and with obviously a great deal of difficulty she spoke.

"My son was asked to leave the program." We all gasped, wondering what in the world he could have done to have been kicked out. She wasn't able to offer any more than that one sentence, and although we looked to the dad for further explanation, none was offered. The mood in the room changed immediately. I leaned over and put my hand on her arm as she bent over and wept. We all now embraced the pain of that parent. We knew it well.

I thought about Justin as we hadn't heard from him in some time and that was never a good sign. I looked around the room and saw red eyes everywhere. I wondered if the family with the good news now questioned if they were doomed to face the same report in the future. *Where was Justin?* I thought to myself. The meeting ended in silence, seemingly everyone already anticipating their next difficulty. This was the roller coaster of emotion we had all come to understand.

CHAPTER 21

The Unexpected News

It was a Wednesday night when the phone rang. The house was quiet, only the muffled sound of the last few minutes of Ashley's television program resonating in the background. I picked up the phone to hear Jim's voice on the other end. He called me nearly every night when he was out of town, but typically it was before bedtime. Tonight was different. Jim's professional tone, the one he usually saved for his crew and passengers underscored the seriousness of every word.

"Pam, would you do me a favor?" his voice sounded almost out of breath.

"Yes, of course!" Was all I could get out before he gave me the instruction.

"I think something is wrong with me. It takes every bit of energy I have just to pull my flight bag from one end of the airport to the other. It's as if I just can't catch my breath. Would you call our family doctor and see if he can see me Friday morning?"

His question definitely filled me with concern. Jim was never one to complain. As a matter of fact, he had only taken one sick day from work in the last ten years. I knew Jim really believed something serious was wrong. I immediately reassured him I would get the appointment set up first thing the next morning. Usually our conversation ended with me trying to be funny. This time I couldn't find anything to laugh about. I was worried, this time about Jim.

Friday morning came not a minute too soon. Jim was definitely having trouble catching his breath. He felt crummy as if he had the flu. A cup of tea didn't interest him, nor did the net gain of the Southwest Airline stock. Everything about his routine changed that morning. I told him I wanted to go to his doctor's appointment with him, but he proceeded to give me some lame reason why I didn't need to waste my time sitting in a doctor's office when I already had enough to do. Before I had a chance to put down my toothbrush, he was out the door. I heard the thud of the garage door slam shut against the cement floor. I threw on my clothes and screeched out of the driveway just minutes behind him.

When I got to the doctor's office, Jim was already in with Dr. Palmer. I thumbed through a few magazines, but couldn't get my mind centered on anything but what was going on behind the closed doors.

Nearly an hour had passed before Jim appeared at the front desk armed with a small stack of papers. He handed me the pile of forms he held in his hands while he reached into his wallet for the insurance card. I quickly shuffled through all the papers and found it to be a stack of orders for tests—lots of tests. While Jim stuffed his wallet into the back pocket of his jeans shorts, I stood silently waiting for him to tell me what happened. He recollected the paperwork from me and grabbed my hand to hurry us out of the office so he could give me a full report.

"Pam, it is serious. He said it sounds like there is a considerable amount of fluid surrounding my heart."

What? I couldn't believe what I was hearing. Jim had always been so healthy. My face told him exactly what I was thinking without uttering a word.

He continued, "I know...this is hard to believe. I can't remember the last sick day I took from work."

I forced a reassuring smile to appear on my face. I kept thinking. God was sovereign. Yes, God knew about all this even before the beginning of time. It was going to be all right. My smile became genuine. "Jim, God is sovereign. I know it is going to be all right."

Jim's furrowed brow and half grin made it clear to me he lacked my confidence.

We spent hours in doctor's offices all over the city getting x-rays and scans. The last appointment was with the cardiologist. He was baffled by the amount of fluid he believed was pressing on Jim's heart. It was time to get to the hospital…immediately!

Past experience prepared us for the slow go of the "admittance" process. We settled into the almost comfortable chairs in the waiting room, completely expecting to get through at least half of "Regis and Kelly" before Jim would be called into one of the little booths. But his name was shouted out within minutes of our arrival. An orderly appeared with a wheelchair and we were whisked upstairs to a private room. Before Jim finished changing from street clothes into his blue cotton Johnny, a nurse came in to give "pre-surgery" instructions.

Our eyes widened when she described the surgery Jim was about to face. They were going to make an incision close to his heart to relieve the pressure caused by the fluid. The hole would act as the escape route for the unwanted liquid. It was very serious. I gently patted Jim on the back as the nurse continued to dictate the next series of events. Our stunned countenance made it clear we were unprepared for the news that Jim was facing heart surgery.

The nurse left us for a minute to collect our thoughts. We were blown away. I kept repeating the one thing I knew for a fact. God was sovereign. He knew about this surgery and the outcome of it before the beginning of time. We could trust Him. Jim was preoccupied in thought. "Jim, what are you thinking?" I said in a soft, almost whispered, voice.

"I don't know what to think. I am going to obviously be out of work for a while. I probably need to call someone and tell them."

I reminded him that he was scheduled off for the next few days anyway, so it wasn't something that needed to get done right that moment. For Pete's sake, I would make those calls for him! The nurse reappeared with a list of questions and further instructions. Jim signed the papers and within a few minutes he was being wheeled into the prep room for surgery. I stayed right beside him the whole time, just hoping he would find it a comfort.

The anesthesiologist entered the area with a cheerful attitude and more things to sign. It was time for me to move to the waiting room. I leaned over and kissed Jim's forehead right before the medicine took effect and he went to sleep. The cold metal door of the surgical prep room swung open and pushed me to the empty hallway.

It was time for serious prayer. I called everyone I knew who would pray sincerely. The first on my list was my sister, then Jim's family and my friends. Everyone was concerned and bewildered at the same time. Jim was healthy. He had always been healthy. All the phone calls kept me focused on the Lord not on my circumstance. I kept uttering "thank you" to the nurses and doctors who kept me posted throughout the surgery. Mostly, I thanked the Lord for His endless mercy and abundant goodness. I sipped on the bottled water I had remembered to stash in my purse, and I smiled when I thanked Him for that too. I sat alone waiting for the doctor's report.

It was hours before the surgery was over. Jim had an extremely serious periocarditis. They took more than 1200cc's of fluid out from around his heart. Both attending physicians were amazed his heart was still able to function under so much stress. I listened and continued to thank God with every word I heard. The surgery was over and Jim had come through it with flying colors. He would be fine. The big question remained. Why had Jim developed such a serious condition? No one had that answer, and it would take days before the tests would take us to that end. I watched as the nurses wheeled my sleeping husband to his room in intensive care.

Ashley was shocked to see all the equipment and tubes surrounding her dad. It was so upsetting. She gingerly touched his arm just to let him know she was right next to him. He opened his eyes and gave her a little smile to reassure her.

"Mom," Ashley spoke quietly into my ear, "why did this happen? Is he going to be all right?"

I didn't have answers to either of those questions. I did, however, know one thing for absolute certain, we could trust God. I drew a deep breath and took Ashley's pretty face into my hands.

"Ashy, I don't have those answers. Right now even the doctors don't know anything. What we do know is that your dad made it through surgery. And the other thing we know is that we can trust the Lord with the answers we don't have."

She crinkled her mouth in a way that had always told me she wasn't convinced God was the one to trust in this situation. I heard her silent disagreement loud and clear. She considered my answer a bit trite and way too simplistic. Her skeptical look spoke volumes to me. We settled into our separate private places. Ashley clung to the scientific and I clung to the spiritual. We sat quietly and watched Jim sleep.

Almost an hour went by before a nurse poked her head around the curtain to remind us of the time. Jim needed to have absolute quiet after such a big ordeal. We should let him have undisturbed rest and attend to our own exhaustion. Ashley and I both agreed with her suggestion but found it hard to get ourselves up from the comfort of our seats. Jim had been asleep for a long time when we tiptoed out of his room. The predictable rhythm of all his monitors coupled with the dimly lit room proved to be just about enough to put us to sleep too. Ashley and I went home.

It took five days before we had any information. Jim went from intensive care to heart care to a regular room. We were encouraged every time they moved him from one floor to the next. It signaled to us that he was getting better. Jim was feeling stronger and was relieved to finally have the heaviness gone from his chest. He did his breathing exercises regularly and loved the fact he could take deep breaths again. Things seemed good to us. We waited for the doctors to tell us what we expected to hear. Jim was healthy and it was a complete fluke for him to have had such a serious case of periocarditis. They would send him home soon.

One morning while I sipped on my chai and Jim finished the rest of his bland hospital breakfast, a doctor we had not yet met walked in. His wrinkled white jacket and scruffy face contrasted with the image I had of a physician. He was the oncologist. He sat cross-legged in a hard chair facing Jim. High water pants and white socks didn't give this guy much credibility. I listened with skepticism. The tests showed Jim had cancer. It was kidney cancer. Jim and I were stunned. Before we could catch our breath, he went on. The tests also showed the cancer had spread to the fluid around the lining of his heart. It was extremely serious. The protocol for such a scenario was sketchy at best. He offered a chemotherapy regime that was so harsh it would probably kill him and if we chose to forgo chemo, Jim would probably have not many months to live.

I couldn't believe how insensitive the oncologist appeared to me. He had the nerve to come into our room unannounced and just lay all that information down at our feet. If he had any people skills at all, he would have certainly picked up on the fact that we were dazed and not following him at all when he went over the tests results. We were stuck on the one word he said early on in his regurgitation of the facts. The two syllables we could not get our minds around was *"can…cer."*

I watched Jim as the oncologist went on and on about one test and another. Jim had checked out. He was in complete shock. I interrupted the doctor and told him that we needed some time alone. We would get back to him at another time. The "matter of fact" manner of delivering such earth-shaking news only punctuated the obvious lack of compassion we felt from our frumpy statistician.

The decision was made on the spot. Jim and I agreed that that doctor would not be our doctor. We couldn't speak. It was as if the word "cancer" became the only word we knew of a foreign language we had not yet learned.

Jim broke the silence with a question. "Pam, what are we going to do?" The news had shaken me to my very core, too. I had no idea what we were going to do in the medical world. I only knew what we needed to do in the spiritual world.

"Jim, we are going to pray. God will show us what to do."

Jim could tell my response was dead serious. God had never failed us with Justin. Even in the middle of the most horrible nightmare of life with a drug addict, God was always there. He would walk this new road with us. I was confident and at peace with trusting God.

Jim asked me if I would pray right that second. I leaned over his bed and thanked God for everything He had done in our lives. I thanked Him for the successful surgery and how He guided the hands of the surgeons. I thanked Him for the fact we now had test results. I thanked Him for the path He would put before us on this new journey. Finally, I thanked Him for the gift of belief. It would be the thing that kept me walking…in hope.

Before Jim was released from the hospital, he had to have a consultation with several of the doctors on the case. The doctors proposed their vision of Jim's "plan of attack." They wanted him to go home and get strong for another surgery. He would have the cancerous kidney removed. Our urologist explained that many patients survive kidney cancer after its removal with the use of mild chemo and/or radiation. Yes, it all sounded so hopeful. Jim came home.

It wasn't long before Jim was up and about. We got in the habit of taking a brisk walk around our neighborhood. Those were times when I prayed aloud about everything and everyone in our lives. I always wished that Jim would jump in and pray with me, but he never did. Prayer always invigorated me. It was as if the Lord gave me a shot of B12 every time I walked into His presence. Those were precious times to me.

CHAPTER 22

The Hospital

My father recently moved to Arizona and my mother and her husband followed shortly after. Their apartments were in the same complex. I visited them almost every day. It was funny to watch my dad interact with the man my mother had married just five years earlier.

My dad was a different man than the one I remembered when I was young. He had a small stroke eight years before he moved to Arizona and it appeared that neurological event snapped all the meanness out of him. His gentle ways and funny habits endeared him to everyone he met. The three most important people to him were "The Big Guy Upstairs," my sister, and me. It always made me laugh when he'd show me the prizes he planned to win after purchasing raffle tickets. He thought Karen and I would love to have new shiny Corvettes, and those were the coveted prizes he longed to win for us. His life had become dedicated to Karen and me and we loved the new place we held in his heart.

My sister had invited Dad to spend time with her at her home in Hawaii. He was so excited. After carefully packing all his colorful shirts and summer shorts, he was ready for the trip. I picked him up and took him to the airport after he had "buttoned up" everything in his tiny apartment. He had never been to Hawaii and couldn't wait to finally see it in person. It was an easy drive to the airport.

When we got into the terminal he stopped in one of the gift stores and bought Karen a box of candy. He knew how much she loved chocolates and was thrilled when he found the perfect chewy treats. With the wrapped box carefully tucked under one arm and me holding his other arm we ambled toward the gate. We were early, so we decided to sit in front of the security area for a while. He put his hand on my arm and looked at me with his crystal blue eyes.

"Pammy," he said with a concerned tone in his voice. "it is going to be all right. Jim is going to be OK. I know this is a tough time for you, but I want you to know one thing, I will be there for you, always. Remember if you need anything, it's yours. Pammy, everything I have I would gladly hand over to you and your sister."

I couldn't hold back the tears that broke free from my eyes and ran down my face. He meant every last word of it. He hugged me and I saw his eyes fill up with water while he stood up and readied himself for the long trek to his gate. The security line was fast filling up, so we decided it was time for him to go. I kissed his wrinkled cheek and hugged him again. I was choked up when I told him how much I'd miss him while he was gone. He smiled and told me he had enough room in his carry-on for me to take the trip too. I laughed. I watched him while he stood in line. He kept turning around to see if I was still sitting where he had left me. I'd wave and blow a kiss. He laughed while he waved with the stiff fingers that awkwardly clung to his gift for Karen.

Security randomly selected dad for the wand search. He didn't mind. My eyes followed him while he hobbled over to a chair to put his sneakers back on. A man with a wheelchair waited for him. Together they left the area and headed for the gate at the far end of the terminal. His baseball cap was all I could see from where I stood. I sure loved my dad. It was hard to watch him leave.

Jim went back into the hospital and had the diseased kidney removed. He was so glad to have it gone! The doctors were very upbeat and hopeful. It appeared as if most of the cancer was gone, but before we really had a chance to celebrate, the tactless doctor we had met early on this road showed up in Jim's room for another visit. The stuffed binder he held in his hands was the same one that had just pronounced the good news.

I didn't dismiss him because I thought he was going to reiterate the positive results we had just learned. In those moments we would have encouraged anyone who wanted to read the file to come in and say that Jim was *cancer-free*. The disheveled man began biting the side of his lip while studying the reports. We watched him intently. After what felt like a long time, though it was just minutes, he revealed the purpose of his visit. The PET scan results had just come in and it revealed more cancer. He wanted to know our plan. Jim looked at me. I took charge of the moment and assured the intruder we would decide a course of action before Jim left the hospital. He appeared somewhat satisfied with our answer and left the room. Jim struggled to sit on the edge of his bed. He wanted to walk. I grabbed his arm and silently we walked in a monotonous circle through the hospital halls again and again.

Just after we passed the nurses' station for the fifth time, my cell phone rang. *Oh darn*, I thought as I struggled to find it in the bottom of my pocket. I was someone who always wanted to follow all the rules, so I was a bit irritated with myself when I pushed send and put the phone to my ear. Jim obviously thought it was either Ashley or one of my friends. He showed no interest in the call.

"Hello," I whispered into the phone.

"Is this Mrs. Cox?" the stranger asked.

"Yes," I continued to whisper. "Mrs. Cox, your son Justin is here in the emergency room. He has had a drug overdose. We are very concerned about his heart. He has had a heart attack. I am calling because he wanted you to know he is OK."

She hung up before I had a chance to say a word. Jim stopped walking and faced me.

"Pam, is everything OK?"

I told him the call was about Justin. Justin was fine. I tried to will the worry lines off my face. It seemed as though Jim hadn't fully comprehended what I said. The pain medication he took kept his thinking a bit fuzzy. I was glad he didn't press me about the phone call. We started walking again and continued until a nurse interrupted us with the suggestion we head back to Jim's room. He had walked enough for one night.

It was time for bed. I made him a cup of tea using the hospital microwave. Jim sipped on it while I talked to him about the funny little personality of our dog. We laughed. It was late and Jim dozed while I watched the last of the 10 o'clock news. I put my hand on his forehead and prayed for him while he fought for a few more seconds before he gave into a deep sleep. The conversation we had about our dog reminded me that Hayden hadn't been outside to go "potty" all day. I needed to get home.

Hayden was glad to see me. His black and white tail whipped back and forth like a windshield wiper set on high. We went through the kitchen slider to the back yard. Hayden dashed around half playing while looking for just the right bush to water. I watched him while I thought about Jim and Justin. Jim was going to do everything he could to live, while Justin was doing everything he could, it seemed, to die. Hayden ran in and out between my legs doing figure eights. He didn't seem to notice how dark it was outside. The landscaping lights cast distorted shadows on the yard's stony surface. My eyes traced the eerie shapes while I watched Hayden. I prayed. "Oh Lord, I need your help. Right now, I don't know what to do for either of them. Please show me how to walk this road. I want to walk this for your glory." Hayden stood in front of me patiently waiting for me to finish.

"And, Lord," I continued, "thank you for this little dog!" I leaned down to pat the head of the precious little guy who always brought a smile to my face. I pushed the heavy sliding door open while Hayden scampered past me into the brightness of a well-lit kitchen. It didn't take long for him to devour his long-awaited treats. He nestled into a small spot beside the cabinet in the living room and soon fell asleep.

Ashley wouldn't be home until right before the last second of her curfew. It was a Friday night, so there wasn't a chance she would be home before midnight. I wrote her a note in case she came home early. It was time for me to go to the hospital, the "other" hospital to see Justin.

CHAPTER 23

The Overdose

I walked into the emergency room and signed in. A pleasant older woman brought me into a makeshift area. There was Justin. His eyes were closed. My eyes traced the open sores that evidenced the amount of toxins circulating throughout his body. Several machines were hooked up to probes lining his chest in single file. His heart raced out of control. My fingers couldn't help but touch the deep scab-covered pits that dotted his arms. It was my cold hands that made Justin aware of my presence.

"Mom, I almost died." His words were pushed out of a cotton mouth.

"Yes. God spared you, Son. He has a special purpose and plan for your life."

I watched tears stream down Justin's face while his body began to twitch like it was responding to the pulsations of a muted drum beat. My throat hurt from the lump that kept my voice silenced. Water drenched the sides of my cheeks and eventually dripped onto Justin's arm as I experienced the depth of my own pain. I dug into my purse and found enough Kleenex for both of us. It seemed all the tissue in the world would not have been enough for us that night. We both cried. A sweet elderly man popped his head around the curtained partition and asked if we needed anything. Justin had fallen asleep. I was busy sopping up the rest of my tears with the bunched up tissue I clutched in my hand while I shook my head no. My throat only permitted me to squeak out an almost voiceless "thank you." The man disappeared out of sight. I dropped my purse on the floor and sat in the black vinyl covered chair positioned right next to Justin's bed. I thought about Jim. What were we going to do? I looked at Justin, and for some reason envisioned his boyish dimples that always melted my heart. I put my head down on the bed's chrome bars that separated us. "Oh Lord, do you hear me? This is too much for me. I don't know where to start.

Please help me!" Long sobs came from the deepest part of my soul. I ran out of tissue and resorted to using the rough brown paper towel from the bathroom next to the emergency room. I wiped my face raw.

It was almost midnight before I actually had a conversation with a doctor. He told me that Justin was lucky to be alive. His heart was on overdrive and it would take a few days before it got back to its natural rhythm. After he flipped the last page of the chart and slipped the clipboard under his arm, he looked at me and in a matter-of-fact tone said, "Mrs. Cox this is your wake-up call. Why haven't you sent him to a drug rehab? Is he going to have to die before you do anything to help him?"

His words took me by total surprise. My first reaction was to haul off and slug him. I reconsidered when I realized that this doc didn't know anything about us. He had no idea what we had been through with Justin. His experience was limited to one drug overdose on a hot summer night. He didn't know about all the other overdoses, nor did he know about all the rehab centers and halfway houses.

The ignorant medicine man stood next to Justin's bed as if he were waiting patiently for me to acknowledge the wisdom of his assault on me. I stood up and looked directly into the bloodshot eyes that were framed by wire rimmed glasses. Strangely enough, I had gotten accustomed to people thinking we hadn't done anything to help Justin. Most of those people made their judgments about us based on the fact that Justin didn't, for the most part, have the "look" of a hard-core drug user. For years, doctors, nurses, and even "drug counselors" accused Jim and me of ignoring Justin's drug problem. That was, of course, before they learned the truth from Justin himself.

One day I sat down and actually counted all the drug rehab centers we had brought Justin to. Certainly I had forgotten some, but I counted at least 15. Then there were the halfway houses, and to be honest, I lost count of them a very long time ago. I cleared my throat to address this uninformed man.

"Doctor, it is obvious that you don't know anything about Justin or his family. Justin has been using drugs for 12 years. Ask him about rehabs." The doctor retrieved the clipboard from under his arm and began to scratch a few notes on the top of Justin's chart. He didn't have anything to say to me. I found that oddly rude, but not unexpected.

"Well, Mrs. Cox, Justin looks like a fine boy. I hope it works out for him. Oh, he will be in the intensive care unit for a couple of days until his heart rate stabilizes. Then we'll keep him here for a day or so just to make sure. After that we'll release him. We'll call you when you need to pick him up."

I cringed at the thought of having to pick Justin up. I wondered if the doctor saw it on my face. I doubted he was very interested in what could be *my* plight.

"Goodnight," was all he said before he handed the orders to the young nurse who had just entered the area. She got busy pushing buttons and adjusting tubes. I don't think she even noticed I was in the room. I bent down and kissed Justin's forehead and said a quick prayer before I said goodnight. He hadn't heard a thing. Short shallow breaths followed by puffs of air pumped unnaturally out of his mouth. It signaled to me he was immersed in a deep drug-induced sleep. It would last a long time.

As soon as I got home, I was met at the door by one worried girl and one small happy boy-puppy. Ashley was upset that Justin would put us through another drug "episode" as she called them, at this time. Jim was very sick and Ashley hated that he would have to deal with Justin's drugs on top of all he already had on his mind. I listened to Ashley while she spewed anger and disgust. She had a lot to say about Jim and Justin. I listened. It had taken a long time for Ashley to finally vent her emotions. It didn't matter how exhausted I was, she needed to get it all said.

Nearly 30 minutes had passed before I walked into my bedroom and almost collapsed onto the bed. Ashley and Hayden followed closely behind. Ashley sprawled out on the gray denim couch close to my bed. Hayden found a comfortable spot right in the middle of his overstuffed doggy bed. I listened while Ashley outlined all the reasons why she was so angry with Justin. I wondered if she wasn't angry with Jim too. After all, he was sick.

She never mentioned Jim, outside of the fact that his illness made it even harder for her to tolerate Justin's antics. It was all completely understandable. Ashley spoke of Justin as if he were an annoying stranger. As she spoke I realized how separate she had become from Justin. It was as if she were an only child. It was a fact that Justin had never been a brother to her. He had stolen so much from her, everything from babysitting money to birthday memories in her camera. Yes, Ashley was hurting too. It was almost 2 A.M. before Ashley had finally come to the end of her tirade. She was exhausted. It took almost all of her energy to climb up onto my bed and give me a big hug and kiss goodnight. I appreciated the effort. I clicked off the light as soon as she disappeared into the hallway. The house was still except for the comforting sound of Hayden snoring at the foot of my bed.

I woke up around 3 A.M. It was not uncommon for me to wake up in the middle of the night. On those occasions I felt the Lord calling me to pray. That morning was that kind of morning. I prayed for Jim and Justin and Ashley. At some point I fell asleep.

Jim was being released from the hospital that Sunday. I made a quick "Starbucks" run before tackling the housework that had been obviously neglected. The tile was scrubbed and clean colorful sheets were neatly tucked into the bed. I even took a few minutes to throw out the shriveled fruit that was beginning to grow hair in the bottom of the refrigerator. After a quick shower, lipstick, and a "potty" trip outside for Hayden, I went to the hospital to get Jim.

He was so glad to be home. He loved sitting outside in the heat of the Arizona sun while inhaling all the news from the business section of the newspaper. Life appeared to be back to normal. The truth was quite different. Nothing was the same. We sat on the patio and talked about what types of treatment options were available. We never talked about the hopeless words delivered to us by the doctor in the wrinkled white coat. We simply chose to ignore his prognosis. There must be something we would find to get Jim through this cancer.

I began to search the Internet. At one point I had stumbled upon the name of a naturopathic doctor with a "cancer" focus. Later in the search, I found information about a man who had devised a non-drug formula for beating cancer. Oddly enough, both men lived in our area. Even stranger to us was the fact that the men worked together on a regular basis. I quickly got on the phone and booked an appointment for Jim. It was a good day, a very good day!

CHAPTER 24

Death, Dying, and Detox

My sister called. Dad was sick. It appeared he had had a small stroke while he was on the flight to Hawaii. She had kept me informed from the minute he landed and we were both hopeful he would be just fine again. But Dad wasn't recovering. He continued to decline. Karen held the phone up to his ear so I could tell him how much I missed and loved him. He couldn't answer. Every day brought another bad report. I wanted to be in Hawaii with Karen and Dad, but it wasn't possible. Jim needed me. Justin needed me. My heart broke when Karen called and delivered the hardest message she had ever given me. Dad died.

I didn't know how I would be able to carry on without him in my life. It was already so hard with Jim and Justin. My dad was the one who offered me "everything he had." He promised he would always be there for me. It hurt to breathe when I thought about him.

Dad lived in a small one-bedroom apartment. I stood in the middle of the living area of his apartment and wailed in pain. My dad had become a loving man, the last eight years of his life. I wanted more years with him. I didn't want to pack up his apartment. All of his stuff looked so precious to me. I touched his coffee pot and peered into the refrigerator where I saw his diet soda and stacks of uneaten desserts. A small, slightly-chipped lighthouse lamp sat on the ledge between the kitchen and living area. He used it as a night light. It was still on. I could hardly catch my breath while I cried. I missed him. I felt alone for the first time in my life. Then I heard the familiar voice whisper into my heart. "Pam, you are not alone. I am the only One who will be with you always. Your dad is with me. Take heart. I will walk every step of this journey holding your hand. I love you."

My heart smiled while I brushed away the never-ending tears that ran down my face. I knew it was true. Dad was with the Lord. I also knew that

I was not alone on this journey. The God of the universe would walk with me until the end. With the last of Dad's things packed into a box, I closed the door to his apartment for the last time. I kept the little lighthouse lamp. For some reason it reminded me of something I had heard from one of the television evangelists. "I don't know what tomorrow holds, but I do know who holds my tomorrow." I would trust God in the dark days to come. He would be my beacon in the storm.

The social worker assigned to Justin called to remind me how important it was for Jim and me to be supportive of Justin at this time. He was going through a hard time. He needed to be in a detox facility for a few days and then admitted into a halfway house. She made it clear to me that I needed to "demonstrate" I cared.

"After all, "she threw in callously, "you only came to see your son the one time." She continued with words like "talk is cheap" and "walk this with him." There were moments in her monologue I would have liked to punch her lights out. What in the world was she talking about? Was she under the impression Jim and I had not demonstrated we cared for Justin? Where had she been the last 12 years of our lives? Her words nearly threw me over the edge. I wanted to lash out in rage at her ignorance. Finally, I took a deep breath and asked the Lord to help me demonstrate His grace. In that moment, I felt the Lord pour His grace all over me. I did what I would not have done on my own; I thanked her for her call and hung up.

Justin was released from the hospital and admitted into "Lark," a detox facility, for a two-day stay. After that he moved into a halfway house. We probably wouldn't have been given all the details of the new residence except for the fact money was involved. He needed $100 to secure a bed in the halfway house. As usual, I was happy to make sure he had a place to go. It sounded as if they had a plan for him. He would have a place to stay as long as he worked at a job. They even had solid leads for him in that department. The envelopes were in the bill drawer in the kitchen. I quickly grabbed one, stuck a stamp on the front, and even before the ink had dried on the check, I dropped it into the mail. It was as if I had done something to help Justin. He called us often and gave updates. Things appeared hopeful.

For months Jim went to a clinic where he received vitamin C treatments and a whole host of other immune-enhancing substances. My daily routine was exhausting. I got up very early, took care of Hayden, collected all of Jim's vitamins for the day, made his protein shake and put together the special items for his breakfast. This all had to be done before I woke him. I smothered cream cheese on Ashley's breakfast bagel while Jim took the first round of vitamins. It seemed as if I was always watching the clock.

There was the bus, the vitamins, meals, more vitamins, and the clinic all before 8 A.M. I was on a tight schedule. No time to waste.

Right after I dropped Jim off at the clinic, I headed for my mom's and her husband's apartment. They looked forward to my visits which always included some food item Mom had just taken out of the oven in anticipation of my visit. Mom scurried around her little kitchen in the always clean and pressed green-plaid apron while she prepared a plate filled with sugary delights. We would laugh in between bites, completely enjoying the sweetness of our time together.

It was about a month after Jim got home from his kidney surgery that life stretched my faith…even more. My mom and her husband, Irving, were at our home waiting for dinner to be served. Jim's food protocol recommended he eat fish at least twice a week. He hated fish, but with lots of fresh organic seasonings and the juice of a freshly-squeezed lemon, he hated it less. I knew Mom and Irving loved fish, but didn't like the smell that cooking it left behind. Every Friday night for weeks, Mom, Irving, Jim, and I sat around the kitchen table eating fish. After dinner, some sweet treat, and coffee, I cleared the table and we played a few card games. It was fun.

One fish night, just when we were all ready to sit down to eat dinner, the phone rang. I almost didn't answer it, but at the last minute decided it might be important. The voice on the other end asked "Are you Mrs. Cox?" I had been asked that question far too often. Immediately I expected the voice to say Justin was back in the hospital. My heart raced while I waited for the woman, who identified herself as a nurse from the emergency room, to explain the reason for her call. The sound of my heart pounding made it hard for me to catch every word she said. What I heard nearly caused me to collapse.

"Your daughter Ashley was in a serious car accident. Please come to the emergency room as soon as possible." I hung up the phone and looked down at the silverware drawer, still open in front me, while desperately trying to arrest the stream of tears that were about to flood over my face.

"Pam, is anything wrong?" Jim sensed there was a problem and prodded me for information. I cleared my throat and said Ashley had been in a little "fender-bender." Jim accepted my rendition of the call without questioning it.

"Why don't I go with you to check on her?" he volunteered. If things were different I would have wanted Jim to come with me. It seemed as if this accident and whatever it meant for Ashley would have been just too much for Jim now. I smiled at him while I struggled to keep my composure and served dinner. I assured Jim it would be best if he stayed home with Mom and Irving. I promised to call as soon as I had more information to report.

Surprisingly enough, he saw some wisdom in my thinking. I grabbed my purse, the car keys, and yelled my goodbyes while Jim, Mom, and Irving sat at the kitchen table casually chatting over fish and seven-layer salad.

The drive to the hospital was the longest 12 minutes of my life. The nurse hadn't given me any information, so I was forced to evaluate the severity of the accident by the tone of voice she used in our brief conversation. It sounded serious. But if it was *very* serious, wouldn't she have said something more to me? All my questions remained questions as I approached the intersection in front of the hospital. The roadway was blocked by yellow police tape. The flashing lights of a fire truck blinked on and off while the men in yellow rubber jackets vigorously swept the last of the rubble. A fireman motioned for me to stop and wait until traffic had cleared from the other direction. My car idled while I surveyed the terrible sight in front of me. What a horrible accident, I thought.

Then, right behind the massive fire truck with the flashing lights, I caught a glimpse of a piece of mangled red metal. I couldn't take my eyes off it. It looked like Ashley's car, her red Honda. I hadn't considered this accident could be her accident. The hand of the fireman was still holding traffic going in my direction when the urge to jump out of the car overtook me. I had to see if that car belonged to Ashley.

It appeared there were two cars involved in this deplorable tragedy. The force of their collision caused one car, an older Suburban, to spin out of control and face traffic in the wrong direction. The small frame of what had been a Honda Civic now stood motionless and stripped of its outer shell. Airbags had inflated and they now clung to the twisted frame of the car like punctured balloons. It was obvious those trying to hurriedly clean up the road didn't appreciate my presence. I kept walking until I touched the car. A page from a notebook blew across the road. I recognized the yellow daisy drawn on the cover. It belonged to Ashley. A fireman had come alongside me seemingly aware of the reason for my blanched, trembling body. He gently ushered me back to my car and personally directed me to the front of the emergency room which was right across the street from the horrific scene. I abandoned the car somewhere in the parking lot and ran through the automatic doors. A kind receptionist immediately took me to the blue cloth partitioned walls of those in serious medical need.

There was Ashley. I quickly stood at her bedside and leaned right down next to her beautiful face. "Ashy, it's mom, I'm here." She opened her eyes and smiled. Her bright green eyes calmed my heart. "Mom, what happened? Do I have the flu?" As she spoke, I silently began accessing her condition. Blood was crusted on her forehead and both arms. I lifted the flimsy blanket and investigated further. It looked as if one of her ankles was broken.

My attention went back to her face. She knew I was her mom, so that must mean her head was all right. Then again she hadn't a clue why she was in the hospital. That couldn't be a good sign. Ashley kept her eyes on me waiting for an answer.

"Lovey, you are in the hospital because you were in a car accident." Her expression told me she didn't have a clue what I was talking about. The thin sheet partition shook and a man stood in the opening.

"She's one lucky young lady." The words came from a mustached man with a receding hairline and a pleasant grin. He flipped through the papers attached to the clipboard at the end of her bed. The stethoscope that draped around his neck touched the plastic picture ID hanging down the front of his chest. He was the doctor.

"Mrs. Cox?" Yes, I nodded. "The tests show no severe trauma to her head. A few fractured bones showed up on the x-ray. Our major concerns are the lacerations to her liver. She will need to be medi-vac'd immediately to Osborne—the trauma center." He reassuringly patted Ashley on her good leg and vanished, leaving the chart to dangle at the bottom of her bed.

Ashley hadn't taken her eyes off of me for a second. It was clear she was trying to register the fact that she was in the hospital. I kept right on smiling. I whispered to her the same words I had spoken to Justin so often. "The Lord will take care of you. He loves you and has a purpose and a plan for your life. I love you so much."

Ashley sobbed while I prayed. Before I could say "Amen" two people with military green flight suits intruded our curtained space. They asked me to leave the small area so they could get Ashley prepared for the airlift. I moved into the hall, but managed to watch them as they transferred her from the soft bed to a hard, silver gurney. They carefully strapped her onto her new carriage and pushed her down the hall and out of the hospital. I followed close behind.

The fury of the helicopter's blades whipped the sand off the tarmac into a small tornado of stony pellets. I squinted and tried to watch the take-off through the veil of dirt. Within a few minutes they were gone. I turned around and almost collapsed onto the wooden and iron bench in front of the emergency room entrance. It was a quiet night. The stars sparkled like sequins on a black velvet dress. I watched them as they shimmered on the dark fabric of night.

My thoughts brought me back to the Lord. I remembered Job in the Bible. He had so many trials. One time he asked the Lord why his life was so difficult. How was all the hardship God's best for his life? Had the Lord forgotten about Job? The Lord responded to his questions by speaking about His awesome Majesty. This was a personal God, who took care of every detail of His creation. The stars in the sky were each suspended in space by the very hand of God. Even the ocean could only lap onto the invisible line drawn in the sand by His Hand. It amazed me as I thought about God...His power and grandeur. God knew everything about Job's life. He loved Job. I smiled when I thought about how much the Lord loved Jim, Justin, and Ashley too. I twisted my head up in an effort to view the vast expanse of stars sparkling above me. They were uncountable to me, and yet each one had been perfectly placed by God.

I kicked my purse with my foot while I adjusted my position to better appreciate the vastness of the sky. Something poked my leg from one of the front zippered compartments of my purse. It was my cell phone. I had forgotten to call Jim. One last time I gave the sheet of lights my focus while I prayed with soundless words. "Oh Lord, I know I have to call Jim and tell him what I have learned about Ashley. Help me say the words that won't cause him to worry about her. I know You, the Lord God of the universe, are worthy of our trust. I entrust her to you Lord. I love you."

I pushed the digits of our house phone into the cell. Jim answered. Carefully I gave the report. Jim seemed comfortable with all the information and asked me if he should go to the hospital with me. I knew his immune system wouldn't be strong enough to handle the sea of germs he'd face in the hospital emergency room. We agreed it would be best if I went alone. After reclipping the cell phone to the side of my purse, I stood up and began my search for the car I had left stranded somewhere in the packed lot. A familiar voice caught my attention.

"Pam, I have something for you." It was my dear friend Diane. I had managed to call her sometime on my way into the emergency room. There she stood, smiling, holding my favorite drink. I sipped on my Starbuck's venti chai tea latte while I filled her in on all the details of the accident. She hugged and encouraged me while I broke into a million tears. I have to tell you, she was the face of the Lord for me. God was very real to me that difficult night.

Ashley had several serious lacerations on her liver. They kept her immobile for three days, carefully watching her liver activity. Finally, after 10 days with all her fractures set in thick white plaster casts and her liver stabilized, she came home.

I loved those days, although they were very busy. Between Jim and Ashley, there was always something that had to be done immediately and barely enough time in the day to get it all done. Ashley was bound to a wheel-chair for a couple of months. She spent much of her day nestled under a chenille blanket on the family room couch, channel surfing or trailing off into much-needed sleep. There were days when Jim and Ashley felt well enough to sit through a video together. They often laughed until they lost their breath. I heard them and missed Justin. I hadn't heard from him in a few weeks. How was he doing? I hoped he knew, wherever he was, that I loved him.

Time was very precious to me. I had very little of it and desperately wanted to use what I had wisely. I took every opportunity to sit and rub Ashley's head while talking to her about the important things in life. She knew the Lord had spared her life for His wonderful purpose. I reminded her at every turn of God's incredible goodness and mercy. It was easy for her to understand that in light of her healing body. What was more difficult for her to reconcile was God's goodness and mercy in the context of Jim's cancer. She had lots of questions.

Why would God let Jim have cancer? Why wasn't he getting better? How was it possible for cancer to be a sign of God's goodness and mercy? One question led to a zillion more. I had only one answer for her. It was the one truth I knew in the very bottom of my soul. God was good. No matter how it felt to us. We needed to trust the sovereignty of God. He knew about Jim's cancer before time began. Nothing slipped by His notice. God would heal Jim. I knew the healing would be one of two kinds; either here on earth or in the heavens. Because of His goodness and mercy, God would never fail Jim. Ashley heard those words over and over again before she faded into sleep each afternoon. I didn't know what comfort they offered to her. I only know it was those words that sustained me. In an unexplainable, incomprehensible way, God was showing His goodness and mercy in all of our lives. I thanked Him under my breath all day long. Praising God brought me closer to Him. I smiled a lot.

The long summer of healing ended for Ashley. She walked into fall on her own two feet. By the end of the year she had finished her certification as a "nail tech." It had been her plan to get that training as a way to get through the daily expenses of life on a college campus.

January was the month of many changes for her. She was going to Arizona State University. Her feather bed, overstuffed comforter, and lap top computer found a new home with Ashley and a roommate in a dormitory on campus. Even though she wasn't that far away from us, she would be very, very far away from the life she had once lived at home

The house was too quiet. It lacked the sounds of a young girl who explored the refrigerator's offerings way into the night. Laughter and chatter had always come out of the bathroom by her room while she got ready to go out with her friends. Every time she left the house I found myself compelled to stop whatever I was doing long enough to pray over the precious blonde girl in the used black cabriolet. I missed her so much.

CHAPTER 25

One More Time

It was March 22, 2003, a day I would never forget. All the protein shakes and vitamins for that day were sorted and stored in the refrigerator ready for Jim. His lunch was neatly wrapped in Saran and crammed in beside his chilling drinks. Jim would be fine alone for a few hours. If he needed me, he knew I would always be available by cell phone. I was ready for the long awaited "fun" planned for that afternoon. Each year Diane and I tried to do something really "girly" on her birthday. We opted that year to spend our time at the spa. I can't think of one woman on this planet who doesn't relish those cucumber facials and seaweed body wraps. It was a great time. We were all giggly and greased up, ready to go home when my cell phone rang.

"Pam," It was Jim. His voice was serious and direct. "Justin called. He needs our help. Would you mind picking him up? I think it is the right thing to do. If you don't want to pick him up, come home and I'll go get him."

What? I couldn't believe what I was hearing. Jim was in no condition to drive, so plan B was out of the question. Why did Jim think it was the right thing to do, *now*? My voice lacked enthusiasm when I agreed to get Justin. I couldn't imagine why Jim would want to deal with the drugs at this point in our lives. It seemed to me our plates were full—overloaded—actually. Jim skipped right over my clearly unhappy tone and gave me directions. I turned the car around and headed for Justin.

There he was pressed up against a building. I made a U-turn and stopped the car right in front of him. It was the scene I had remembered from so many times before. I hated being in that same place with him over and over again. Justin ran to the car and jumped in. I watched while he fumbled for a place to store a dirty brown paper sack. He wasn't satisfied until he had it smashed on the floor in front of his legs.

He looked exactly as he had looked every time I went to rescue him. I couldn't help but study his face. Dark circles underscored the hollowness of his dull, lifeless eyes. His skin was stretched so tightly over his protruding jaw bones that it looks ready to split into long oozing lines of pus. He never looked at me. He kept his gaze straight ahead.

"Oh Lord," I pleaded in soundless anguish, "I am so angry. Help me." I bent my head over the steering wheel and quietly sobbed.

"Mom," Justin whispered, "I am going to be different this time. I promise."

I looked over at Justin through a curtain of tears. Things were the same. The jerking arm gestures and never-ending bouncing leg confirmed that fact. It was the same story over again. Justin was coming down from a high with no money and nowhere to go. I resented what sat in front of me.

"Well, aren't you going to say anything to me?" Justin said using a familiar self-righteous tone.

"Justin, I am mad. I am mad at you and I am mad at your dad. I didn't want to come and get you."

There I had said it! The awful truth was out in the open. Justin didn't have anything more to say on the drive home. My mind raced. How was I going to take care of Jim *and* Justin? The two undisturbed hours of rest I counted on each night would be gone. I sighed while I wrestled with all the sadness and the impossibility that lay before me. We were almost at the stop light at the bottom of our street when I heard a small voice speaking in my heart.

"Pam, all things are possible with Me."

I knew that voice. "Yes, Lord" I said to myself, "all things *are* possible with You." I remembered what I had heard as I packed my dad's apartment. I was not alone. The Lord would accomplish all of it. This war would be won. I found myself smiling while I sniffled.

"Pam, stay focused on the battle plan," I said to myself. It was going to be all right, I now knew it. After I inhaled deeply and slowed down my breathing, it seemed important for me to speak to Justin before we entered the house.

"Justin, forgive me. I have believed with every breath the Lord would walk us through this. God is going to win this war. I know it." Justin nodded his head as if in agreement. We pulled into the garage and entered the next part of the journey.

As soon as I shut the door behind me, Jim called out to Justin. While propped up in bed, he once again delivered the house rules. I watched Justin as he held his old, torn sack tightly to his chest. It was as if it contained his most precious possessions. The way he clung to it made me very curious about what lay hidden inside. Jim spelled out the way life would be while he was in our home. Justin would have to sleep at the foot of our bed, on the mattress we would bring in from the garage. He would have to spend all of his time with me.

When Jim said that, I felt as if he had punched me in the stomach. In amazement I looked up at Jim. His nod assured me Justin would be fine, this time. Somehow I mustered up a smile and agreed with the mood in the room.

"OK, Lord" I silently said while I excused myself from the room. "This is something You are going to have to do for me! I don't have time to baby sit Justin and take care of Jim." Calmness came over me. I knew the Lord had already taken on this task for me. It would be all right!

To be honest, I don't think I can recall five weeks that had more meaning in my life. It took Justin about a week to completely come down from the drugs. His outbursts lessened as the days went by which were relatively easy compared to the nights. Some nights were frightening. On the mattress at the foot of our bed Justin squirmed and moaned. It was in the blackness of those times I was reminded about the spiritual battle we were in. I sat up and prayed against the enemy—every night.

Each day Justin shadowed me. He held the small blue glass dish while I dropped Jim's daily dose of vitamins into it. We carefully guided Jim as he walked up the stairs to the clinic every morning. No matter what I had to do, Justin would do it with me. In some strange way it felt that I had another crack at being a mom to this son. He had been gone for so long I hadn't realized the depth of my ache for him until he stood beside me.

Justin found a job and he was thrilled. It was working at a grocery store in the deli section. Jim and I were as excited as he was about this new opportunity. In the morning I'd get Jim settled into his daily routine while Justin scampered around the house trying to find his always "missing" green apron and name tag. Daily, I'd drop him off and pick him up from his workplace. On one of Jim's good days, we met Justin for lunch. We always looked forward to hearing all the stories he had to tell about his day. Sometimes I laughed so hard my stomach hurt. When Ashley came home from college for a week-end, we'd all bunch up together and watch a video. We were a family. The bitter sweetness of those moments were beyond my imaginings.

On Justin's second payday the past crept back into our lives; his co-worker was close to his age. "Hanging out" with this kid was all he could think about. My gut told me the reason. It was drugs. I resented this new "friend" even though I really didn't know anything about him. While I waited for Justin to finish work I wondered why he would ever want to go back to that life. The pock marks had only left a few scars on his arms. His face was now bright with sparkling clear eyes. He was clean and we were a family. I wanted to somehow protect all of us from having to experience that dark life ever again.

Justin interrupted my thoughts by thumping on the side of the car while he tried to break free from the strings of his apron. He jumped into the car with the fidgety anxiousness I had seen so many times before. He was excited about his plan for the night. His new "friend" had invited him over to his apartment to watch movies. I hated the plan.

Justin pointed to the car parked across from us. It belonged to this new boy who was going to follow us home. I started the car and kept tabs on the old road-worn vehicle that followed closely behind us. I wondered, as I caught a quick glimpse of the face of the driver, if this kid was the threat I had perceived him to be. As soon as we rolled into the garage, Justin practically ripped off his seat belt while trying to escape its clutch on him. He was incredibly nervous. Finally with one quick tug the seat belt released and he bolted from the car into the house. I sat in the car for a minute longer while the new friend casually wandered past me.

"Oh Lord," I prayed, "please don't let this kid be a druggie." Before I even pushed the button to close the garage door, Justin and the friend ran right by me. They laughed in between Justin's "Bye, mom," and the kid's, "It was nice meeting you." Car doors slammed and they squealed down the street. It all happened so fast.

I walked into the house and went straight to our bedroom. The room was tidy, not a sign of the napping man I expected to find. Where was Jim? I found him sitting outside on the patio. He looked as if he was in deep thought. The sound of the screen door scraping on its frame caused him to look straight at me.

"Jim, what do you think about that kid and the whole movie thing? It doesn't feel right to me." I blurted the questions out so fast and furious, I wasn't completely sure Jim had heard one word. Disappointment was clearly written on Jim's face as he spoke to me.

"Pam, we are right back at square one. That kid is a druggie. I don't think we will see Justin for a while."

I hated knowing what we both knew to be the truth. I fell into the swivel chair that faced Jim and shook my head. Justin's bright green deli apron had been dumped on the outside table. My eyes focused on the nametag facing me. I bent my head and felt the warm drops of fresh tears race down my cheeks. It was important to me that Jim didn't see me cry. I didn't want to burden him with my worry.

In silence I cried out to the Lord. "Lord, your Word says You will keep all of my tears. Please take these. You know exactly what Justin is doing. Lord, show him who You are in this moment."

Jim leaned back in his chair, unknowingly disturbing my prayer time. "Pam, we can't do one thing about Justin. He is going to do what he is going to do. The saddest thing about his choice though, is that it could kill him." Jim spoke each word slowly with obviously great deliberation.

I didn't say anything but wondered if Jim had been thinking about something else. We never spoke about death, and yet I knew we both thought about it all the time. It was too hard to be that honest about what was on our hearts. I took a deep breath, excused myself, and made dinner.

Justin didn't come home that night. It wasn't until late the next day that he called us from some unknown part of town. He wanted to come home. Once again we caved under the delusion that having him home safe-guarded him from drugs. He was alive and that seemed good enough. As always, Jim and I went to his rescue. We found our barefoot boy standing dazed in front of a hotel. He climbed into the car and we began the long road to sobriety, once again.

CHAPTER 26

The Explosion

Jim quit going to the clinic. The treatments weren't offering him the relief we had anticipated. He was in more and more pain. Eventually his new "best friend" was the drug-saturated "pain patch" that I faithfully stuck on his back every three days. I continued to count out the vitamins and made the protein shakes every day. Each meal was strictly "organic," painstakingly made entirely from scratch. Night after night I explored the Internet into the wee hours of morning to find answers for Jim. There were no answers. I begged God to show me how to keep walking a walk that seemed impossible.

Even though the long nights got longer and the days started earlier, the Lord continued to give me the energy to walk the walk. I had learned on this journey not to rely on what standard medicine could offer, and eventually came to the place where it was clear alternative medicine didn't have the "magic bullet" I had hoped for either. Every place we turned was a place of discouragement. There was Someone, though, who never failed us. I leaned more heavily on Him with each passing day. My trust completely rested in the Lord. Though our lives appeared to be headed down the road of utter despair, I didn't see the depth of the tragedy others observed. I knew only hope, and it wouldn't come from chemotherapy, organic food, or unpublished cancer cures out of Poland. The one true hope we had, was in the God who held life in His hands. I knew that God's plan for our life was absolutely flawless.

After months of late night Internet searching, I gave up on what the world had to offer. It was strictly a spiritual thing. I began to redirect my thoughts at every turn. I quit trusting in medical reports. I had to go deeper than that, to the ultimate place of comfort…at the feet of Jesus. I knew He would help me with Jim and Justin. After all, He knew all about Jim and the cancer. He knew about Justin and the drugs. He knew it all. Even more amazing to me was the fact God loved Jim and Justin more than I could ever love them. He would take care of them. As for me, the true work at hand was quite simple. I just had to keep believing God would work His plan. It would be a journey that required me to walk into the unknown, blindly holding onto the hand of the Holy One.

Usually, by afternoon Jim was exhausted and went to bed, so it wasn't strange when Jim climbed under the sheets early on that particular day. I tucked him in after he gulped a mouthful of water with two small orange morphine pills. He seemed to always be in pain. No matter what I did to stay ahead of the it, the pain seemed to always find a way to break through. Justin stood in the doorway and appeared as helpless as I felt. It was hard watching such suffering. It didn't take long before the drugs dulled the pain and Jim dozed off.

Justin backed away from the middle of the doorway, so I could close the double doors of the bedroom. I pressed my ear up against the door one more time just to make sure Jim was settled before I walked to the other side of the house. Justin followed me, raising his voice with each step we took toward the kitchen. My watch kept me on schedule. It was time to sort vitamins into the blue glass custard cup. The sound of the pills bouncing against the glass before they settled at the bottom of the small dish caused Justin to become highly agitated. He began pounding the wall with one hand while holding himself up with the other. I went right on counting pills as if nothing was happening.

Within a few minutes Justin began to scream out unintelligible words. It took me by surprise at first, and honestly terrified me. Every so often, I left Justin's tirade to run to the other end of the house to check on Jim. I desperately hoped he hadn't heard the ruckus coming from the kitchen. I quietly cracked the door open so I would have just enough space to squeeze into the bedroom.

Jim seemed unaware of what was going on down the hallway from him. He drank his shakes and sipped on water, never once addressing the madness I thought *must* have slipped under the crack in the doorway. FOX news had always captured Jim's interest in the past, so I clicked on the television and prayed it would be a distraction from whatever lay ahead for me on the other side of the house.

Justin's ranting went on for several hours. He paced back and forth on an invisible path he followed from one end of the house to the other while I grated fresh vegetables for dinner and prayed out loud.

"Oh Lord," I said in a tone falsely suggesting I was calm, "I call on your name Jesus, the name of power, to protect Justin from the presence of the enemy. Protect us Lord!"

Justin continued to pound his anger into any surface his fist contacted. I stood over the pile of shredded carrots with my eyes closed and begged God to be close to us. My prayer produced no visual difference in Justin but that didn't matter to me. God was in control. He was at work even though it appeared to be a chaotic nightmare.

I collected myself, wiped off the mascara that had smudged halfway down my face and searched for the bright yellow lemon I had stored in the bottom bin in the refrigerator. A small voice in my heart told me not to worry, it would be all right. I smiled while I drizzled the juice from the freshly squeezed lemon onto the chicken. It popped and sizzled while it baked in the oven.

Justin stormed out of the kitchen to his bedroom where he began pounding so hard on the wall, the house shook. I wondered if the fresh drywall and stucco on his walls had given way and exposed the gaping fist holes hidden underneath from days gone by.

The wonderful smell of lemon-glazed chicken floated all around the kitchen. I hoped its allure had made its way down the hall into Jim's room. Jim was in a deep sleep and didn't budge when I stuck my head into his room to check in on him. It amazed me to think he had escaped Justin's racket. I shook my head while I asked myself why we had willingly brought the explosions back into our home, again.

While Jim slept, I crowded the kitchen counter with the bright colors of fresh, organic produce. We were going to have green beans, carrots, and a raw cabbage salad to complement our dinner. The sound of water rushing over the dirt-covered veggies was barely audible over the noise Justin generated by slamming his bedroom door, over and over. The door's frame cracked under the pressure.

When I had just about finished scrubbing the last bit of garden grime off our dinner, Justin appeared before me. He towered over me as he hurled words of contempt into my face. The poisonous cocktail of drugs he had taken, left him filled with hate and loathing. I prayed aloud. "Lord, this is Justin, my son. I know you love him more than we do. Please help him see You."

The impassioned disgust in Justin's hardened countenance seemed to disintegrate right before my eyes. In that moment he threw his arms around my neck and begged me to keep praying. I prayed and prayed. The beeping timer for the chicken brought us back to the moment.

Jim ate dinner propped up on soft down-filled pillows that lined the back of his bed. He didn't really eat his dinner, he just moved it around on his plate to try and fool me. It was becoming more and more evident Jim wasn't going to eat. Even when I helped with the fork, his small bite always ended up scrunched in between the layers of his paper napkin. This deeply worried me.

Justin strolled into Jim's room as if nothing had been going on in the kitchen and plopped himself down on the edge of the bed. Jim stopped chewing, carefully put his fork down on the plate and focused on the boy who sat in front of him.

"Justin are you all right?" Jim asked, obviously knowing Justin was not all right. Justin didn't say anything for a few moments. He scooted Jim's left leg over a bit, so he would be able to sit more comfortably on the bed beside him. I watched as Jim studied Justin. His glasses magnified glistening pools of water that hovered under the green of his eyes. In one blink they let loose and spilled down his face. Justin put his head on Jim's shoulder and cried.

"Dad, I hate this. I don't want to live like this anymore." The contrast in the scene before me gripped my throat. Jim's frail arm reached around Justin. They held each other and cried. I cried too.

"Thank you Lord for this moment, for it is by Your hand," were the words I whispered.

Life had changed for all of us, even Ashley. She had gone away to ASU for a semester but decided it would be best if she came home. She could always go back to school. We loved having her with us again.

"Mom!" It was Ashley. She had managed to come into the house without anyone's notice.

"Ashley we're in the bedroom," I said so she would know I had heard her. A blonde bunched up ponytail bounced as she walked into the room. It was apparent something emotional had just taken place, as we were all sniffling and wiping our noses. She never asked what happened. It was as if she hadn't seen anything out of the ordinary.

"Hi Dad, how are you doing today?" Her presence always made Jim smile.

"I'm doing better, Dolly." He spoke as if he were just getting over the nuisance of a cold. Her bright eyes twinkled as she walked past me to hug Jim. She completely ignored Justin. It was as if he wasn't even in the room.

"Mom, did you ask Dad?" I knew instantly what she was talking about and I had simply forgotten to mention it to Jim.

"Ashley, we really haven't had much time to talk. I promise I will ask him later. OK?" A look of total disappointment spread over her face.

"Pam what is Ashley talking about?" Jim had clued in and wanted to know why Ashley was upset.

"Well, Ashley would like a puppy." I never would have thought to ask Jim for another dog, but this was a different time. It seemed to me a puppy would bring new life into our home. It could be a good thing for all of us.

Jim appeared to be thinking about the unexpected request. "Pam, what do you think?" he asked.

I looked over at Ashley and said, "I think it is a good idea. Hayden might not be too happy about it, but I think a puppy will bless all of us." With that Jim nodded a "yes." Ashley screeched with delight while she skipped out of the room. Jim and I smiled, happy to see her eyes sparkle with delight.

CHAPTER 27

The Scam

It was a Friday night. Ashley had done all the research and found a breeder with the perfect puppy. We would call her "Tilly." Ashley, Tilly, and I spent the afternoon getting all the stuff our new addition needed to make her more comfortable in her new home. It was such fun. Justin had agreed to sit with Jim while I was at the store. My cell phone rang as I stood in the checkout line at Pets Mart. It was Jim.

"Pam, Justin has a terrible toothache. I found a dentist who will meet you at his office tonight. Would you take Justin or should I?" I couldn't believe my ears.

Jim was in no condition to drive Justin, or anyone else, anywhere! I convinced Jim it would be best if he stayed at home while I drove Justin to his dentist appointment. Although he was not happy with the plan he knew it was not reasonable for him to think he was able to drive. Ashley, Tilly, and I gathered all of our purchases and hurried home.

Justin was lying on the bed bedside Jim, groaning. It was almost 6 P.M. and the appointment was scheduled for 7 P.M. There was a lot that had to get done before I would feel comfortable leaving the house. Ashley volunteered to give Jim all his vitamins and nighttime medications and stay with him until we got home.

I kissed Jim, Ashley, and Tilly "goodbye" while Justin put on his shoes. At that time the top of my convertible had a serious malfunction. It was an old VW Cabriolet I had inherited from Ashley when she got a new Hyundai Tiburon. The canvas top wouldn't move up or down. Unfortunately, it had broken when the top was down, and I had scheduled to get it fixed in the coming week. Usually Arizona weather is quite predictable, not so at that time. We had record steamy heat, torrential rain, and an atypical night chill.

I felt it all with the top down. I warned Justin about the problem with the car before we left the house. Justin didn't seem to mind.

As we traveled in silence down the 101, I wondered if this whole dentist trip was for real or just another scam. Obviously Jim bought it, but it seemed odd to me. Maybe I had become too skeptical over the years. It certainly was possible to develop a toothache even if you hadn't had one all day. Those things happened.

I was reminded of a time in my own life when I had a horrific toothache. Yes, an abscess had just sprung out of nowhere. Maybe this time my cynicism was unwarranted. I glanced over at Justin and silently apologized to him for being such a suspicious person. He looked into the night without one word, appearing to be preoccupied in thought. We were about to get on the 202 West when Justin informed me we were not going to the dentist. I kept driving, hoping he wouldn't notice we were not far from the office. "If you don't take me to Camelback, I will jump out of the car." His face told me he was dead serious. My heart started to race. I wasn't going to take him to his drugs. I couldn't do that! The thumping sound of my heart grabbed my attention. My grip on the steering wheel grew tighter and tighter.

"I'm not kidding," he said in a nasty tone of voice. For a moment I blocked out his hostile presence so I could get my bearings. If my memory had served me correctly we were just a few streets away from the dentist. As we neared the office, Justin yanked the steering wheel out of my hands. I tried to rip his fingers off the wheel while struggling to keep us on the right side of the road. He overpowered me and guided the car onto the off ramp. There was nothing I could do. I never let go of the wheel, nor even eased my tight grip. We were exactly where he wanted to be. The car coasted into the parking lot of a Walgreen's. I kept my foot on the brake until I could turn off the ignition. People were laughing and talking all around us while they ambled in and out of the drug store. I sat paralyzed.

Justin leaned over me. "You know what happens next. You give me money." I sat dazed by what had just transpired. His demand shook me. I was not going to help him get the drugs.

"No!" I said in a deep guttural, controlled voice. Fear prevented me from making even the slightest move.

"If you don't give me the money, you will be sorry." His last four words stung me. It was as if Justin had turned into one of the hate-filled strangers I read about in the newspaper or had heard about on the late news.

I turned and looked into his blank eyes. Was it possible he had said what I thought he said? Would he really hurt me? My eyes kept focused on his icy glare. Somehow I managed to muster up the boldness to ask the question on my heart.

"Are you going to hit me? Would you really hurt me?" My brazen question shocked me. It seemed to shock him too. He looked at me as he contemplated his next move. Thoughts flooded my brain.

OK so what if he hit me. I would be able to handle it. The sound of an older lady fiddling with her car keys right beside us, brought me back to the reality of the moment. What craziness had I just contemplated? What if I had to go to the hospital? Who would take care of Jim? Most importantly, I realized it would devastate Jim if Justin hurt me.

"I want money" were the words that jarred me back into the moment. I dug around in my purse and found $20 and handed it to him. He jumped out of the car without even opening the door. I watched him while he disappeared across the street into the night. The lights from the "Walgreen's" cast a strange greenish glow onto the parking lot. My heart continued to hammer at my chest. I couldn't find anything to wipe my tears but an old Starbuck's napkin that had been shoved into the side pocket on the door of my car.

The growl of a motorcycle idling caused me to look up. It was a cop. I jammed the crumpled wet napkin into my purse and took off after him. Within a minute or two I was behind him flashing my lights. His hand motioned for me to follow him into a nearby, empty lot. Surely, he would help me.

It quickly became clear this cop had no time for me. I tried to relay the events of the night. Justin was going to use drugs with money he had taken from me. Why didn't the cop want to help me help Justin?

After my last words were spoken, I waited for the policeman to respond. "Ma'am, may I see your driver's license?" It didn't seem like a relevant question, but I was desperate. I handed him my license with one hand and pointed in the direction Justin was headed right before I lost sight of him. The cop didn't even look up. He said, "Oh, I see you are from Scottsdale. Now, let me get this straight. You drove your son in this convertible all the way from Scottsdale to this location, gave him money, and now you want me to go find him to stop him from taking drugs. Do I have it right?"

I bent over the steering wheel and sobbed. "Mrs. Cox, I have seen this situation over and over again. Send him to rehab. Don't drive him to his drugs and give him the money to get them!" His voice was indignant. It was impossible for me at that point to stop crying.

When I was able to somewhat collect myself, I watched the policeman as he snapped the chin band of his helmet, mounted his motorcycle and sped away into the blackness of the long unlit lot. He didn't care about me or my son. Obviously I just looked like some pathetic woman too stupid to even know what role I had played in the events that had unfolded in front of me. I sat in the darkness in complete disbelief. The cop had judged me, just like I had been judged so many times before in my life. A part of me thought I should have stood my ground with Justin and waited for his fist to swing at me. Would that have been better? Maybe Justin was bluffing and he had no intentions of laying a hand on me?

The truth haunted me because I knew what I knew. No amount of rationalization would ever be able to deny the utter contempt I saw in his face. In that moment I experienced Justin's hatred. He was focused on one purpose and only one purpose. He needed money for drugs. I had fallen into the trap I had stumbled into so many times before. Justin never had a toothache. I hated being right. He wanted drugs and it didn't matter who he had to hurt to get them, and it could have been me.

I turned the key in the ignition to start the car. Nothing happened. The car had a security system with a weird fluke. The key had to be in a certain half-on position before the three chirp-like sounds would fire up the engine. That feature had always bugged me, and every time I had the oil changed, I promised myself I would get that system removed. It seemed fitting to me with all the events of the night, I would be stranded in a jet-black parking lot. I turned the key several times and nothing happened. The car would not start.

Off in the distance I heard several men yelling what sounded like, "Hey, baby." They started running toward me and within a second or two I saw the shadowy frames of three men getting closer. My fingers trembled so much I wasn't sure I'd ever be able to get that car to start.

"Lord," I cried out. "Help me!" After the third try, with the approaching men only yards away, the car started and I sped past them into the traffic. They tried to follow me, shouting obscenities into the night. I found my way back onto the highway all the while trying to remember to breathe deeply and pray. It was going to be all right….somehow.

I was almost home before I remembered to call the dentist to cancel Justin's appointment. Jim had penciled the phone number on a scrap of paper he had found in the computer desk. I searched the car with one hand while I drove with the other. Finally, I found the doctor's phone number. The sound of the evening traffic made it difficult to have a conversation but I was too afraid to stop the car. I carefully punched the digits into my cell phone and strained to hear as it rung.

First a click and then, "Hello." I asked if I had dialed the right number. His agitated tone made it even more difficult to talk. I apologized for inconveniencing the doctor on a Friday night, but Justin would not be at his dentist appointment. I didn't know what I expected to hear, but what I heard was absolutely *not* what I would have ever expected. The doctor literally screamed into the phone, lambasting me for being such an irresponsible person. He was incensed that I had disrupted his personal time with his family. All of my apologies went unheard. I hung up the phone and cried again.

I didn't call Jim. The night's chill felt good on my face as it blew my tears dry. I spent the drive home thanking God for His mercy and grace. I was safe. It was important to me that I kept my focus. My circumstances were causing me to become distracted. I reminded myself out loud to keep focused on the truth. The truth was the same in the good times as it was in the impossible times. God was at work. He would take care of it all, right down to the last detail. Thoughts of the goodness of God made my heart glad. I smiled while I closed the garage door, ready to face Jim.

CHAPTER 28

Tilly's Lesson

It was obvious Jim was getting sicker every day. His once vital six-foot-two-inch frame had become an emaciated skeleton of skin and bones. Even though I kept myself on the schedule that had dictated my life for so many months, Jim quit the routine. He wouldn't drink the protein shakes and it became more and more difficult for him to take all the supplemental vitamins, so that eventually stopped too. Finally, he hardly ate a thing. Small bites only happened after I distracted him with idle conversation while I fed him. The "pain patch" wasn't enough any more. We struggled to find the right amount of morphine to keep the pain at bay without getting lost in its effect. All the days melted together.

One day while he stood and held onto one of the posters at the end of the bed, his legs literally collapsed under him. It was time to go to the hospital, even though he protested. I scooted him across the floor on a hassock with wheels and balanced him on my back as he unsteadily hobbled to the car. We rushed to the emergency room. Within a few minutes of our arrival, he was plugged into an array of machines that blipped, beeped, and buzzed at different speeds. I peered over the technician's shoulder as he examined the blurry red and blue patterns on the EKG machine. He tried to divert me from asking any questions regarding the bright colored masses that danced on the screen in front of me, by talking to Jim.

"How are you doing, Jim?" The concern in his voice seemed genuine.

"So, what are you seeing?" Jim replied while studying my face.

"Oh, I am only the tech person here. The doctor will be in soon. Then you'll get all the answers you want." As he spoke he jotted something onto the once blank page of Jim's chart.

Jim kept his eyes on me. I knew he was trying to get a sense of the situation by how I responded. I leaned down and looked directly into his eyes. "Lovey," I spoke quietly, yet firmly, "I know it's going to be all right. You are safe in God's hands." My smile came directly from the heart. I stroked his hair. Jim closed his eyes and went to sleep. I watched him while listening to the daunting melody made by the machines. A small voice spoke to my heart.

"Pam, it *is* going to be all right. You are safe in God's hands too." I nodded and half-smiled while warm drops of water raced down my face.

The doctor arrived. She was cheerful and a bit surprised by how much I seemed to understand about Jim's condition. Her large frame caused her white jacket to ride up as she explained the fuzzy images on the screen of one of the machines. All the data pointed to one thing. Jim was seriously ill. She instructed a nurse to move him into a private room on the "heart" floor of the hospital. A pleasant young orderly appeared and proceeded to get Jim ready for the journey to the next floor. The doctor asked me to step out into the hall with her.

"Mrs. Cox, your husband is extremely ill. The fluid we drained from around his heart is back. There is nothing we can do about it. We can't drain it, because it is thick like gelatin. Mrs. Cox, I am so sorry. Jim isn't going to live much longer."

Her words almost stripped me of the confidence the Lord had just given to me moments before we met. She stared at me while she waited for my response.

I cleared my throat and said, "Dr, I have heard what you said. I completely understand what you have just told me. Though, what you have told me is important information. That is all it is to me. God is in charge. He is the giver and taker of life. I trust Him with Jim."

Right after I spoke the last word, the doctor grabbed me into her big arms and hugged me. She called me "brave" and encouraged me to talk to someone from Hospice before we left the hospital.

I called Karen. I needed her. She caught the first flight out of Hawaii and landed in Phoenix within 24 hours. Karen had always been there for me my whole life. This was a time I needed her more than ever before. She waved to me from behind security. Her big smile melted my heart and caused me to unexpectedly shatter into a million broken-hearted pieces. Her warm embrace and love-filled face carried me along way. We collected her bags and headed for the hospital to see Jim. He was almost as happy to see her as I was.

Jim was released from the hospital after only a couple of days. They weren't able to do anything but perform additional tests and deliver more bad news. The cancer had spread to his bones and brain. For some reason, it seemed Jim either never heard those results, or he just wasn't able to accept them. In any event, we never talked about them. We just went about the business of living every day.

We didn't hear anything from Justin for weeks. Karen anticipated she would hear Justin's voice every time the phone rang. It was never he.

While Karen visited us, we were in constant motion. The tremendous workload was shared. She pitched right in and took care of Jim while I handled other business. We found ourselves laughing hilariously over memories from our past, while we chopped and shredded the fresh ingredients of dinner. Often we blamed the onions for making us cry, when clearly we were giggling for so long our stomachs hurt and our eyes winced with water. Jim often sat in the family room enjoying the energy of two happy women.

What we both looked forward to the most each day was holding Ashley's little Tilly. At not quite two pounds she was just about the size of the palm of your hand. Her little body was covered in tiny, caramel-colored baby curls. She loved to snuggle close and squirmed her way right up into the crick of your neck whenever it was possible. No one ever minded. The sound of her gentle breathing and occasional sighs, made life so much better. We all loved Tilly. Late into the night when everyone was asleep I'd tiptoe into the kitchen, scoop her up into my arms and bring her to bed with me. It was often such a disappointment to find that Karen had already kidnapped Tilly for the night.

Potty training went smoothly. Oddly enough, I even looked forward to getting up with her in the middle of the night. She seemed to know how tired I was, and for that reason got her business done before I was even fully awake. Hayden quickly learned to accept the bouncy, baby Tilly. She made us all smile.

Karen went back to Hawaii. She hated saying goodbye to us, especially to our sweet little Tilly. Within days of her departure, Tilly developed a hacking cough. We had noticed traces of it before, but nothing like this. Immediately we went to the vet. Special medicine would be the ticket for her complete recovery. She continued to cough. It alarmed us to watch her body heave under the pressure of a hack much bigger than she was. At night we no longer even considered putting her into her crate to sleep. She slept nestled in someone's neck, completely at peace, until her little being unwillingly gave in to the disruptive spasms.

The medicine didn't work. When we took Tilly back to the vet, she was so sick. Our wonderful vet Bonnie saw how special Tilly was to our family. She tried to deliver the harsh news as delicately as she could, but there was no easy way to say what needed to be said. Tilly was seriously ill, and after many tests it was determined that she had "distemper." There was only a small chance that her tiny body would be able to pull out of the devastation of that disease. I sat in the vet's office and stroked the miniature presence that had become such a giant in our home.

I instructed the vet to do "everything" she could to save her life. I sat in the animal hospital parking lot for a long time trying to collect myself. I begged the Lord to take care of our precious Tilly. Certainly He loved this little dog more than I loved her. I reminded myself of the words the Lord had given to me so many times before. Things would be all right. God was sovereign and His grace and mercy would reign even in the life of our little Tilly.

Ashley was very excited when the doctor called with good news. Tilly was responding to the treatments. It appeared she would be ready to come home on Monday. We spent extra time completely disinfecting our home, just to make sure all remnants of the "distemper" were destroyed. Ashley and I cleaned everything from top to bottom. We threw away the small blanket that had been her bed when she wasn't snuggled in our arms. It was definitely a labor of love.

Monday showed up full of sunshine. The phone rang early that bright morning. It was the vet. Tilly had taken a turn for the worse. She was not going to come home. The words of the doctor caught me off guard. I cried right into the phone. It was as if I had just been told one of my children was about to die. Ashley and Jim were still asleep. I sat alone in the kitchen and wept. Hayden heard me cry and encircled my feet as if to remind me he hadn't left me. I rubbed his tummy and cried and cried. I thought about heaven. The Scripture talked about horses in heaven, so maybe puppies would be in heaven too. Tilly would love to nuzzle the neck of Jesus, I thought. Jesus would love that too, I knew it. It amazed me how much I wept over that tiny puppy.

Ashley and I could hardly breathe through the pain of losing Tilly. I called Karen and she sobbed while she tried to offer consolation. She reminded me of an important truth. We thought Tilly had been with us to bring life into our home. We were wrong. Tilly had a special purpose. She would show us death.

I went to the vet's office to pick up Tilly's belongings. Hurriedly, I got back into my car and dumped out the contents of the manila envelope into my lap. Her pink diamond collar appeared even smaller than I had remembered. My heart throbbed while I thanked the Lord for giving Tilly to us even if it was for such a short time. She had accomplished the plan God had for her. Her job was done. I smiled when I recalled all the joy that itty-bitty thing had brought into our home. I held her collar close to my neck and thanked God for how He would use this in my life. It hurt so much, but I knew I had to still keep focused on the truth, not the pain. The truth gave me peace.

Jeremiah 29:11 came to my heart. "'For I know the plans I have for you,' declares the LORD, 'plans to prosper you and not to harm you, plans to give you hope and a future.'" I loved contemplating the first nine words of that verse. How amazing it felt to realize God continually thought about me. He was thinking about me right then. In that moment, I just wanted to snuggle into His neck where everything would be fine. He was truly my safe haven in what felt like a shipwrecked life. It would be all right because God would make sure of it. Without any warning, I found myself singing one of my favorite old hymns. Life was wonderful.

CHAPTER 29

Should I call 911?

The nights and the days were all mixed up to Jim. He slept most of the day and wanted to be up most of the night. I rested on the couch across from his bed because it made it easier for me to jump up and get whatever he needed. Often my biggest role was just trying to keep him comfortable while he tossed and turned in the shadows of the night-light. This way of life went on for months.

It had become almost impossible for me to find time in the day to take a shower. It's not really that time was the problem, it was a safety issue. Even with a motion detector beside him, and the metal hospital railing encircling his bed, I never felt comfortable being too far away from Jim. Sometimes he managed to swing his leg over the chrome bars in such a way the motion detector failed to signal his activity. Those times frightened me.

Ashley tried to help but she was very intimated by the whole situation. She didn't know what to do when he became agitated and it seemed to happen often when she was on duty. Jim appeared irritated, but I believed he was simply frustrated. He wanted to get up, but when we finally got both of his feet planted on the floor he inevitably wanted to be right back in bed. What a vicious cycle. It was too much for Ashley to handle alone. Often several days went by before I found a way to take a shower. I knew it would all work out somehow…and it did.

My dear friend Diane was always available for me in those days. She listened to me and offered comfort by praying with me. One day Diane asked me an important question. Would it help if she moved in with us? I was blown away by her selflessness. Here's a woman who worked full-time, had her own home and health issues, yet was willing to put it all on a back burner to help me. I loved the idea, but wanted to make sure Ashley was on board with it too. Ashley agreed it would be a great help and encouragement to have Diane live with us. She moved in and brought a wonderful balance back into my life. Often times, she'd come home from work with her hands juggling a Starbuck's along with her heavy briefcase. We'd laugh until our sides hurt as we talked about our individual quirkiness. Diane volunteered to watch Jim while I managed to take a quick "undisturbed" shower. We all settled into our new lives together.

It was almost 10 P.M. when the doorbell rang. I couldn't imagine who could be at our door so late in the evening. My heart pounded while I squinted and pushed my eye up against the peep hole. It was Justin. He kept one finger on the doorbell while he leaned up against the iron frame of the security door.

The sound of the chime echoed past me all the way down the hall. I ran to make sure the unceasing noise hadn't penetrated the quiet of our bedroom. Jim slept undisturbed. Diane cracked the wood blinds in her bedroom to get a better look at Justin. The front porch light revealed the ravages of drug use. He looked awful. Filthy jeans shorts almost fell off his too-thin body. It took him at least five minutes to realize it didn't matter how long he pressed on the ringer, I was not going to respond. He backed away from the door staring at the metal cut-out images of the newly-installed security doors.

Diane watched him pace around the small cement entrance, moving in and out of the shadows. Dirty feet blended into the faded color of his flip flops. He kept pulling at the bottom of his already stretched out T-shirt. A ragged kerchief was wrapped around his head like a baseball cap without the rim. I pressed my ear up against the door, as Diane saw Justin mouthing what seemed like words. Justin was speaking into the blackness of the night. He wanted in.

For years I assured him that he could count on always getting two things when he came home; a sandwich and a shower. He wanted them both now. My hand desperately wanted to grab the chrome handle of the shiny varnished wood door that stood between us. Should I let him in? Diane reminded me of the danger of the situation. I had to remember Jim was only a few yards away, completely helpless. I could not compromise him.

I moved away from the wood barricade and thumbed through the numbers in my phone book. Whom should I call? Diane thought I should be calling the police. I fingered through the alphabet until I came to the name of someone who had helped us before—Ryan. Ryan was a really good friend to Justin. He was a leader in one of the church youth groups and Justin respected him a great deal. Ryan had already seen Justin drugged out a few times before. Actually, it had been only one month before that I had enlisted him to babysit Justin while I attended to the needs of Jim.

I punched the digits into the phone. It almost surprised me when he answered the late night call on his cell phone. Once again, he came to my rescue. Within a few minutes an SUV was parked in front of our house with the window rolled down. Diane and I watched Justin casually stroll up to the opened window. Ryan pushed the passenger door open and Justin made his way into the front seat of the car. They drove away. Even though I felt relieved, my heart didn't quit racing until much later into the night.

Jim no longer wanted to get out of bed. He kept his eyes closed. Most of the time, I wasn't sure he even heard me when I spoke to him. It didn't really matter that he heard me. I just kept right on sharing life with him as if he understood every last word. Each morning I'd pull the shades wide open, so the sun would light up the room with its brilliance. Whenever I went to the store, I always brought home vibrant bunches of fresh cut flowers, often having more flowers than vases to put them in. I'd read the paper to Jim in the morning while I sipped on my Starbucks chai. I watched a video with him in the evening. The most important room in the house was Jim's room. I'd laugh with Ashley about her day, fold the laundry, and create the next day's shopping list, only few feet away from him. It was not a quiet room waiting for death. It was an alive room awaiting a miracle. It finally happened.

CHAPTER 30

What Do You Love About Me Best?

July 16, 2003, was an ordinary day. I had hired a few caregivers to fill in for me when I had to run errands. Charlotte had been with Jim for a few hours that afternoon. When I got home from having the tires rotated and oil changed on the car, Charlotte gave me her usual rundown of what she had done for Jim. She was a genuinely caring woman, so I always felt he was safe with her when I was gone. That day she had washed his hair in the waterless cap Diane had found at the drug store. He refused to eat, even though she offered him everything and anything she thought might be an enticement. No luck. It didn't interest him to drink anything either. She tried several juices, water, and even a homemade milkshake—all to no avail.

I smiled as she relayed her attempts to find something that pleased him, only to come up empty-handed. That frustration was something I knew first hand. I walked Charlotte to the door and hurried back to Jim. I picked up the water glass that was right beside his bed and pushed the tip of the bent straw into his mouth reminding him how important it was for him to drink something. He pursed his lips to disable any fluid from traveling up the straw. I leaned down over his face and told him how wonderful he smelled with his newly washed hair, while I planted a kiss on his forehead. My fingers traced the lines on his very thin face. In those moments he looked more like the young handsome 31-year-old man I had married, than the cancer-ravaged 58 year old he had become. His skin was smooth and clean-shaven. I kept my face very close to his, and for some reason started a conversation with him as if he heard every word.

"Jim," I started, "you have not answered this question in a long time. And I have let it go up until now, but I'm not going to let it go any longer. So… what is it you love about me best? I know you have had lots of time to think of a good answer." It made me smile to think about how many times I had asked that question in the past. Jim opened his eyes. It was the first time he had looked at me in months.

"Pam," he said with great effort, "I love the way you...breathe."

With those words he closed his eyes. Who would have thought to say such a thing? It was the most beautiful thing I had ever heard. It wasn't about all the running around I had done for him or the meals I had spent endless hours preparing or the protein shakes accompanied by the hundreds of vitamins that had to be sorted and dispensed...no it was something so simple. I closed my eyes and put my head on his chest and wept. My ear caught the sound of his heart beating. I looked down at my watch to count the beats like I had done so many times during the day. It was fast, too fast. His heart raced with 154 beats in one minute. I ran for the phone and called the hospice nurse. They told me not to worry. A nurse would be right over. I waited, watching the time and counting the beats of his heart. Jim groaned and grabbed the air as if trying to find something. I took his hand.

"Lovey," I said while my own heart raced, "it's going to be all right. I am right here and God is right here with us. You are safe." As I spoke, Jim tightened his grip for a few seconds, then he let go. My head dropped to his chest. I listened. There was no sound, no pulse. He was gone. In that moment, I realized Jim was standing in the presence of the Lord. I grabbed his hand and stood in complete silence trying to comprehend the moment. The warmth of his skin faded quickly. I looked around the room as if I expected to see the angels God had chosen to usher him into heaven. Jim was finally healed.

So many people have asked what those last moments felt like to me. It was an amazing time. I felt I had run a race with Jim and we ran it to the end, together. It was as if we both held a banner and when we came to the final moment, Jim ran into the heavens while I held it here on earth. We both won. I knew in my heart that for the very first time in my life, I had finished something important to God. I had come to the end of a marriage and had finished in victory. Jim had gone on to glory while I stood in the shadow of this great triumph. It was a blessed time.

CHAPTER 31

The Memorial Service and Days After

Diane put together the entire memorial service. I didn't know where to start and honestly felt quite overwhelmed with all that had to be done. She stepped right in and went to work. My job was to make decisions based on all of her many hours of legwork. She is a friend I will never forget.

Our financial planner Bob took care of all the rest. He filed all the paperwork and carefully walked me through all the details of the mountain of forms he diligently collected for my review. He helped me stay centered in the middle of the storm. I will be forever grateful to Bob.

The phone rang. It didn't make me jump like it had in the past. I thought it was the caterer, Diane, Bob, Kinko's, or maybe a well-wisher. It wasn't any of those people. The unfamiliar protocol of a phone call from a prison made me strangely silent. The prisoner was Justin. I accepted the charges and heard the voice of my lost son. There was so much to say, but no time to get it all said. Justin was in prison. I took slow deep breaths as I engaged him in conversation while trying to get a grip on that new reality. The memorial service was the first Saturday in August. The prison system might allow Justin to attend his Dad's funeral. Time would tell.

I can't remember if it was sunny that day in August. It felt cloudy. The chapel was filled with crisp blue Southwest Airline uniforms and the chatter of friends and family embracing each other. At the far left of the chapel sat one isolated boy dressed in an orange jumpsuit flanked by two prison guards.

I approached the guards and was quickly reminded I was not permitted to touch the "prisoner." Those words hurt me deeper than I could have ever imagined. They were talking about my son. I nodded to them with ambivalent understanding and proceeded to the front row to take my seat.

Ashley had finally come back to take her place in the chapel, too overwrought with pain to stay seated until the service began. Her best friend Kelly walked beside her. They took their seats close to me. I examined the program for the memorial service. It amazed me at what a great job Diane had done putting it all together. When I had just about finished reading the last words on the back cover, I felt someone standing right over me. It was Justin. He had been given permission to sit with us. The shackles on his wrists and ankles clanged as he wiggled into the vacant space the girls made beside me.

The service began. A dear friend, Dave, officiated. He spoke of Jim's life in surprising detail, everything from his navy days to his final days. Jim's sister Becky sang beautifully while her friend accompanied on the piano. Another of Jim's sisters, Carolyn, read a letter Jim had written to the pilots of Southwest Airlines not long before he died. I got up and said a few things, followed by some friends and family members. Without warning Justin leaned over to me and asked if he would be able to say something too? I was delighted by his request. Before he got up, he looked me right in the eyes, very closely and said, "Mom, are you ashamed of me?" I patted his leg and told him I was actually very proud of him.

"But Mom, how can that be? I am sitting here in this orange prison uniform."

I shook my head and whispered "Justin, you are no different from me or anyone sitting in this room. We are all sinners. We *all* fall short of the glory of God. Your sin is just more visible than the sins of the rest of us, and that is why I am so proud of you. It takes courage to stand up in the face of sin. Your dad would be proud of you, Son."

Justin dropped his head into his bound hands and sobbed. After a few minutes he stood up in the front of the room and spoke. I watched as he shifted his weight from one restrained foot to the other. The chains rattled while he tried to find a way to balance his stance. His close-cropped hair amplified every expression on his face. He spoke about how much he admired his dad and how he wanted to be just like him. With downcast eyes he lamented over the fact he had caused Jim so many, many years of pain. He was very sorry.

I am not sure what else he said, except I knew beyond a shadow of a doubt that God was still at work in Justin's life. In the quietness of my heart, I thanked God for His mercy and goodness. Yes, it was going to be all right. Actually, it was already all right because God was in control of all of it.

Weeks after the memorial service, people repeatedly asked me two specific questions. How had Jim's death affected my life? And secondly, how was I dealing with the fact that Justin was in prison? I spent hours pondering how I really felt about those two very different, yet both extremely poignant, questions.

First of all, Jim's death signaled both the end and the beginning. I knew with God's help, He would enable me to embrace both. In what way was it the end? Well, obviously it was the end of a marriage. I had been married nearly 27 years—more than half my life. The subtle comfort of married life was gone. I had never before grappled with the immense shift the death of this marriage would mean to my life. My own identity needed redefinition. I had never been someone who struggled with my role as wife. Now, as a result of the death of "husband," came the death of "wife." Honestly, I felt naked, stripped of the "Mrs." I had often hidden beneath while life roared by us. There had been many difficulties in our lives, but I took comfort in the fact I was part of a couple. Somehow together we would walk through whatever the Lord had planned for our lives.

It had all changed. I was no longer one-half of a couple...I was half of nothing. What a very strange feeling. It felt as if I had lost my footing in life. The familiar rhythm of my gait was gone and everything about life was unrecognizable. I had to reconcile myself with the truth of the situation. Jim's death wasn't about me or how it affected me, it was about God. That fact was hard to fathom. God had a specific purpose for Jim's life and it only took 58 years for that to be accomplished. Though the last year of his life was difficult, like the harshest winter ever, that season was over. I had to look to the Lord for the springtime.

I had a new title—"widow." Let me tell you, it was an uncomfortable word for most people. It certainly would be easier for the world if I were "divorced." There was something about the idea of a divorce that had more appeal to people. A "widow" has something unsavory attached to it. Someone had to die so that you could get the title, and that part made folks ill-at-ease. Friends that had once been so relaxed around me, staged ways to include me in dinners filled with awkward conversations. Ashley often stayed away from me. Being around me reminded her of the loss. It was a strange new life.

So how did I handle life as a "widow"? There were only two choices: retreat or dig in. I dug in. Every chance I had, I spoke to women about God's faithfulness. I taught a "widow's" Bible study at the home of one of the widow's in our church. Week after week the teaching centered on the joy we had in Jesus. It was a blessed time for me. I also made some great "widow" friends like Mary, Bonnie, Lee, and Nancy. They have enriched my life greatly.

Though I had never expected life to turn out as it had, I found it was surprisingly full of new and exciting opportunities. Whenever I heard about someone in financial need, I easily responded with a check. The adult "singles" group at our church was jammed full with broken-hearted people. I enjoyed reaching out to them. I loved the great spontaneity of this new life. Ashley and I traveled to New England, Hawaii, and Vail, Colorado, in that first year, often snuggling together while we laughed and looked with great hopefulness to the plans God held for us.

People pressed me to talk about how I felt about Justin being in prison. It took me a long time to fully wrap my mind around my feelings about Justin. I was never ashamed. In some ways I was relieved to know he was "somewhere" and no longer wandering the streets. I prayed for him all the time. The local news reported endless stories about the deplorable conditions of the Arizona prison referred to as "tent city." It was touted as one of the harshest prisons in the system. It was always in the news because of the tough approach Sheriff Joe Arpaio took to those sentenced to time in prison. He served the inmates rancid green bologna sandwiches and issued pink boxers as standard prison attire. It was unquestionably an undesirable place by all reports. I listened and kept right on praying for Justin. I hoped he was safe in such a dangerous environment. When I prayed for him, I hardly ever mentioned the drugs that had brought him to that point in his life. Night after night, I'd fall asleep in the middle of long conversations with God begging Him to reveal Himself to Justin. The only One Justin needed...was the Holy One.

When people asked about Justin, I spoke honestly about him. I never worried about what people thought of me, or him. I had gotten accustomed to being judged by those who felt their walk with the Lord somehow insulated them from that kind of difficulty. It just didn't matter to me what anyone thought about me. After all, Jesus had been judged. He was my role model and the reason I kept looking up to the heavens. I knew behind the steel-laden cement blocks of prison, God was at work, and that brought me great peace...and joy.

The day came when Justin was released. I can't honestly remember how he got from jail to the halfway house. I had spoken to one of our pastors at church about his release, but how it all played out was unclear.

Over the months, I had gotten comfortable in living life "solo." When I was a little girl my dad told me life would be best for me if I never married. In a strange way, I wondered if maybe my dad had been right from the beginning. Don't get me wrong, I was blessed to have had such a great life with Jim. But when I became a single person, it seemed I needed to reckon with the notion that maybe I had been pre-destined to "singleness." After all, even though I had been married for so many years, I had ended up "single." There were times, however, when I would let myself wonder, and even speculate with friends, about what life would be like with another someone special in it. Even in those times, I felt as if I were betraying the dream my dad had designed for me. He believed I would have my greatest opportunities in life… alone. So be it.

CHAPTER 32

Just Joe

I had no idea how much my life would change. It was just lunch. We talked for five hours straight that afternoon while we chewed on chicken salad and sipped iced teas. Our time together that day didn't end until after we sat on a bench barely aware of the squeals of little children as they ran through the spraying water of a fountain in the middle of the courtyard.

We talked about everything. Conversation with Joe was easy. There wasn't one thing I felt I needed to hide from him. Our connection was completely unexpected. The most important person in our lives was Jesus Christ. It was from that foundation everything else found a comfortable place. I told Joe everything about Jim, Justin, and Ashley. We had no secrets. Our relationship was so transparent we had "dirt" day once a week. This was a time we shared every sin that had impacted our lives in some way. There was nothing that exposed ugliness quicker than putting personal sin under a microscope for someone else to examine. We learned a great deal about each other and ourselves from that unusual practice. One lunch led to many dinners.

Sometime in October of 2003, I planned a February trip to Colorado with Ashley and our friend Erica. Another close friend, Darcie, convinced me Vail was a winter wonderland in February. She planned on joining us a few days into the vacation. The girls wanted to learn how to snowboard and I wanted to take a stab at snowshoeing.

It was nearing evening when our shuttle pulled into the village of Vail. The trees were wrapped in a blanket of freshly fallen snow, laced with small glistening white lights. Narrow, winding streets entwined chalet-styled hotels and shops. A-framed glass fronted buildings invited us to enjoy the warmth of the fireplace we saw ablaze from the windows of our van. The sight was breathtaking—like it had come right out of a dream. We settled right into our hotel and the fantasy. It was a memorable time.

Two days before we had to pack up and head for home, my cell phone rang. Justin was on the other end, completely frantic. It was the first time I had spoken to him since his release from prison. It took me a minute to understand all he said. In a nutshell, he needed money immediately or he would be thrown out of his residence. The tone of his voice was panic-stricken. He screamed into the phone as he delivered his plight to me. My body shook while I listened intently to the jumbled message.

What I came to understand was that Justin now lived in a hotel with a girlfriend. He had been there for almost two weeks and didn't have the funds to pay the bill now due. His voice grew louder while he calculated the amount of money he owed. I hung up and prayed while calling Joe. He would keep me centered. I needed him. Joe encouraged me to follow my heart and help Justin this time. I gathered up my courage and called the hotel. The hotel manager answered the phone and reemphasized the gravity of the situation. Either Justin would pay up or he would be put out on the street. I convinced the hotel manager I was trustworthy and would pay the bill as soon as I returned to Phoenix. He agreed.

Joe picked us up from the airport. I was excited to be back home with him, but dreaded the whole hotel situation I needed to face that night. I warned Joe about the vile attitude Justin had when he used drugs. It didn't matter to Joe, he refused to consider letting me go to the hotel without him. We prayed as we drove toward Grand Avenue.

The hotel was in the worst part of town, completely run down and smelled of mildew. The manager was a skinny man with a deep voice and large framed glasses held together by a small piece of black tape. The keys that hung from his belt jangled while he walked behind the counter to find out exactly what Justin owed for the room. I paid the bill and gave extra money to be used in the so-called restaurant attached to the hotel. Joe and I walked toward Justin's room. A toothless woman smiled at us in the hallway while she tugged at the arm of her small daughter with one hand and balanced a mop and bucket with the other. Plaster had crumbled off the wall leaving small piles of white powder all over the threadbare rug that lined the hall.

We stood in front of Justin's room. My stomach went into knots. I closed my eyes and hung on to Joe when he knocked on the door. A young girl with braces opened the door. She greeted us with a smile and pointed to Justin. My eyes surveyed the scene. The room smelled of stale air and dirty clothes. Justin sat on a bed that was covered by a faded, ripped spread. His leg bounced while he kept looking down barely aware of our presence.

Joe walked right up to Justin and introduced himself. Justin glared at him with the same contemptuous look he had flashed at me so often in the past. Joe didn't miss a beat. He engaged Justin in conversation while I stood silenced by what I saw. Justin looked as though he hadn't had a meal in weeks. His bones poked out of his filthy, torn T-shirt. Blood-encrusted scabs covered his face and arms. I had never seen Justin so desperately near death.

Joe held my hand tightly while he focused on trying to understand the words Justin was struggling to form. My heart started to pound in my chest with such force, I had to take deep breaths aloud just to keep from passing out. Justin casually asked for help. There was no conviction in his plea. It was as if he knew he'd have to say something to get what he wanted from us. We knew they must be hungry, which was the real reason Justin promised us he would not use drugs anymore. I looked at the bent shoulders of this boy, my son, and wondered if he would even see the dawn of a new day. Drugs had nearly destroyed him.

Joe sensed how dramatically the scene had affected me and put one arm around me and drew me close to him. My heart found safety in his embrace. Justin and his girlfriend walked behind us while we headed toward Joe's Silverado in the parking lot. They echoed their pledge to stay clean as Joe opened the truck's door and I climbed into the front seat and shut the door. Justin stood with his hands in his pocket and nodded a goodbye while the young girl faked a smile and a half-hearted attempt at a wave.

I was sick. Tears exploded from my eyes as my heart went right back into its familiar pattern of slamming at my chest while I tried to find the air to breathe. Joe was very concerned about me, about Justin, and about the young girlfriend. He reassured me over and over again. God would do a mighty work in everyone's life, and "one day your family will be restored." I wanted to believe him, but I came very close to giving up.

The phone calls came more often than usual from Justin. He needed a plan and we all knew the hotel wasn't going to be a long-term fix. Joe had an idea. He had such a refreshing optimism that it was contagious. I felt as if once again I could roll up my sleeves and dig into life with Justin. Joe helped me not give up, and I thanked the Lord every minute for bringing him into our lives.

It was time that Justin lived in an apartment away from halfway houses and people who used drugs. My young friend Erica, who was in the apartment leasing business, found a perfect place for him. Joe and I checked it out and agreed it would work. It was a one bedroom within walking distance to plenty of work. The majority of the residents in the complex were families with lots of children. I liked the feeling I had when we were shown around the property. A woman came out of the laundry room holding a basket of clothes while two small children danced behind her as they headed back to their apartment. Two older kids rode their bikes in the parking lot while they laughed and tried to "pop a wheelie." The manager was a gentle young man who clearly had a heart for hurting people. I signed a six-month lease. It all seemed perfect.

Joe and I visited Justin and his girlfriend at least once a week. We tried to offer them a sense of family by taking them out to eat, bowling, or going to the movies. Every week we brought them to the grocery store where they filled their basket with food and supplies for apartment life. We paid for it all, while they searched for jobs. My sister sent me the video series "A Purpose Driven Life" which we incorporated into a weekly Bible study with them. We even volunteered to take them to church with us each Sunday. Joe was as committed to helping Justin and his girlfriend find a way out of the drug life as I was. We thought we were finally on the right road.

It wasn't long before we saw the darkness of the drug life entangle them once again. We actually wondered if the drugs had really ever left. Our visits were not as welcomed as they once had been. On several occasions Justin answered the door so hyped up on drugs Joe was concerned for my safety. It went from bad to worse.

CHAPTER 33

The Phone Call

Life for Joe and me, on the other hand, was really quite wonderful. We loved our time together. It was clear to both of us that God had orchestrated this union. Springtime had arrived in my life. Joe asked me to marry him and I said yes.

The week before we were to be married, the manager from Justin's apartment complex called me. He was very sorry, but Justin had to be evicted. Justin had been involved in a series of drug deals gone bad. The residents were afraid for themselves and the safety of their families. Justin had overdosed and was in the hospital. His apartment needed to be evacuated and assessed for damages. Joe took the news in stride while I got sick to my stomach. Would this drug war ever end? I had to remind myself to keep focused on God's promises. They held me up.

It was a Friday night. We had been given permission to get into Justin's place before the apartment manager would inspect it. It was appalling. The floors were completely invisible under the thick layers of shredded paper, clothes, and books. Many torn video box covers were thrown on top of the never-ending heap of junk that filled every inch of the small apartment. Black and neon pink graffiti stained the once bright white walls. Black magic marker drawings were etched onto the surface of every fixture. All the towel racks from the bathroom and clothes racks from the closets were ripped from their anchors in the walls and tossed on the floor. The kitchen overflowed with stacks of food-encrusted dishes. Even the kitchen baseboard had been yanked from the wall and piled onto a mountain of rubble.

We had never seen anything like it. It was hard to know where to begin the clean-up. After we filled no less than 20 plastic bags with garbage and hauled them to the huge trash receptacle in the parking lot of the apartment complex, we decided to tackle the walls. I stood at one end of the wall while Joe stood at the other end. I cried and blew my nose while I tried to rub the imbedded images off the wall. At one point, after we had been scrubbing for some time, Joe stepped over the remaining trash on the floor and wrapped his arms around my waist. I stopped and turned around to face him. He took my hands into his and reminded me how very much he loved me. I threw my arms around his neck and cried from a depth I didn't know existed.

Our wedding was beautiful. The small old chapel in the heart of red Sedona rock was filled with family, old friends, beautiful flowers, and the echo of the love we pledged to one another. It was a magical day though neither of my children was present. I knew it would be too painful for Ashley to attend, so I asked her to stay at home. She was relieved.

Justin was still in the hospital. His heart had stabilized as the drug's poison reluctantly pushed out of his body. His voice sounded strong when we spoke on the telephone. I almost laughed, however, when his counselor called me and insisted I consider sending Justin to "rehab." He had little patience for a mother like me, "who was clearly too busy with her own life to consider the life of her son." In years past those words would have hit me like a sledge hammer. Not so anymore. I knew the truth. I had been there for Justin from the beginning, and I would be there to the end…no matter what.

Joe and I cruised to Alaska for our honeymoon. Blue chunks of glacier ice smashed into the sea while we observed their magnificence from the deck of our vessel. Sea lions glided between the rippled patterns of our moving ship. Whales jumped into the misty air from fresh pools of ice cold water. It was spectacular.

We went on many small excursions and enjoyed everything about our trip. We had sightings of a grizzly bear as we journeyed on a small, creaky, yellow school bus through Denali National Park. Miniature ships puttered around secluded bays where we glimpsed the orca and the hump back whales as they engaged in battle in the unseen war zone at the ocean's floor.

Our cell phones had very sporadic service, if any at all. One afternoon when we were about ready to leave the dock on a small fishing boat, my cell phone rang. It was Justin. Joe and I were amazed that the signal found us in the middle of nowhere. Justin announced that he was going back to "Teen Challenge." He was tired of living a life he couldn't stand to live anymore. I strained to catch every word he said over the sound of the boat's motor as it sputtered its way into the bay. I chided myself for thinking he was calling with some unspoken agenda. He was just calling to tell us he had had enough of the drug life, and that was it.

The phone started to cut out and I thought for sure I would lose the signal. Justin kept right on talking unaware of the skips in his sentences. I asked him to repeat himself so that I could make sense of the conversation. That's when I heard the real reason for the call. He needed money. He explained that it would be pointless for him to go to the "Teen Challenge" in Phoenix, he needed to be out of state and he didn't have the funds for the bus fare.

I sighed, disappointed by the motive behind the call. Joe and I agreed that Justin needed to find his own solution, without me. After all we were in Alaska, in the middle of Glacier Bay, far away from civilization. The only thing I would be able to do for him at that point would be to worry and that wasn't going to help.

Justin wasn't happy with me and tried to make his problem mine. He would certainly fail if he had to stay in the Phoenix "Teen Challenge." I took a deep breath and prayed silently before I told Justin that it was time he solved this dilemma in his own way. If he needed to get to another state, then somehow the Lord would provide the way for him. Before I could finish my thought, the call was lost. I tried calling him back, but couldn't get a signal. *OK.* I thought while I dropped my useless phone into my purse, I had to do the one thing I knew was the right thing. I had to trust God.

The "what ifs" lined up in my head and took turns taking potshots at my resolve. I wavered while Joe stood firm. He reminded me what was really going on. This new situation with Justin was not about me and Justin. It was about God and Justin. It was important to keep focused on that undeniable truth. There was a spiritual battle going on…still going on…and I had to stand firm.

I took my place of defense in the Lord and prayed while our little vessel navigated between small land masses and sea animals. It was such an irony listening to the naturist as she explained the unseen war raging under the calm surface of the glassy water. Looks were deceiving. Yes, so it was in the spiritual world too. Justin was still embroiled in battle, though at times, it appeared calm on the surface. Joe took his eyes off the narrator and looked at me. He knew what I was doing—praying. He wrapped his arms around me and prayed too.

CHAPTER 34

The Court Date

Somehow Justin got to the "Teen Challenge" in San Jose, California. A court date in Phoenix brought him back to Arizona for a day after being away for months. Joe and I hurried to the airport to pick him up. It was exciting. We waited patiently on the hard plastic chairs in terminal four as Justin made his way down the long corridor past security into our line of vision. He looked so handsome. His blue eyes twinkled while he flashed us a big white smile. *Oh yes,* I thought, *God has done a great work!* Joe shook Justin's hand while I stood on my toes to be able to get my arms around his healthy six-foot-four frame. In that brief hug I praised God for His endless mercy and goodness. The long battle with drugs appeared to be over. My heart was overwhelmed with the joy of this great, great victory. God won, of course.

It was an amazing day. Joe, Justin, and I held hands while we prayed through the unknown trek of the court system. The Lord calmed our hearts. I was moved as I listened to Justin call upon the name of Jesus. The depth of his faith was striking. There was no doubt that Justin was a new creation. After we paid the bond and Justin pocketed the contact information for a public defender we left the intimidating cement walls of the municipal building. It was over for now.

Ashley, Justin, Joe, and I met for lunch. I enjoyed watching Justin and Ashley connect as a brother and sister. They laughed and poked fun at each other the way siblings do when they love each other. Joe and I smiled at the new relationship we saw growing right in front of us.

It was time to get Justin to the airport to make his flight back to San Jose. After we scrambled to resolve the minor crisis involving the loss of his identification card, we pulled onto the airport parking ramp. Unexpectedly, Justin put his hand on Joe's shoulder and said; "Joe, I just want to thank you for loving my mom. I think God has restored our family." Joe caught my eye and smiled. Yes, the Lord had done it by using Joe. I would never have dreamed that was possible. Yes, I thought, we serve a God of the impossible.

Another court date was set for Justin. He would have to fly into Phoenix again to make an appearance in front of a judge with his public defender. All I knew about the case was that he was being charged for "theft." It was entirely plausible for the judge to put Justin back in prison for the crime. My stomach churned as I thought about the possibility. Joe continued to remind me of the truth. God was still in control. What did that really mean to me? It meant that the outcome of the judge's decision was in the hands of the Holy One. Maybe Justin would have to go back to prison, although I tried not to dwell on that verdict. My mind raced when I considered how the thought of going back to prison might unravel Justin. In the past he would have gotten so stressed dealing with the potential of a harsh sentence that he would have run away. Would he run now? I begged the Lord for peace while I wrestled with the unknown.

The new court date came and went without a phone call from Justin. I spent most of the day in prayer. My heart's desire was to trust the Lord, but my head was in another place. I just wanted to know what went on in the courtroom. I sat at the kitchen table with my head in my hands feeling very uneasy. Joe hated watching me worry so he suggested I get on the phone and call Teen Challenge. They would have all the answers.

I seriously thought about it, though I wondered if my "need to know" was more a testimony of my lack of faith than anything else. Once again I began to rationalize my concerns. It's not as if I was trying to take control. I just wanted to know what had happened to him. Was Justin in prison? Did he skip town and his court date? Did he go back to the drug life to escape real life? The questions piled up in my head like heavy bricks almost impossible to carry or set aside. I brought my thoughts to the Lord and pleaded for His direction. In that still quiet voice He spoke to me.

"Pam, do you trust Me?" I was disappointed by the question. Certainly the Lord knew I trusted Him. "Pam, why do you need to know an outcome before you have peace? What will it take for you to understand that you will never find peace in your circumstance? I AM your peace."

I shook my head completely ashamed. Years ago I thought I had figured that out. Peace would never be found in the circumstance. I knew that! The only place I would ever find peace was when I looked past the trial into the face of the Lord. He was my peace! I chose not to call Teen Challenge. I had gone too long on this journey with God to give in to my fears now. I needed to stand in victory regardless of the outcome. It was still tough for me to do, even after so many years.

I shook my head and laughed at the simplicity of life with Jesus. He had given me the perfect battle plan. I just needed to be strong in the Lord, put on the full armor of God, stand firm, and take up the shield of faith, the helmet of salvation, and the sword of faith. Pray, pray, and pray. Be on the alert and stand still. The irony of this plan was certainly that every bit of what appeared to be "my" part was accomplished by Him alone. All I had to do was just…believe. God was and would always be in control of all things. I had to make a choice. Was I going to engage in pointless worry, or was I going to surrender Justin to the Holy One, again? It only took a little while for me to decide that time. I refused to indulge in all the "what if's" that spun around in my head. I smiled and thanked the Lord for the unsettling space of the unknown. It was time to stand in the unseen victory and simply…dance in the kitchen.

Epilogue

What were some of the life lessons on this journey? The most important thing I learned was that everything in the Christian life boils down to one basic component—belief. I had no idea how much work that would entail. It required me to dig far down into the roots of my faith to expose the thin thread of "true" belief that lies woven into the thick fabric of years of spiritual "assumptions." It was in that uncovering that my small faith stood naked in front of me for the first time. The depth of the question the disciples asked Jesus in John took on life-changing meaning to me.

> Then they asked him, "What must we do to do the works God requires?" Jesus answered, "The work of God is this: to believe in the one he has sent."
>
> (John 6: 28-29)

It was difficult for me to stand spiritually undressed before the Lord, stripped of all the principles I had been taught throughout the years. I hadn't truly believed, in my heart, many of the teachings I lived by for so long. It was a time to spiritually realign because it wasn't possible for me to "try" to believe any more. What became my lifeline was the small portion of faith I did have. Through that journey, God in His grace and mercy built in me a great fortress of faith in what had been an unstable shack of religious platitudes. Faith didn't come by wishing for it or pretending I had enough until it showed up to rescue me. Faith came by "hearing and hearing by the Word of God." I had to embrace God's Word and run with it. I was living in the midst of something I had never identified before—spiritual warfare. The enemy was after Justin and the closer I got to the battlefield, the more I found I was a target too. My source of encouragement, direction, and hope got quickly narrowed to one thing, the Bible. I recognized my true calling in life. It was simple…just to believe.

Our Lord became intensely personal to me. His "still small voice" brought me great awareness of my enormous need for Him in my life. I watched Him answer prayer in ways that only our awesome, magnificent God knew how to do. His hand guided, comforted, and protected me at every turn. His presence was overwhelming as He walked with me.

> For the LORD your God moves about in your camp to protect you and to deliver your enemies to you. Your camp must be holy, so that he will not see among you anything indecent and turn away from you."
>
> (Deut. 23:14)

No matter how impossible the struggles were in life, God demonstrated His amazing love. He kept me focused on the truth when I tried to wander off into despair. His hope kept me anchored.

> Who shall separate us from the love of Christ? Shall trouble or hardship or persecution or famine or nakedness or danger or sword? No, in all these things we are more than conquerors through him who loved us. For I am convinced that neither death nor life, neither angels nor demons, neither the present nor the future, nor any powers, neither height nor depth, nor anything else in all creation, will be able to separate us from the love of God that is in Christ Jesus our Lord."
>
> (Rom. 8:35, 37-39)

I learned to trust the Lord to accomplish His perfect plan in my life and the lives of my loved ones. God was good, though what I had expected God's goodness to look like and what it actually looked like were disarmingly different. His holy righteousness was apparent at the worst of the worst moments with Justin. It was clear in those uncertain moments right after Ashley's accident. It was evident in the short life of our little Tilly, and it was unmistakable in the journey with Jim through cancer. God is good, no matter how it appeared to me. That brought me great comfort.

> "For I know the plans I have for you," declares the LORD, "plans to prosper you and not to harm you, plans to give you hope and a future."
>
> (Jer. 29:11)

A walk with the Lord meant that I needed to expect the unexpected. His ways were not my ways. I struggled as I clung to His battle plan. It was the only way to walk through drug addiction, though it appeared absurd at first glance. I was called to disregard my ways and trust His. I needed to put on the full armor of God. I had to stand firm, take up the shield of faith, the helmet of salvation, and the sword of the Spirit. Finally, it was imperative to pray and stay on the alert. A small faith grew strong as I fed on God's nourishing Word.

> "For my thoughts are not your thoughts, neither are your ways my ways," declares the LORD. "As the heavens are higher than the earth, so are my ways higher than your ways and my thoughts than your thoughts."
> (Isa. 55:8-9, NIV)

On this road, I experienced the fruitlessness of worry. Don't get me wrong, I desperately tried to pencil "worry" in on my daily planner, as if it were the most important item on my emotional to-do list. The more worry I accomplished, the more defeat I felt. Worry always failed me.

> Do not be anxious about anything, but in everything, by prayer and petition, with thanksgiving, present your requests to God. And the peace of God, which transcends all understanding, will guard your hearts and your minds in Christ Jesus."
> (Phil. 4:6-7)

I learned that things were never as they appeared. My world seemed as though it were spiraling down a path of doom. After all my son was a drug addict, my husband was dying of cancer, and pain and suffering had taken residence in my home. God taught me not to be deceived by what it may look like to the naked eye. My sister once reminded me that we serve a God of order. It was as if He put the ingredients of my life into a funnel and as they all swirled around, into what appeared to be a chaotic mess, He was working them together to create something beautiful.

> But the LORD said to Samuel, "Do not consider his appearance or his height, for I have rejected him. The LORD does not look at the things man looked at. Man looked at the outward appearance, but the LORD looked at the heart."
> (1Sam. 16:7)

God became real to me in unanticipated ways. When I scrambled to find answers and couldn't, He was my *El-Shaddai* (The All-Sufficient One.) On the bench in front of the hospital after Ashley's accident, I experienced the magnificence of *Elohim* (Creator). When I stood by Jim in the face of death, *Jehovah-rapha* (The Lord that Healeth) brought me to the unseen finish line filled with joy. When I learned of the death of my Dad, God reminded me that He was my father. *El Olam* (The Everlasting God) was the One there for me…always. When Tilly died, *Jehovah-shalom* (The Lord is Peace) comforted me. When I thought I couldn't take one more step, *El Elyon* (The God Most High) carried me.

> Jesus looked at them and said, "With man this is impossible, but with God all things are possible."
>
> (Matt. 19:26)

> Ah, Sovereign LORD, you have made the heavens and the earth by your great power and outstretched arm. Nothing is too hard for you."
>
> (Jer. 32:17)

When life tried to suck me into despair, I focused on Jesus. When I almost got caught up in the desperateness of what "seemed" to be my circumstance, the Lord brought me to the ultimate place of truth—the foot of the cross.

> Finally, brothers, whatever is true, whatever is noble, whatever is right, whatever is pure, whatever is lovely, whatever is admirable—if anything is excellent or praiseworthy—think about such things.
>
> (Phil. 4:8)

> You will keep in perfect peace him whose mind is steadfast, because he trusts in you.
>
> (Isa. 26:3)

Another amazing truth I learned was about drug addiction. It wasn't simply about chemical dependency. It was far more than that. Spiritual warfare was its root. Pills from psychiatrists or clever ideologies from a rehab program wouldn't provide a victory. The battle would only be won using God's methods, in accordance with His perfect timing.

> The weapons we fight with are not the weapons of the world. On the contrary, they have divine power to demolish strongholds. We demolish arguments and every pretension that sets itself up against the knowledge of God, and we take captive every thought to make it obedient to Christ. And we will be ready to punish every act of disobedience, once your obedience is complete."
>
> (2 Cor. 10:4-6)

Stand firm then, with the belt of truth buckled around your waist, with the breastplate of righteousness in place, and with your feet fitted with the readiness that comes from the gospel of peace. In addition to all this, take up the shield of faith, with which you can extinguish all the flaming arrows of the evil one. Take the helmet of salvation and the sword of the Spirit, which is the word of God. And pray in the Spirit on all occasions with all kinds of prayers and requests. With this in mind, be alert and always keep on praying for all the saints."

(Eph. 6:14-18)

I experienced the abundance of God when I felt empty. When life was hard, it was time to praise God. When life was completely impossible, I praised God more. And when I thought I wouldn't be able to get through another day, I praised God the most. It was through those times He delivered me from the barren place of hopelessness.

Let everything that has breath praise the LORD. Praise the LORD.

(Psa. 150:6)

I learned about prayer. It wasn't a foolproof formula I could use to plug into a problem for a solution. Nor was it a tool I could employ to manipulate God. It was a real communication between the Most Holy Lord God and me. Most importantly, I learned that it wasn't about getting a result. It was about developing a relationship. I talked to Him all the time, about everything. He became my lifeline.

1 Thessalonians 5:17 says, "pray continually."

In the same way, the Spirit helps us in our weakness. We do not know what we ought to pray for, but the Spirit himself intercedes for us with groans that words cannot express. And he who searches our hearts knows the mind of the Spirit, because the Spirit intercedes for the saints in accordance with God's will."

(Rom. 8: 26-27)

I experienced the depth of my own despicable heart. Every fiber of my flesh cried out against what I knew was the right thing to do. I was rebellious over and over again. The most frightening thing about it was that I realized the pull disobedience had over me. Even when I saw its destruction in my own life it did not alter my behavior. The Bible reaffirmed the importance of obedience. It had a great purpose. It was the vessel the Lord used to pour out His enormous blessings into my life. I learned that I had to trust God for everything, even for my obedience.

The most important thing I learned about life was that it wasn't all about me. It was all about the Lord. At the beginning of this journey, I believed what happened in the physical life was the direct consequence of what was going on in the spiritual. Meaning, when hard times hit, it was related to my walk with God. He was either disciplining me or teaching me. It had been all about me. I found the truth to be astounding.

Yes, it was possible to experience hardship for the purpose of discipline and teaching, but not for the reason I thought. God was not in heaven carrying a big stick to keep me in line. He knew I would fail on my own every time. The purpose of everything that happened in life was to draw me into a closer, deeper relationship with Jesus Christ. It was all about Him. I learned the importance of keeping focused on His perfect plan. Simply put, to walk the victorious life I had to press on… in Him.

Parenting took on new meaning. Honestly, I had always thought that kids reflected their parents. So often I heard Christian parents discuss the tried and true techniques they used to create their "great" kids. I learned something completely unexpected about raising daughters and sons. Parenting was not about children at all. It was about the reflection of my relationship with the Lord. The closer my walk with the Lord, the more the fruit of the Spirit poured out of my life into those around me. Raising godly kids was completely out of my control but I could, however, be the best parent on the planet when my life exuded the fruit of the spirit. I quit trying to be what the books called a "good parent." Instead, I focused on loving God, knowing the best I could ever do for my children would be to reflect Him.

That brought me to another stunning fact. My children were not born Christians just because I had given birth to them. They were born lost until the Lord Himself, called them from death into life. I was never given the power to do that. It changed how I viewed both Ashley and Justin. I found myself more compassionate as I understood the mission field that existed in my own home. The only thing I could do was to continually expose them to the Light. I prayed the Lord would choose them, like He had chosen me, but I didn't assume He would. I kept my eyes on Him thanking Him for His goodness and mercy. God was good, always.

I learned that life was filled with judgments, especially from Christians. Often Christians whispered about our flawed parenting behind closed doors while others were bolder and leveled their blatant accusations right at us. There were times I felt as if we were standing in the middle of a firing range taking hits for crimes we didn't even know we had committed. When Justin ended up in the hospital, staff members, doctors and nurses formed an opinion about us before we even met them. The same indictment was harshly hurled at us. "If we loved our son, then why hadn't we put him in a drug rehab?" No one cared to dare think we might have done something for Justin without their intervention.

We faced judgment at every turn and it changed my life. I realized that I had been a "closet" judger myself up until that point. It had been easy for me to find the insufficiencies in other people until I faced my own. The truth became clear. I was never called by God to judge, just to love. That was why the words of Jim's mother's caregiver stuck to my heart like glue. "When things got difficult with a person, I would love them more. After all who could resist that?" I never judged Justin for using drugs. I just loved him more.

I learned about sin. The world wanted to call drug addiction a "disease." A "terminal" condition without any possible cure in sight. Often I heard people rattle off the years, months, and days from their last drug use, as if the "time" wall they were building had the power to keep them clean. "AA" meetings and "NA" meetings were considered the ticket to a good life.

The church wanted to call "drug addiction" a different kind of sin. It appeared "safe" to chide or excuse the drug addict from the pulpit while the rest of us sat in the undisturbed quiet of the other sins we just didn't talk about. Sin was sin. Drug addiction was a sin, just like gluttony, and lusting over a neighbor's wife. There was no difference.

Finally, I experienced a completely unexpected life filled with hope and victory in the midst of enormous difficulties. I studied the women in the Bible and found that the unnamed faceless ones had so much to teach me. In the Old Testament it was the common practice of the women, whose husbands had gone to war, to live triumphantly long before they knew the outcome of the battle. They couldn't contain their exuberance as they danced in the streets celebrating the unknown victory. I, too, learned to proclaim victory just like those women. The war over drugs had been won in Justin's life though the battles may continue. The fight for Jim's life was finished. Jim now stands healed at the right hand of God, singing His praises. Even though my Dad wrestled with death, it was powerless over him. He is alive in heaven, for all eternity. Our little puppy Tilly is finally at rest after a wearisome struggle, curled into the neck of the Holy One, breathing in His sweetness. Joe continues to hold me, love me, and challenge me to keep my eyes on the unalterable Truth. God is good, always.

"Call to me and I will answer you and tell you great and unsearchable things you do not know" (Jer. 33:3).

Are you in the middle of a crisis? I know it's hard, but just take this moment to breathe in God's grace and mercy, to grab hold of His unfailing promises and join me while we dance in the kitchen…together.

Printed in the United States
81129LV00001B/94